Social Work and Social Exclusion

The Idea of Practice

MICHAEL SHEPPARD
University of Plymouth, UK

ASHGATE

© Michael Sheppard 2006

Published by
Ashgate Publishing Limited
Gower House
Croft Road
Aldershot
Hampshire GU11 3HR
England

Ashgate Publishing Company
Suite 420
101 Cherry Street
Burlington, VT 05401-4405
USA

Ashgate website: http://www.ashgate.com

British Library Cataloguing in Publication Data
Sheppard, Michael
    Social work and social exclusion : the idea of practice
    1. Social case work 2. Marginality, Social 3. Social policy
    I. Title
    361.3'2

Library of Congress Cataloging-in-Publication Data
Sheppard, Michael.
    Social work and social exclusion : the idea of practice / by Michael Sheppard.
      p. cm.
    Includes indexes.
    ISBN 0-7546-4768-4 (hardcover : alk. paper) -- ISBN 0-7546-4770-6 (pbk. : alk. paper)
     1. Social service. 2. Marginality, Social. I. Title.

    HV40.S58246 2006
    361.3'2--dc22

2006012017

ISBN-10: (Hbk) 0-7546-4768-4   (Pbk) 0-7546-4770-6
ISBN-13: (Hbk) 978-0-7546-4768-3   (Pbk) 978-0-7546-4770-6

Printed and bound in Great Britain by TJ International Ltd, Padstow, Cornwall.

Contents

Preface

This book is presented both as an original contribution to the understanding and practice of social work, and as a text of general interest to a wide audience in social work and other related areas such as social policy. Its originality (I hope) lies in its central theme – that the social location of social work may be identified in relation to social exclusion and inclusion, and, in particular, how this specifically emerges around central and enduring characteristics of social work. Its general interest lies in its exploration, in pursuit of this theme, of a whole range of areas of key interest in social work, including social work values and knowledge, empowerment, authority, choice, need, evidence-based practice, reflection and reflective learning, judgement and decision making, social work and 'art' and social work as 'science'.

It is in the relationship of the central theme of social exclusion to these enduring themes in social work that its originality, such as it is, lies. It is in the sense or way in which social work is concerned with social exclusion and inclusion that we can, it is argued, understand social work. However, in exploring these central themes, and that of social exclusion, it is hoped that the book is of wide interest in social work and allied disciplines. It is difficult to imagine that a social worker could be deemed competent (to use current jargon) without understanding issues such as empowerment, need, reflection and authority, and being able to incorporate them in practice. However, these also help us to understand social work itself and its enduring themes in their societal and social policy context.

Chapter one

Introduction

It is the contention of this book that social work is characterised by certain enduring themes and concerns. It is possible to identify these, and from them to construct a picture of social work, not the subject solely of political whim or of mere practical activity (although it *is* a practical activity), but one which has durable and stable characteristics by which it can be identified, despite the developments and changes which do occur.

Our title gives away our twin themes: that social work is founded on notions of social exclusion and inclusion (indeed cannot be understood without these notions), and that ideas and practice are closely related. Social work practice is permeated with ideas, and social work ideas can only be rooted in practice. Hence our title: *Social Exclusion and Social Work: The Idea of Practice*. We might encapsulate all these elements (social work, social exclusion, ideas and practice) in terms of the idea of social work.

At the heart of this are the notions of *social exclusion and inclusion*. It is perhaps ironic that a term of relatively recent origin – it has been widely used only in the past two decades – should be a cornerstone of an enduring notion of social work. This is not, however, as problematic as it may seem. The issue is about finding a 'language' to express some of social work's central themes and concerns. Although the term 'social exclusion' is of only recent origin, it gives expression to some of the major issues which have long been a concern of social work. This is important in two key respects. It is concerned, as is social work, with the relationship between the 'mainstream' and the 'marginalised', and social work has long occupied a place between the two. Second, and underlying this, are notions of social solidarity and a belief in a broad consensus about key elements of social organisation and societal values. The assumption of value consensus is one which has generally characterised the practice of social work (if not always the writings of those interested academically in social work).

Social exclusion, as a result, encapsulates elements of inequality and disadvantage, factors that have long been the context for social work practice. Its expression gives voice to the concern that people can experience themselves as 'outsiders', through a range of possible factors, not just about economic disadvantage but through ethnic group, health, disability, even personal characteristics, and so on. Underlying this is an assumption of the dignity and worth of human life which permeates social work.

Social exclusion, then, provides an anchor upon which to secure the idea of social work. However, this is far from enough to identify the idea of social work. We have to be able to identify characteristics which both unify its different forms (what is it that makes different areas and forms of social work part of the same overall thing that is social work?) and which differentiate it from other activities (what are the facets of social work which, together, distinguish it from other activities, such as nursing, teaching, counselling or policing?). This requires us to take an in-depth look at a range of aspects of social work which are widely regarded to be important and central to its discipline.

Our journey, in this respect, will involve us seeking to answer a number of important questions. The first involves us asking exactly what is meant by social exclusion (and inclusion), and why might it be considered relevant for social work. This is the subject of chapter two. We follow this up with a further question: what is it about social work which so closely aligns its nature and purpose with that of social exclusion? In this we examine some of the characteristics which create this alignment. This is the subject of chapters three and four. In particular, some of the concerns with social solidarity and consensus create a very close relationship between social exclusion, as it has been widely espoused in official and governmental documents and in social work.

However, we are also concerned with further related issues: what is it that determines the *focus of social work* on some areas of social exclusion, but not others? This is very much about the social construction of social work – the processes by which it is involved with some areas of concern and not others. However, if there is a concern with social exclusion, which places social work between the mainstream and the marginalised, we need to 'fill this out' with a more detailed analysis of those aspects of social work which provide its '*social location*'. This involves examining social work as operating on the cusp of a number of areas of social life (as well as between the mainstream and the marginalised). Such cusps run between the public and private spheres; between the social role and the humanised person; and in an interactional context.

Through this we will seek to establish both *social work's focus* (or foci) and its social location. In order to obtain a deeper understanding of social work, however, we need to move on to consider some themes which have become of major importance. One key issue (at the heart of this book) is the extent to which we can consider social work to have an enduring and real status. This takes us directly on to the realm of values and the need to consider the issue of postmodernism, widely prosecuted as a legitimate 'lens' through which to view social work. In chapter five we confront this issue directly. Postmodernism, it is argued, is not simply inappropriate as a way of viewing social work; it is actually antithetical to the possibility of an idea of social work at all. It operates, in other words, with assumptions which contradict the very idea of social work. The idea of 'postmodernist social work' is incoherent. This leads us towards recognising the centrality of some objectivism in social work (that it treats the world, and the problems with which it deals, as real and independent of our perceptions of them) and of values and morality to social work.

If social work treats its concerns as being 'real', we may then ask: what is it that social work is responding to? This leads us to another area of huge importance in social work, the focus of chapter six: that of *need*. Beyond this, a further issue arises from the 'material' of social work practice – its concern is human beings, who are (in principle) capable of making decisions and choices. In dealing with need, how far are clients able to determine the direction of practice? Under what circumstances are choices primarily those of the client, and under which are they predominantly those of social workers? This involves two further issues of major importance in social work: those of *authority* (the powers that social workers have, and the mandating of those powers) and *choice* (a central concern in modern society, as well as in social work).

In carrying out these processes, what are social workers (and what is social work in general) trying to achieve? This question leads us (yet again) to a major concern of contemporary social work – that of *empowerment*. This notion is closely examined, and found to be rather problematic and grandiose, despite its widespread use and popularity. Alternative concepts – less popular, but apparent from earlier writings on social work as integral to its practice – are then examined. These involve *maintenance* (of the client and society), *social functioning* and *coping*. Though rather more modest than empowerment, these notions come out as rather more robust for the purposes of social work. These are examined in chapter nine.

Once we have sought to understand what it is that social work seeks to achieve, we need to look at what social workers *do*. What lies at the heart of social work actions? What form must social work take? Yet again, this leads us to issues of transcendental importance in social work. Is social work *art*? To what extent does it rely on *reflection*? Is social work, alternatively, a *science*? If so, how adequate is the notion of *evidence-based practice*? On the other hand, is it largely a tool of management – social work being a simple technical activity, which involves a series of relatively straightforward *competencies*? These issues are the focus for chapters ten and eleven.

The question of *judgement and decision making* is never far from the surface in social work. It is asked every time there is a child death tragedy, and frequently in the day-to-day contexts of practice. How, then, we must ask, can social workers make judgements and reach decisions? How can these be as rigorous as possible? This leads us to look at some of the most up-to-date issues in social work: those of *reflexivity* and *process knowledge*. This, in turn, involves the close examination of social work as being a matter of practical reasoning, a demanding task, requiring practical intelligence. This is the subject of chapter twelve.

Our penultimate chapter (thirteen) requires us to focus again on the 'material' of social work? How does social work 'construct' human beings? What are their core characteristics? Does social work have a notion of *human nature*? Some of this is alluded to earlier, but some of the core elements are examined here: humans as purposive beings; as social beings; and as having a conscious, but also subconscious and preconscious, state.

Our final chapter (fourteen) moves towards the recognition of social work, not just as a practice form, but as an *academic discipline in its own right*, separate from, but existing alongside other social sciences, such as sociology, psychology and politics. The chapter sketches out the paradigm which needs to be adopted for social work to be a distinctive discipline (the practice paradigm). In relation to understanding the world (including the social world) it requires a core of objectivism (the recognition that the world 'out there' is real). In relation to human beings, it requires the recognition of a 'limited voluntarism' – that is, that people are capable of being autonomous, self-directing beings, making their own decisions. Thirdly, there is – broadly – an 'order' or consensus view of society. These together provide us with key elements by which knowledge appropriate for social work may be judged – that of practice validity. Forms of knowledge appropriate to social work are (in part) valid, to the extent to which such knowledge is consistent with the assumptions outlined in the practice paradigm. This is examined in terms of *the discipline of social work*.

The final comment that should be made is of considerable importance. Some writers have sought to suggest that social work is an ambiguous thing, subject to change. We can agree that the *situations* confronted by social workers can frequently be ambiguous. We can also agree on the 'surface-level' changes to which social work is, from time to time, subject. However, it is the position of this book that social work is an enduring entity, with underlying characteristics which are consistent over time. These are apparent in its enduring themes. This will provide the overall position of the book, to which we can now turn.

Chapter two

Social exclusion and social work

In recent years a burgeoning interest in social exclusion has developed in the realm of social work. This is perhaps not surprising. On the one hand there have been extensive policy initiatives and discussions on the issue of social exclusion – in Britain, the European Union and wider afield. On the other there is an intuitive appeal in the idea that a concern with social exclusion is the very stuff of social work and marks a theme of continuity in its history. This surely cannot be a coincidence: social work's concern for those marginalised and with little power presents a consistent theme in social work writing.

This notion of social exclusion – taking this intuitive viewpoint – merely represents a conceptual way of bringing together many – perhaps all – the key themes of social work's enduring concerns. As such it would be tailor-made as an idea representing the central purposes of social work. Social work, this view would have it, works with those who are, in some respect or other, socially excluded, and seeks to increase their opportunity, through a range of means, for inclusion. The concepts of social exclusion and inclusion – two sides of the same coin – then, provide both the clientele and the purpose for social work.

This interest is evident from a growing series of publications on the topic, many of which, while focusing on social work, regard social exclusion and inclusion to be so central that the term is included in the title (Barry and Hallett, 1998; Dowling, 1999; Jordan, 2001; Nahri, 2002; Pierson, 2002; Ferguson, 2003; Smale et al., 2000). Likewise, a cursory examination of social work qualifying courses on the Web shows the importance of social exclusion to the curriculum (for example: http://www.lancs.ac.uk/users/acadreg/pubs/00ass.htm; http://www.stockport.ac.uk/CourseSearch/course_search_page; http://www.anglia.ac.uk/health/social_prospectus/structureandsequenceoftheprograme.htm).

The Association of Directors of Social Work (ADSW) has stated that 'the overriding aim which should guide social work into the new millennium is social inclusion' (ADSW, 1997, p. 4), while the Scottish Office White Paper (1999) comments (para 1.2) that:

Social work services can make a key contribution to social inclusion … Social work services can also help to promote social inclusion, by supporting family and friends in ways that help people to remain active members of the community, and by helping offenders to become better integrated into a purposeful way of life.

If we consider social work's key purposes, Smale et al. (2000), for example, consider social work should be 'working towards social inclusion', and that it is central for 'social work to address issues of social inclusion when responding to individual needs' (Smale et al., 2000, p. 29). Jones (2002, p. 7) comments that 'social work in Britain and elsewhere is immersed in poverty and social exclusion'. Martinez-Brawley, in suggesting social work has a heritage of seeking to be 'life-enhancing', was alluding to its capacity to encourage social inclusion (Drakeford, 2000), while whole conferences have been dedicated to the idea of social work 'as a means of social inclusion' (for example: http://www.elsc.org. uk/socialcareresource/tswr/seminars.htm (2000); http://www.icms.com.au/ social99/Highlights.asp (1999); http://www.ifsw.org/Info/SWAD2003-1.info. html (2003)).

Likewise, where poverty and social exclusion have been so closely associated, there is a strong case for the clientele of social work to be highly socially excluded. Jones comments (2002, p. 7):

> The overwhelming majority of those who use, or who have social work imposed on them, are poor and drawn from the most disadvantaged sectors of the population … it is often poverty and the associated absence of social and political influence which serve to corrode the lives and well being of individuals.

This is not just a modern phenomenon. Social work emerged in the nineteenth century out of a concern with the poorest in society – including amongst their number, and memorably referred to in Britain's main metropolis by one author as, *Outcast London* (Stedman-Jones, 1971). The ideology and purpose of these early social workers may be put under the microscope – to identify whether they had only humanitarian philanthropic concerns or whether they were reacting to the problem of order and maintenance in society – but the focus of individuals such as Octavia Hill and bodies such as the Charity Organisation Society and the Oxford Movement was nevertheless on those who were poor and excluded from civil society. Poverty and associated problems, including what would now be called social exclusion, has been a perennial concern of social work.

Those in poverty, however, are not necessarily the only groups which may be considered excluded, and a description of such groups expresses a litany of those populations with which social work is centrally concerned. Dowling comments (1999, p. 246):

Social exclusion suggests an isolation which is not necessarily connected to financial hardship. Those who are, for example gay or female, or working class or older, or who have disabilities or are from a different ethnic group can be excluded by individual prejudices and by the stigmatising policies and structures of the wider society.

The intuitive case for a central concern with social exclusion and inclusion on the part of social work would appear, therefore, to be strong. This, though, is not straightforward, and this relationship will be explored in greater detail later. However, our immediate concern should be to map out the main dimensions of social exclusion, in order that we can understand better to what, exactly, this intuitive case commits social work.

The nature of social exclusion

Social exclusion, in fact, has a variety of possible meanings and of foci. Perhaps the best definition which gives us a sense of the meaning of social exclusion was expressed by the Child Poverty Action Group (Walker and Walker, 1997). Social exclusion 'refers to the dynamic process of being shut out, fully or partially, from any of the social, economic, political and cultural systems which determine the social integration of the person in society'. This definition gives the sense that some people are 'outsiders', unable to participate fully in society, and that the problem is systemic, in that it involves – whatever the cause – social systems. Nevertheless, the range of meanings and foci which lie behind this general notion of 'outsiders' means that, if we are to consider social exclusion in relation to social work, we must understand what people are being excluded from.

Unemployment

One key approach to social exclusion and inclusion is that which focuses primarily on unemployment and reintegration into the workforce. People, it is argued from this perspective, are excluded primarily because of unemployment, and society should, therefore, focus on reintegration into the workforce as a means for extending social inclusion.

In Britain, France, Germany and The Netherlands, social exclusion policies have emphasised this issue of unemployment and re-employment. At the end of the twentieth century, the European-wide awareness of major social and economic structural change (within which higher and longer-term levels of unemployment arose) provided the background to this concern with unemployment as a source of exclusion (Commission of the European Communities, 1992).

The prominent role ascribed to social exclusion – in both the rhetorical and policy senses – in Britain, has been reflected in the establishment of the Social Exclusion Unit. While there have been a number of foci, the emphasis again has been on unemployment, and reintegrating (in particular the long-term) unemployed into the workforce. However, both here and elsewhere, unemployment has often been used as a practical and shorthand proxy for poverty and its effects. Britain's Prime Minister, Tony Blair (Atkinson and Davoudi, 2000, p. 435), argued that social exclusion is 'a shorthand label for what can happen when individuals or areas suffer from a combination of linked problems, such as unemployment, poor skills, low incomes, poor housing, high crime environments, bad health and family breakdown.' One interesting factor here was that Blair identified social exclusion not just as a property of individuals, but of geographical areas – particular areas or regions may suffer exclusion because of their economic and social disadvantage, exemplified by unemployment and poverty.

Realising human potential

Clearly, here, unemployment is not the only issue, but also its effects on the experiences of individuals, families and areas which suffer such disadvantage. It both encapsulates, and provides the context for, social exclusion. A less narrow basis for examining social exclusion and inclusion emerged through the idea of human potential and the right to be given the opportunity to realise it.

This is a rights notion. Social exclusion occurs where there is a denial, or non-realisation, of rights (Berghman, 1995). These are rights which are (or ought to be) accorded universally within society, and hence to all individuals and groups. To the extent that these rights are not achieved, people are suffering social exclusion.

The European Union had very idealistic notions of what exactly these rights were: no less than the right to be, or to achieve, what any person could, potentially, be (Comité des Sages, 1996, p. 26):

> The object of the Union is to enable every citizen to realize his/her potential in conjunction with his/her fellows, bearing in mind the necessary solidarity with future generations, and that legal rights and economic and social progress must be subordinate to this aim.

This is no isolated commitment, but one reiterated by Gordon Brown (1997), the British Chancellor of the Exchequer, who suggested that 'all deserve to be given an equal chance in life to fulfil the potential with which they are born'. Unemployment, and poverty, of course, could provide the context for the denial of these rights, but the issue focused more on the multi-dimensional disadvantage to which a variety of groups could be vulnerable, particularly where such disadvantages are persistent and long-term. These can include health, disability, gender, age and so on.

These direct us less to the individual or group as the architect of their own exclusion (though that can be the case) than to the social constraints which prevent them from achieving their rights as citizens. Hence the European Commission (Commission of the European Communities, 1992, p. 8) were concerned with the multi-dimensional nature of the mechanisms by which individuals and groups were excluded from 'taking part in social exchanges'. They pointed to the fields of housing, health, education and access to services.

This, in turn enables a focus on key societal systems, as providing the context for inhibition of the achievement of potential: these were identified by the Commission (1998, p. 21). Social systems included the family, labour market, neighbourhood and society. Economic systems included monetary resources and markets for goods and services. Institutional systems were another dimension, such as the justice system, education, health, political rights and bureaucracies. Those relating to territory involved migration, transport and communications and deprivation. Finally, 'symbolic references' – the ideational elements of exclusion – included identity, social visibility, self-esteem, basic abilities, interests and motivations and future prospects.

Social solidarity

Atkinson and Davoudi (2000) comment on the strong emphasis on the issue of social solidarity as a means for understanding social exclusion and inclusion. This is a concept which helps bring together both the 'citizenship' (and hence rights) argument and the systems within which such rights are achieved. One way of viewing this is that the solidarity is manifested as a practical consequence of the strong social and community values through which inclusion may be achieved.

The idea here is that all individuals are integrated into, and participate in, a national social and moral order. Social exclusion is primarily concerned with relational issues – the dynamic processes which lead to the breaking of social ties and the marginalisation of groups in relation to the society as a whole. Those who are socially excluded are marginalised groups and those whose social ties are damaged.

Spicker (1997) puts forward two notions of solidarity. On the one hand, it refers to solidarity *within* groups. This entails the forms of reciprocity and mutual aid that underlie the development of social insurance systems characteristic of market-oriented social democratic societies. This can justify differences *between* groups. On the other hand, there is a societal solidarity. This refers to the common moral and social order that transcends individuals or particular groups, including class and ethnic groups, and regional interests.

These two notions do not necessarily coincide. It is easy to see, for example, how the interests of particular groups may clash. Where there is a shortage of housing, those without houses may find themselves in a conflict of interest with those already in housing but who do not wish to see the expansion of housing into what they may regard as areas of beauty around their area of residence. In extreme circumstances – for example Northern Ireland – different social groups can show high degrees of internal solidarity, such as Roman Catholic and Protestant groups, although this has led to high levels of conflict with other groups. Where this happens, the sense of social solidarity in the society as a whole could be replaced by a sense of differing interests, and even profound conflict.

How can this solidarity be disrupted? If, for example, we take territorial systems – a focus on the geography of groups – many of those suffering from social exclusion are located in particular areas. These are generally identifiable by their degree of disadvantage. Their deprivation 'excludes' them from the rest of society, producing what Kristensen (1995) refers to as 'excluded spaces'. In these excluded spaces the different dimensions of social exclusion interact. This in turn intensifies the whole process, creating a 'spiral of decline'. Such would be the case in 'sink estates'.

Likewise, it is possible to see how individuals, families or groups can find the degree of exclusion intensified by multiple layers of disadvantage and deprivation. Attempts at social inclusion in such cases would reasonably focus on the individual, family or group. Where, however, we are focusing on 'excluded spaces', the approach cannot focus merely on these levels, but also on the geographical area or community as a whole.

Meaning of social exclusion

Socially excluded groups, therefore, are those who are:

- suffering poverty, unemployment and associated multiple disadvantage;
- who are deprived of their full rights as citizens; or
- whose social ties are damaged or broken.

Each of these conceptions provides a different emphasis, though the links between each are also apparent.

Implicit in much of this are issues of:

- identity – the extent to which the person (or group) is able to identify him or herself (or themselves) with the aims and processes of the wider society;
- humanity – the degree to which the person is able to live a full and productive life;
- values – the degree to which individuals or groups are able to achieve their rights as citizens, and the value placed on humans which underlie this;
- their experiences – the extent to which their life is seen as positive, or they feel they are being ground down, isolated, detached from a sense of community which could help sustain their psychological well-being.

All these reflect, to some degree or other, themes underlying elements of social work practice. While, therefore, *all* aspects of social exclusion may be beyond the realms of social work, *some* would appear to reside within it. This, of course, is a provisional comment, which needs to be subject to refinement as we go along. What, however, of some of the societal assumptions underlying the issue of social exclusion?

Themes in social exclusion

While unemployment (or poverty), exclusion from citizenship or limitation of citizens' rights and disruption of social solidarity are deemed facets of social exclusion, there are various themes as to the origins or causes of social exclusion. Levitas (1999) has provided way of looking at this, some of which are reflected here.

Two key foci can be identified, one being the way in which inequality works to exclude, particularly drawing upon the concept of relative deprivation or need, and the other being the value, attitudes and identities of individuals and communities and the concept of citizenship.

Relative deprivation and social exclusion

One theme has been that social exclusion reflects and emerges in the context of (not simply) poverty or unemployment, but in an unfair distribution of material resources. The poverty itself is not some absolute state, but can only be considered relative to the income and wealth of a society, and this can, of course, vary across societies. It is a concept of relative deprivation, in which the relative absence of material resources becomes enmeshed with other factors which serve to exclude individuals and groups from the mainstream of society.

Much of the work developing theories involving relative deprivation and poverty were carried out in the 1970s by Townsend and Runciman. The latter's work drew on a range of influential theorists, particularly on the work of John Rawls (1973). Runciman (1972, 1990) was interested in developing a notion of the 'just society', one whose distribution of income, wealth and status could be justified to all individuals and groups within it, and as a model of the 'good society'.

Runciman noticed that there were times when quite large differentials in income, wealth and power did not excite discontent, particularly when perceived by individuals and groups to be outside the common experiences, or reference, of any particular population. On the other hand people could be very concerned about relatively small differentials, consider such differentials unjustified and find them a cause for resentment. Thus, for example, manual or skilled workers may be concerned very much with income differentials affecting them, as compared to other manual or skilled workers, but less so in relation to, say, professional workers. A plumber may feel that he or she should be rewarded similarly to an electrician, but may be less concerned by comparison with a doctor. His solution was to call upon the concept of reference groups, suggesting that what determined people's sense of justice and fairness in the distribution of income, status and wealth was their reference group. In this example, the reference group comprised manual or skilled workers rather than professionals.

On a wider basis, he felt that individuals and groups were more likely to take as their reference groups those in their own society, rather than those in other societies. However, the key in both situations was the sense of *relative* (as opposed to absolute) deprivation felt by individuals and groups. People, in other words, took their yardstick for measurement of their own circumstances, not from some abstract or absolute idea of deprivation or adequacy, but from what they saw around them.

This Runciman felt to be both understandable and appropriate. He was unconvinced by some absolutist concept of need, but felt it had to be defined it in relation to the varying circumstances of different societies and different historical epochs. What in Edwardian or post-war societies might have been regarded as adequate was unlikely to be considered sufficient in the changed circumstances of a more affluent society. The adequacy of this relativist argument on need should not detain us at this point (we shall consider it later). Rather its importance lies in its implications for the division of resources in society. Such a relativist notion suggests that such division of resources would not be the same as societal affluence changed.

His concern, then, was to look at circumstances which justified inequality and the scale with which such inequality should occur. Crucial to his argument was his view that societies could not and should not tolerate unlimited inequality. There should be limits to the degree of inequality experienced by individuals and groups in society.

Instead, therefore, of accepting inequality as automatically justifiable – as somehow an unavoidable element of the human condition – Runciman set out to argue that it was only justifiable if certain principles were followed. He identified three major areas: need, merit and contribution to the common good (Runciman, 1972, chapter 13). He suggested that, under the conditions of the model, 'it is hard not to visualise substantial provision being made for redistribution according to need' (Runciman, 1972, p. 307).

Crucially, his perspective was underlain by two key themes which have relevance for the redistributivist position. First, he suggested that these decisions should be made in the context of societal income and wealth, and that this could differ, as we have seen, at different times. Secondly, he suggested (similarly to Rawls, 1973) 'the test of inequality is whether they can be justified to the losers, and for the winners to be able to do this, they must be prepared, in principle, to change places'. In effect this emphasised the importance of the context on income and wealth but also a tendency to place limits on the extent of acceptable inequality.

Townsend picked up on this notion of relative deprivation and applied it to social policy. His highly influential study of poverty (1979) aimed to define poverty away from an objective, sustained condition, which was based on falling short of a threshold of needs required to keep 'life and soul' together. Such an approach would ask: what is the minimum required for a household to buy sufficient food? How much do they need for fuel, gas or electricity? What is required for clothes, rental of accommodation and so on? Added together this would yield a minimum acceptable level of income. Townsend's intention was to redefine poverty as an objective condition of relative deprivation. Rather than focus on an absolute income level required for subsistence, Townsend was interested in whether individuals, families and social groups had sufficient resources to participate in the ordinary life of society, and to fulfil what was expected of them as its members.

In this he was drawing upon some of the key principles expressed by Runciman, in particular, the sense that as societies changed, so what might be reasonably expected also change. However, it was not just about income or wealth, but what such financial circumstances gave people in order that they might participate in social life. Townsend, in effect, went beyond narrow financial circumstances to their implication for people's capacity to participate in, to feel part of, society. This involved a notion of normal living which would change with changed societal circumstances – hence his use of the term *ordinary*: 'they are, in effect, excluded from ordinary living patterns' (Townsend, 1979, p. 32).

What were these 'ordinary living patterns'? Townsend only defined them loosely but they involved the customs, social activities and use of amenities to which people generally expected access. This could reach a point, where the scale of disadvantage was sufficient, whereby there was not just a reduction in participation or capacity to participate, but complete exclusion from these ordinary patterns of social life. The 'lived lives' of individuals would be fundamentally different and more psychologically (as well as materially) impoverished than those of people not suffering from poverty – in effect, in mainstream society. Poverty is multi-faceted, involving restriction of social horizons, at times emotional hardship, as well as (potentially) alienation from prevailing values in society. The emotional toll of this disadvantage, with its inevitably demoralising impact, has been attested by the well-established relationship between social disadvantage and mental ill health.

In very practical terms, poverty was at the heart of a nexus of social evils which had excluding effects: homelessness, inadequate levels of food and nutrition, poor health (both physical and mental), deprived social environments, and the creation of circumstances which made it, in effect, even more difficult for those able to maintain their hope and motivation to re-enter mainstream society. For example, homeless people, without an address, would find it difficult to claim benefits or to find employment.

The consequences of this analysis were quite radical, inviting societal and political levels of intervention. It would be no good to work on individuals and families, although it was often at this level that exclusion could be most strongly felt. Political action, leading to redistribution of income and wealth, was necessary. In effect, this position advocated a greater equality (or as Runciman would put it, limits on inequality), not just in relation to *opportunities* but in relation to *outcome*. Society should not just be concerned with the degree of opportunity to achieve but with the material (and social) circumstances which were the outcome of those achievements.

Townsend, in effect, recommended a practical version of that which Runciman had presented more theoretically: societal-level action was necessary, such as incomes policy, full employment, higher social security benefits and a more redistributivist tax structure. Action was required, in other words, at the levels of social policy, and involved reducing the proportion of income and wealth in the hands of those who were best off in society and placing it in the hands of those least well off.

From redistribution to employment

As Levitas (and others) note, the redistributivist agenda, particularly inherent in Townsend's work, subsided under an agenda which focused more on reducing unemployment, both as a means of dealing with poverty and as a means for gaining greater social inclusion. Of course, the redistributivist implications of both Runciman's and Townsend's work transcended just employment, and included state benefits.

This is significant because, while the implications of deprivation were maintained, it enabled solutions to be developed which provided less of a challenge to the existing distribution of income and wealth, except in so far as this was achieved by higher levels of employment. The relative deprivation of those who were disadvantaged by poverty was to be reduced and this was to be achieved through programmes of incorporation into the workforce of those who were previously unemployed.

Furthermore, by focusing on unemployment, its importance as a definer of, and context for, social exclusion was affirmed. The significance here was on the psychological implications of unemployment and the sense in which employment was able to engender a sense of participation in society. In this respect, the link between social circumstances of relative material disadvantage was made with their psychological implications, in the sense of the sense of disadvantage it engendered. One does not have to feel (relatively) deprived simply materially but, more generally, socially. For example, the sense of esteem generated by participation in paid work could be significant in developing the feeling of involvement in 'ordinary living patterns' identified by Townsend (see above).

Moral renewal

A rather different theme characterising social exclusion is the extent to which it reflects prevailing attitudes amongst particular individuals or groups in society. This theme, by placing such an emphasis on attitudes, makes their moral content, at the level of individuals and groups, much more the focus. Whereas the value content of relative disadvantage stressed societal-wide distributions of income and wealth and problems associated with poverty, this placed the spotlight much more on individuals, and groups, who could be criticised for their attitudes and behaviours. There were those, in effect, who were morally upright and those who were morally reprehensible, or at least that was the subtext of the message.

This view of exclusion was of something in which individuals and groups may be said to have actively participated. They might well be influenced by particular social circumstances, but the individuals and groups made decisions, and these had the effect of marginalising and excluding them or, at the least, contributing to their marginalisation. Such individuals and groups clearly existed in a social context, and that social context greatly influenced their possible decision making. But these were individuals and groups who were nevertheless able to choose. They were, at the very least, in some measure, self-excluders – they took part in their own exclusion.

At the same time, there was concern that the adoption of certain attitudes would undermine the workings of society – in effect presenting a threat to it. Etzioni (1995, 1998), in a series of writings, expressed a concern for the importance of community, with a shared moral commitment, as a necessary element of the good society.

He expressed a concern at the development of what he called 'social anarchy', which had emerged in the increasingly individualistic culture of Western societies. He saw anarchy as the absence of order, regulation and normative guidance. More than this, there is an absence of commitment to those rules which could be the basis for such normative guidance and order. This, in effect, undermines the sense of commitment to the society as a whole, since a key characteristic of social life – indeed a necessary condition for social life – is a commitment to certain basic moral positions which enables people to coexist and show sufficient levels of cooperation.

This growth of anarchy was evident in a number of societal features. He expressed concern about the dangers of crime in public places, of the loosening and decline of traditional sexual expectations and values (the more permissive strain in sexual behaviour), corruption in public life and the decline of traditional notions of the family. It was expressed, also, in an overemphasis on rights at the expense of responsibilities, of expectations that could be placed upon society by individuals at the expense of expectations that could be reasonably made *of* individuals and groups for the good of society.

He was particularly concerned about the young – as the people who would develop and be part of future society. The extent which they were not committed to a moral system represented a future threat. This he attributed to a parenting deficit, which arose because of the absence or lowering of parental involvement in childcare. His views were that parents were central, and as they take up paid employment, or for some reason do not commit themselves appropriately to childcare, so moral deficit emerges amongst the young. Substitute care was not necessarily the answer, for it could be inadequate.

The absence of a moral commitment amongst the young emerged in children and young people's involvement in crime, drug abuse and other anti-social behaviours. This was the long-term result of a widespread neglect of proper care for, and involvement with, children, by some parents. However, some families were particularly vulnerable – or culpable, according to whichever way you viewed it – and these were single-parent and broken (particularly divorced) families. It was sufficiently widespread that it had created a class of 'outsiders', of those who were excluded because of what amounted to inadequate socialisation.

This, of course, could be taken as a critique of a slide from values which emphasised traditional role stereotypes and the place of women in the home. However, this was by no means a necessary corollary of Etzioni's position. It was perfectly possible for developments and changes to occur within society, provided there was the right balance between rights of the individual and responsibilities to others and society in general. What was needed was commitment to *a* workable moral order, rather than any one particular order.

At the heart of this was the importance of socialisation. What was important was that those norms which could be externally represented as ties binding society together as a community would be internalised by individuals who were properly socialised. This does not – ultimately – represent suspension of all critical appraisal, but it does involve commitment to those mores which help sustain and create appropriate development in society. Such commitment, furthermore, is important, since it is the difference between experiencing belonging and involvement in community, and a sense of alienation, of those norms being externally imposed. Furthermore, it was not a growth of individual or group autonomy which was the problem; it was 'bounded autonomy' which was sought – one which recognised the framework of societal norms in which to consider alternative options and possibilities.

The most important fact in socialisation of children was the family, and parents in particular. It would be necessary for children to be parented adequately in order that they might develop into 'good citizens'. This meant that parents had certain duties, and their moral education was of considerable importance amongst these. They would need to make appropriate arrangements so that the age-related needs of children were appropriately met. This included work and social arrangements, the former of which could be facilitated by employers.

Moral underclass

The moral underclass theme, associated with Charles Murray, also emphasised the affirmation (indeed reaffirmation) of societal morals. His, however, and those of others, was more overtly individually judgemental. It was more clearly conservative and right-wing. The concerns about a moral underclass echoed some of those presented by Etzioni.

At the heart of this position was a view of an underclass in which the 'moral and cultural character of the poor' (Levitas, 1999, p. 15) was put in the spotlight. At one level, the underclass – although, like so much in this area, difficult to define – could be identified without overt reference to their moral inadequacies, as those beneath the working class 'whose roles place them more or less permanently at the economic level where benefits are paid by the state, to those unable to participate in the labour market at all' (Runciman, 1990, p. 38).

At another, however, the moral inadequacies of this 'underclass' were highlighted. One of the more colourful – yet representative – of these descriptions identified characteristics of 'laid-back sloppiness, association in changing groups and gangs … hostility to middle-class society, particular habits of dress, hairstyle, even drugs or at least alcohol' (Dahrendorf, 1987, p. 13). While this sounds like the moral outrage of a retired colonel from the Home Counties, it does bear characteristics in common with other writers on this issue. Writers like Murray (1994) and Field (1990, 1996) write in terms of the morally problematic nature of this underclass.

The problem, for Murray, was twofold: that there was the emergence of an underclass, where more and more people were making the wrong moral choices (and thus entering this class), and that welfare policies, specifically social security benefits, were creating 'perverse incentives' (Alcock, 1994, p. 42) for them to do just that.

This group had characteristics which in some respects are reminiscent of Etzioni's concerns. There was no question that poverty provided the context for this underclass. It was not, however, the poverty *per se* with which he was concerned, but rather with the '*attitudes and responses* [my italics] of poor people'. While he was prepared to accept there were poor people whose circumstances were neither of their making nor reflected this moral bankruptcy, there were large numbers in poverty who were part of the underclass. (In this he reflected the distinction, going back to the Charity Organisation Society in the nineteenth century, between the 'deserving' and 'undeserving' poor.)

The development of the underclass was nurtured by (and expressed in) the levels of illegitimacy/one-parent families, crime, and those who dropped out of the labour force (Murray, 1994). There were, however, two key dimensions in the emergence and maintenance of the underclass: child illegitimacy and welfare dependency.

He was concerned about the relatively short-term nature of cohabiting relationships which provided a less stable basis for child rearing than marriages. These relationships, both financially and in other respects, he believed, tended to be poorer, creating a correspondingly worse environment for the developing child. He also linked growing illegitimacy with other social problems, in particular poverty, unemployment and criminal behaviour. Where familial environments are relatively poor and less stable, and emotional relationships are correspondingly less certain, children are more likely to grow up with anti-social behaviour.

Welfare dependency sustained the underclass. He suggested that the welfare system actually encouraged single parenthood. Many lone parents, he suggested, abuse the state benefit system by taking advantage or defrauding it. Furthermore, the system itself encouraged lone parenthood, perhaps particularly amongst the more naïve and young, by giving the impression that, once the child is born, housing as well as financial benefits will be available. As such, it can encourage teenage pregnancy and motherhood. However, even without abuse, the system was designed to be more generous in welfare payments to lone parents than those in couples. Thus it was actually a disincentive to dual-parent families, despite, in his view, their importance in securing social stability.

Frank Field, a veteran campaigner for the Child Poverty Action Group and former British government minister, also felt the threat from the underclass, but was less completely condemnatory of its membership. Their position was, to some degree, understandable. While retaining the emphasis on the moral complicity of individuals in the underclass, Field (1990, p. 155) is more gentle on them. Their status on the economic margins meant, he thought, that they were liable to take on the attitudes and values of the outcast: 'it should come as little surprise that some of those who feel they have no stake in "official" society react in a way that demonstrates their exclusion'.

Field distinguished three groups. The first, the very frail and elderly, could hardly be considered complicit in their own poverty and exclusion. Their position was dependent on government policies on pensions, and on the extent that these were inadequate, so these already vulnerable people would be in poverty: 'no one in their right mind believes this group has volunteered for membership' (Field, 1996, p. 58).

The other two groups were single-parent families and the unemployed. He commented, of these, that 'there is no question that the vast majority of both these groups initially viewed membership of the underclass with disdain' (Field, 1996, p. 58). Like Murray, he was concerned at the way the benefit system encouraged single motherhood. He commented that the fastest growing group on welfare was single mothers. In countering this trend practical education was most important. They needed to learn that having a baby did not lead to queue jumping in relation to public housing but to 'sink council estates'. Such knowledge could act as a disincentive to teenage pregnancy.

He commented, of unemployed people, that there were many who were willing to take almost any job. However, he observed that some, particularly young adults on government training schemes, were on them to obtain more time on welfare rather than entry into the labour market. In many of these cases, the experience of being unemployed and on welfare eroded the motivation to seek for and obtain paid employment. Indeed, he commented that many had criminal records, making the prospect of gaining full employment a 'near impossibility'. For many of these, their attitude to gaining employment veered between jaundice and contempt.

Amongst those who write about the underclass there is a theme of moral complicity and personal responsibility on the part of those who were in the underclass. While on the one hand the moral condemnation may be (in the case of Murray) unfettered by a sense that some of their disillusion and 'unconventional' values were understandable, others (like Field) mitigated their negative views by observing the way their circumstances could cast them as outsiders.

However, whether there was considered to be a structural component or whether behaviour and attitudes were primarily manifested in individuals, the potentially corrupting impact of the underclass on 'mainstream society' had to be combated. Even for Field, this contained personalised elements in which, rather than deal simply at the level of social policy, direct involvement at the personal level was important (for example, educating teenage girls about the dangers of pregnancy and the myths of benefits).

Citizenship

A third theme in relation to social exclusion and inclusion is that of citizenship. To the extent that social inclusion involves participation and involvement in society, individuals and groups are enabled to do so to the extent that they are citizens. In relation to social exclusion, it is the diversity of society, and the disadvantages which can accompany that diversity, which prevents individuals and groups from being able fully to be citizens. Of particular relevance are the comments noted earlier, about the capacity of individuals to achieve their potential. What is it about their social circumstances which can inhibit such achievement? How can equality of opportunity – which as Levitas (1999) notes, is the dominant discourse of equality in relation to social exclusion – be achieved?

However, it incorporates a further dimension, that of the underlying notion of achieving potential. The equality of citizenship rights is dependent on an implicit notion of the equality of value placed on humans in society. Young (1990) emphasises the importance of the 'universality of moral commitment to the moral worth and participation and inclusion of all persons, which underlies a notion of citizenship'. It is because of a belief in the moral worth of individuals that we are able to develop an inclusive idea of citizenship.

Diversity and disadvantage are two key related concepts – and facets of society – in this context. The diversity of modern society yields up groups which, for a variety of reasons, may be disadvantaged in some way. One major element is, of course, poverty, but diversity is expressed in the range of groups, any of whom may experience some form of disadvantage through, for example, gender, disability, physical and mental health and so on. How, for example, can we be sure that women receive equal treatment in the workplace? Or that those with learning difficulties are provided with an environment in which they can achieve maximum involvement in esteem-enhancing activities, such as paid work? Such questions could be applied to a diverse range of groups.

This is, in some respects, an issue of justice, some key elements of which were discussed earlier in relation to poverty. However, while poverty is often the accompaniment to diversity and disadvantage, the issue has wider focus than just economic disadvantage. The link between diversity and disadvantage may occur because of the failure of systems in society or because of the statuses of the particular groups. In this context, there is a collective obligation, alongside that of individual and group rights, for a response to be made to that diversity-associated disadvantage.

The forms taken by this disadvantage may have generic elements, and those specific to particular groups. For example, young people, in the context of a changing labour market, may find participation in society and achieving their rights as citizens more difficult. Race and gender can be associated with discrimination (including in the workplace), lower income and higher levels of poverty. Older people, likewise, with an absence of involvement in paid employment, can suffer poverty and possess a sense of having marginalised status, because they are no longer perceived as economically productive.

Citizenship transcends simple material issues or economic inequality. It emerges, for example, in the prejudice and stigma suffered by some groups, a prejudice which can affect their life opportunities, negatively affect their sense of identity, and encourage low self-esteem. These are widely understood, where issues such as race, gender and mental health status can engender widespread negative differential treatment. As Sayce (1998) comments, in relation to mental health problems, such discrimination can have far-reaching excluding effects. The wide-ranging nature of responses which, she argues, is required indicates the scale of societal responsibility for inclusion. These involve: anti-discrimination law, strategies to enhance work opportunities, influencing media coverage of mental health issues, public education campaigns and funding local work to enhance opportunities for inclusion for people with mental health problems in communities of their choice.

Social citizenship

Social citizenship is of particular importance here, and the starting point for this is usually Marshall (1950). In advocating this concept, Marshall was seeking to promote social stability, a key element in the agenda to combat exclusion. His construction of social rights serves to confirm the close relationship between citizenship and social inclusion. This was wide, from economic welfare and security to the right to share in the social heritage and 'to live the life of a civilised being according to the standards prevailing in the society' (Marshall, 1963, p. 74). It meant that people could be treated as full and equal members of society (Kymlicka and Norman, 1995).

Social citizenship is of particular importance, because it is concerned with the welfare of people as citizens. Marshall distinguished social from civil rights by arguing that the former involve them as receptors of services which respond to their needs. The latter, on the other hand, involve the use of power with the potential to create political organisational forms, which can include groups, associations and movements. In a society where areas of diversity could be characterised by disadvantage, need becomes a relevant issue, one which can enable those not fully able to exercise their social rights to do so.

For example, in the case of an individual is suffering from long-term unemployment, what exactly do they need in order to obtain paid work? Likewise, where a woman has previously taken on full-time childcare responsibilities, and is now interested in paid work, what is it necessary for her to do? As Marshall originally conceived matters, citizenship entailed everyone being treated as full and equal members of society. Citizenship stood as a means for curbing the excesses of the market, the dominant economic force in modern industrial (capitalist) societies. Such societies produced inequalities which, left to themselves, would be socially divisive. The welfare state became a key means through which the divisive effects of the economy were contained, and through which citizenship rights were to be achieved.

Marshall saw these citizens' rights as very much to be achieved through state provision, and as containing three key dimensions. First, they were collective, rather than individual rights. They were not about individuals enforcing their rights, so much as the collective provision of services (Plant, 1991). The state had a general duty of provision, and this emerged in the form of health, education and personal social services. However, while the obligation may have been collective, the corresponding right – in so far as it was aimed at individuals – was individual (Pierson, 2002). Such collective obligations entailed the provision of services which enabled individuals to pursue their life plans. This is particularly emphasised where, typically, many of the services were characterised by individualised interventions (doctors dealt with patients, social workers with clients, and teachers with pupils).

Second, the rights were universal, rather than residual. Marshall (1965) was concerned that these services ensuring citizens rights were not simply a matter for marginal groups, the most deprived in society. The rights were characteristic of the whole society and, in the sense that citizenship was something to be enjoyed by all members of society, this was necessarily the case. However, services designed to ensure those rights were inevitably going to be targeted at the most deprived groups, since it would be they who needed those services in order for their rights to citizenship to be manifested.

Third, social rights were largely to be assumed passively rather than actively. The state was the 'caretaker', ensuring their rights by looking after their interests. What this meant was that, in the case of welfare services (such as social work), it was the expert who defined, and determined response to, need. The service recipient, on the other hand, was passive, receiving the help they needed. In this respect, the duties of the state and the right to citizenship were to be achieved, in the individual instance, through a dominant and disinterested professionalism (Keane, 1988).

Marshall's concept of social citizenship, however, most significantly limited individuals to 'passive recipients'. The capacity of individuals to act on their own behalf, or to be enabled to do so, recognises their capacity to resolve their own problems (at least in part) and be involved in civil life. However, it draws on a *civic republican* tradition which emphasises the *obligations* of citizens to their community (Lister, 1997). This civic republican tradition paints a picture of a much more active citizen, able both to solve their own problems and to contribute to society as a whole.

The tradition can take a variety of forms. The obligations of individuals, in the form of their attitudes and behaviour, has already been referred to as a counterweight to the developing 'anarchy' identified by writers such as Etzioni. One way in which this could be manifested is associated with the right wing of politics – in the form of reducing public provision and encouraging voluntary and private provision for those most disadvantaged. Here, we have the worthy active citizen, who takes part in local life, taking responsibility for those less fortunate, and who ensures that excessive resources are not used (Oliver and Heater, 1994).

Another way in which this is manifested is in the day-to-day rights of those who are service recipients. They are able both to ensure the services they receive are adequate and to operate as a result, in effect, as a quality assurance mechanism for the service as a whole. The practical manifestation of this was in a citizen's charter, through which standards of service expectations were set, and the right to complain and obtain redress was given (Cabinet Office, 1991; Labour Party, 1991). A raft of further measures relating to the quality of health and welfare have been taken.

A further dimension lay in the capacity of citizens to define and act upon their own need. One form relates to service recipients. In this case, there was a change in the balance of power between provider and receiver of services, exemplified in the notion that service users were generally 'experts' in relation to the assessment of their own need. No longer were the professionals seen as the sole experts, and a re-balanced relationship which was more equal, or even balanced towards the service user, was explicit (Smale et al., 1993).

Another form refers to local communities. In this case disadvantaged people come together in groups, actively to improve their own lives and the lives of those in a similar position to them (Holman, 1993). This is a matter of people doing things for themselves, rather than as service recipients, or as the beneficiaries of the philanthropic activities of the worthy active citizens, outlined above. No, of course, some of those in the most disadvantaged position may find it most difficult – because of the effects of their disadvantage – to actually *be* active citizens. One only has to think of the esteem-reducing, energy-inhibiting effects of depression, which so often accompanies disadvantage, to understand the dangers of expecting too much. Nevertheless, one does not stop being a citizen because one feels unable to act – that is, the rights of citizenship are not taken away because the individual is not taking up this active role. What, however, occurs when the individual or group is active, is that they are taking up and enacting those rights – they are fulfilling their potential (or going some way towards it) in the way outlined at the start of this section (Bulmer and Rees, 1996).

Conclusion

The notions of exclusion and inclusion, together with the themes associated with these concepts, reveals a range of ways in which they are constructed. On the one hand, we have very practical notions, like poverty or unemployment;

on the other we have more abstract notions like the achievement of human potential. The themes presented draw attention to structural causes, contract rights and moral degeneracy as sources of exclusion.

However, as Levitas (1999) and Bowring (2000) point out, the whole idea of social exclusion is underpinned by assumptions of a widespread commitment to common values. There is an assumed consensus about the desirable state of society, the ends to be achieved and the values which should be held by individuals or groups. It is assumed that both included and excluded should aspire to the same things – a just distribution of income and wealth, reduction of unemployment, certain expectations of attitudes and behaviour, the achievement of human potential and so on. The notion of universal citizens' rights suggest there is consensus as to what those rights should be.

Behind this, we can also see concern for the problem of order. Where individuals or groups are excluded from mainstream society, they can present a threat to that society itself. If inequality becomes too great, then those most disadvantaged may feel their aspirations are not attended to, that it is unfair, that they have no commitment to, and seek to undermine, the social order. Where mendacious attitudes and behaviour characterise an ever-growing substratum of society, they too represent a threat to its good functioning.

Bowring (2000) sees the consensus to be a misrepresentation, to cover up the dominance of 'mainstream' values (the notion of a mainstream and consequent residual groups in society he contests), and that those groups who are excluded may have their own ideas about what they want to achieve and what the 'good society' looks like. He believes that behind the notion of social exclusion is a commitment to market capitalism whose operation is such that there is bound to be inequality and losers. Why on earth should such people be committed to the values of 'mainstream society' – values which are responsible for placing them in this excluded and unequal state?

Yet, as we shall see, social work has, as an enduring theme, been concerned with the interface between 'mainstream' and 'residual' elements in society. It has likewise been concerned with the interface between the individual and society in its culture and organisation. While some of the more right-wing formulations, where they appear to conflict with ideas of human dignity, may be too much for social work, the themes of social cultural and individual dimensions to social exclusion are consistent (again) with enduring themes in social work.

Clearly, though, there are diverse themes to social exclusion. However, there are here 'themes within themes' which are highly relevant to social work. These include, for example:

- The issue of disadvantage, and helping those who are disadvantaged, provides one such 'theme within a theme' which chimes with consistent concerns of social work.
- The idea, so important to action to tackle social exclusion, of a universal moral worth to be attached to people is another which marks continuity within social work.
- A recognition of personal and group responsibility, as well as more societal explanations for behaviours, would be recognisable to all social workers.
- The importance of morality – societal and individual/personal – closely associated with both individual actions and societal responses is enmeshed in social work.
- Systemic and structural inadequacies are also recognisable as a context within which social work operates.

Levitas (1999, p. 178) comments that social exclusion, as a concept, facilitates a shift between the different discourses in which it is embedded – by which she means different perceptions of its extent, nature, cause and solution. This indicates the range of ways in which it can be understood and the range of ways to which it may be responded. Thus, if we ask again: 'which social exclusion?', it draws us to look in more detail at social work itself. What are the key dimensions of social work? How do these dimensions draw us towards the idea of social exclusion? And, of course, does it encapsulate certain elements of social exclusion, and if so, what are they?

We shall now turn to some of the enduring dimensions of social work, in relation to which we can begin to excavate its concern with social exclusion.

Chapter three

Social work and social exclusion

While there is a clear interest in social exclusion amongst those engaged in social work, and social work academe, and we can show also that some themes chime with traditional core social work concerns, there remains some debate about its significance for practice. Indeed, there are three themes about the relationship between social work and social exclusion:

1. Social work is appropriately and centrally concerned with social exclusion, and is engaged in ensuring inclusion and integration.
2. Social work *could* (and should) be involved in enhancing social inclusion – indeed its traditions would lead to that expectation – but it has been marginalised.
3. Social work is itself exclusionary. It cannot engage in integration and inclusion because its innate functions involve labelling and marginalising people.

One could add a fourth theme – hardly surprising in the light of this – that social work is paradoxical, encompassing both inclusive and excluding functions.

While, therefore, there are some differences, one common feature emerges – a concern to examine the connections between social exclusion and social work. At this stage, it is worth looking at these positions.

Social work as an excluding activity

At a conference specifically intended to explore the ways in which social work acted inclusively, and which included service users and service user groups, a rather vociferous objection to this very idea quickly emerged (Drakeford, 2000). Interestingly, it was predominantly from the user groups. The very heritage of social work was called into question (as indeed were the assumptions of the conference), and the claim that it was 'life-enhancing' was rejected:

> Did the history of social work, it was asked, really measure up to such a proposition? Might it not be equally claimed that social work had often been used as a means through which straightforward excluding actions had been undertaken? (Drakeford, 2000, p. 524)

Another person, representing a coalition for inclusive living, suggested that, for many people, the notion of 'social work as a means for social inclusion' would appear to be a contradiction in terms. In practice it was tied up too much with systems encouraging the free market and 'bureaucratic centralism', and was rejected in favour of more direct action undertaken on the part of excluded, or potentially excluded, groups themselves.

This is not a position widely reflected in the professional literature (an interesting disjunction between the perceptions of some service users, at this conference at least, and the professionals, and writers on the profession, who purport to espouse the cause of these service users). Nevertheless, there are some authors who draw attention to the exclusionary possibilities of social work.

Barry (1998) and Silver (1994) point to the excluding potential of the term 'social exclusion' itself, and that in adopting this term social work can itself potentially exclude. A discourse emphasising social exclusion can 'ghettoise' those so labelled, thus distracting attention from the more general rise in social inequality experienced within society as a whole. The analysis of social exclusion amongst employed people, for example, they claim, is rare compared with those who choose to leave or stay outside the labour force.

Hartnoll (1998), while recognising social work's enduring role with marginalised groups, suggests that this association itself undermines its capacity to work productively with such groups. She points both to the labelling process which stigmatises marginalised groups and to the fact that, by working with them on their own terms, social work itself may be stigmatised. This can act as a disincentive to working with marginalised groups on their own terms (Hartnoll, 1998, p. 43): 'Social workers who seek to speak up for them, or encourage them to speak up for themselves, are liable to be branded as troublemakers and marginalised in their turn.'

The link with labelling points to a long-standing concern about the labelling potential of social work. Schur (1973) – who wrote before the advent of the term 'social exclusion' but whose writings have profound implications for it – has argued that the labelling process inherent in social work actions goes further than stigmatising individuals. It actually makes them more likely to act as deviants. As such, social work is achieving the opposite of its intentions. Schur argues that, in being labelled, an individual takes on the 'deviant identity' in such a way as they are more likely to act in a deviant manner. Thus, for example, the effect of bringing a young person to court, where they are convicted, is to give them the 'sense' that they are a criminal, not someone who has simply stolen a CD player. If they see themselves as a criminal, they are more likely to undertake criminal behaviour.

Social work, he suggests, is an integral part of the labelling process, which creates 'outsiders'. By labelling people as criminals, child abusers or mentally ill, social work, in effect, creates groups of socially excluded individuals. There are major implications for social exclusion and inclusion. Rather then being engaged in a process of social *inclusion*, social workers are directly involved in social *exclusion*.

Barry (1998) also suggests the term 'social exclusion', furthermore, may be so general that it does a disservice to the complex range of disadvantages subsumed under that heading. The advantage of providing such a general heading to cover a range of concerns, from disability and homophobia to poverty and racism, all of which provide a focus for the interest of various writers on social work, may be overwhelmed by its disadvantages. The term may mask the different mechanisms underlying each process, dehumanising the different groups and trivialising the individual disadvantages subsumed under the general heading of social exclusion.

Humphries (2000) suggests social work can have an exclusionary role in relation to immigrants. Social workers are often expected to check out the immigration status of service applicants before offering a service. This, she suggests, is part of the 'second-class treatment' of minority ethnic groups, not just in Britain and Europe, but across the world. This takes the form of exploitation in employment, denial of access to education and wealth, discrimination, harassment and violence. Such people are amongst those who have been admitted to a country but who are denied social and citizenship rights. Many live on the margins of society, vulnerable to poverty and ill health.

Humphries (2000) also points to the difficulties in social work's attempts to be radical. She notes that it stood out as an occupation seeking to combat racism and sexism, defining itself (in some quarters at least) as primarily challenging inequality. However, she suggested that it was not 'well grounded' in a set of values which could sustain its position when 'trouble brewed', particularly with more right-oriented government: 'Values which challenge the roots of social systems are out of place, they sit uneasily with what is required of modern practice' (Humphries, 2000, p. 109).

However, these comments fail to take account of the consensus assumptions underlying the notion of social exclusion, and which have been considered in the previous chapter. Such assumptions precisely do not involve a challenge to dominant values – and where groups are seeking actions which do involve such a challenge, they are likely to be disappointed. Thus, to the extent that social work reflects the very assumption underlying the notion of social exclusion, they are liable to incur the opposition of such groups.

It is important also to recognise the imperfection of the practical activity of social work. While its central concern may be with social exclusion, social work may not always manage to work inclusively for a whole host of reasons, ranging from the limited competence of some practitioners to the financial restrictions on local authorities. Just because doctors do not always cure all their patients, this does not mean they have no concern with health and illness.

Social work marginalised from social exclusion

While the theme of social work as an excluding activity has been pursued by some, others have emphasised a potential for combating exclusion and increasing inclusion, one which (however) has been unrealised. This is of particular concern where recent social policy agendas emphasising inclusion offer new opportunities for work in this area.

Jones (2001, 2002) has drawn attention to the tension which exists between underlying causes of social exclusion, and the dominant forms of practice by social work. Casework perspectives, he has argued, meant that social work practice has tended to individualise social problems, and underplay the hard material realities – derived from societal level inequalities – about client needs. Of course social work cannot eradicate poverty, but there was widespread belief, he thinks, that casework could help poor families to manage their poverty in ways that were less anti-social, or that could provide them with insights and values which would ensure their children might be in a position to have long-term productive and self-sustaining working lives, rather than drifting into crime or long-term indolence.

However, he suggests that social work has been marginalised from the large number of initiatives which have been launched by the British government in seeking to combat exclusion. The result is that social work is 'accorded little or no positive value as a positive strategy for combating social exclusion' (Jones, 2002, p. 14).

This is a theme taken up by Bill Jordan (2001; Jordan with Jordan, 2000). He considers a dual process in which government policies on choice serve to reduce opportunities for poorer groups of the sort of most concern to social work, while reducing social work to a largely regulatory function, in which concerns about issues like child protection and severe mental health problems predominate. Choice has encouraged 'mainstream citizens' (the more well-off, 'savvy' members of society) to be geographically mobile in pursuit of 'positional advantages'. They seek the best schools, the best health services and best neighbourhoods to live in, and these become beyond the means of poorer families. Less well-off people are left in districts with the worst public services, highest rates of crime, drug use, violence and other social problems.

At the same time, employment, rather than traditional welfare, became the heart of the government's policies to combat exclusion. The strongest emphasis in these inclusion policies was placed on increasing employment levels and facilitating the process of returning to paid employment. By focusing on barriers to employment, it was suggested, social work seemed to be relegated to a peripheral role because, since the advent of the welfare state, social work has not been involved in economic and employment issues.

However, Jordan felt this did not have to be the case. It had 'become obvious' (Jordan, 2001, p. 531) that there was little faith in social work amongst those making policy. On the one hand, a new range of public sector agencies and occupations were developed, such as New Deal personal advisors, asylum support workers, and so on. On the other, through various funding sources a whole range of civil society organisations were spawned at the local level. Despite all these new organisations and occupations employing methods of work and skills traditionally associated with social work, social work itself was not a direct part of these arrangements.

Instead social work remained confined to a specific range of traditional tasks, often regulatory in nature, focusing on child protection, youth justice and adult care. These were undertaken, furthermore, with client groups with less access to the best services, because the processes of 'exercising choice' favoured the better-off, leaving poorer population groups less well served.

Evans and Harris (2004) suggest this, more regulatory, set of functions have been emphasised, paradoxically, in the context of a stress on greater autonomy in service user rights (discussed in the previous chapter), as citizens. The new rhetoric of empowerment has emerged in the context of citizenship in which citizens were not simply passive recipients of services arising from social rights, but were active participants in defining and responding to their circumstances.

However, the exhortation to recognise service users as rational agents, capable of action in their own interests (Howe, 1996), has masked a continued commitment to professional power for regulatory purposes. While, on one hand one view of rights – the 'autonomous will' view – reflects the choice of the rights holder (in this case service user) to decide when and how to exercise his or her rights, on the other hand – using a different 'need-based' conception of rights, there remains a duty to respond to need and an obligation to meet that need. The latter provides grounds for an obligation to respond to need, whatever the wish of the service user. Evans and Harris quote the Social Services

Inspectorate (1991, 3:35): 'ultimately, however, having weighed the views of all parties, including his/her own observations, the assessing practitioner is responsible for defining the users' needs'.

Hence, the marginalising of social work from the social exclusion agenda, particularly in its emphasis on regulatory functions, can be seen in relation to two dimensions. The first is a citizenship notion, which continues to emphasise needs at the expense of choice, and which limits the capacity of service users to act autonomously. The second arises from the tendency to equate exclusion to unemployment, while simultaneously excluding social work from those new arenas where social workers could legitimately practise their skills.

Some of these criticisms, again, may be misplaced. Because social work is not involved in *all* areas of social exclusion, and all actions to combat it, does not mean that it is not concerned with some aspects. It may be (to some) unfortunate that social work is not involved directly with issues of unemployment, but that does not mean it does not have a place elsewhere (nor that unemployment is not an issue in much of social work practice). The key, then, is to understand how it is that some areas of social exclusion fall under the auspices of social work while others do not (an issue for the next chapter).

Social work as an inclusive activity

The majority of commentators have emphasised the capability of social work to combat exclusion, and to work, in its own ways, with the agendas for social inclusion. A key theme in understanding the ways in which social work may contribute, according to Barry (1998), is the distinction between micro and macro contexts. These are systemic concepts, relating to different 'levels' of society. The former involves societal level of analysis – the factors which operate in causing and giving meaning to social phenomena. The latter tends to focus on the individual, familial and, at most, local levels.

The macro, in this context, she thinks, relates to the overall concept of social exclusion, its theoretical underpinnings and policy implications. Micro issues, on the other hand, tend to relate more to the delivery of social work services within the context of social exclusion and the problems that social work experiences within an ever-changing political, conceptual and policy framework. It is necessary, therefore, to understand that social work can make a micro-level contribution, and to judge it on that contribution, rather than to judge it on macro-level considerations.

Barry points to a feature of social exclusion, furthermore, which enables social work involvement. Its political attraction, she suggests, is in part because it diverts attention from the possible need for radial change and encourages compliance with the status quo. If social work is to engage with this agenda, and can only do so, as she suggests, at the micro level, then radical change, which would need to occur at the macro level, would seem to exclude social work.

Hartnoll (1998) points also to the need for a symmetry between the aims of social work and the social policy context in which it operates. Social work cannot combat exclusion where social policies castigate those out of work as scroungers (close to the 'underclass' theme outlined earlier), and if the relationships between economic and social change and ill health and poverty are denied. Social policies designed to 'cushion' the worst consequences of the market provide a context in which social work services may contribute.

Within these frameworks, there are two broad dimensions to a social work contribution, from which the details of the practice action can emerge. One approach involves the *notion of citizenship*, particularly securing those rights which enable people to function acceptably within society. This, Barry (2000) thinks, is facilitated by social work's position or 'place' within society. It operates at the interface of, and hence mediates between, advantage and disadvantage, self-determination and dependency, integration and marginalisation.

Dowling (1999), for example, notes the structural causes of poverty, yet (like Barry), argues that pragmatic social work actions can enable people to secure their rights as citizens. Social work is in a potentially particularly helpful position because of the capacity to claim benefits. She points, in this respect, to their capacity to claim for users through the Social Fund, and that not to do so – arising from some misguided view that because poverty is structurally caused, only macro-level action is appropriate – is not to act in the interests of those in poverty themselves. The same goes for the provision of funds through the family support elements of the Children Act 1989. In both cases, social workers can enable those in poverty to alleviate its effects by claiming for or providing money.

Dowling also suggests that paying heed to financial matters is part of an holistic approach to social work, one which (because of its attention to the whole person) is liable to be more in their interests than some, more compartmentalised, approach. Poverty and financial difficulties are often aspects of larger life problems, to do, for example, with the family or childcare, divorce and unemployment. Citizenship is also enhanced, furthermore, where people, particularly those in disadvantage, have the information required to function more effectively in society, and secure their rights. Frequently, the experience of poverty and deprivation has not equipped service users well to deal with the range of officials, and officialdom which they are likely to encounter. In such circumstances social workers are able to act as advocates.

Dowling's comments fit well with social work's traditional approach focusing on individuals and families. Hartnoll (1998) comments on the range of ways in which people may be excluded, which are not just about poverty or unemployment. Individualised work can contribute to life enhancement of those with physical disabilities or chronic ill health, with dementia, mental health problems, learning disabilities or childcare difficulties.

Such approaches enable social workers to ameliorate the worst aspects of poverty and disadvantage. However, social work can go beyond this, Lister (1998) suggests, and encourage *active* citizenship. Here service users become involved as the autonomous agents which have marked out more recent conceptions of citizenship. The autonomous active agency of active citizenship is, she thinks, often most frequently enhanced, in the context of disadvantage, by self-help groups. The kind of self-help groups could be those based on poverty, gender ethnicity or neighbourhood.

Holman's (1998) strongest advocacy is for neighbourhood work. This is exemplified, within practice, in community social work (NISW, 1982), which made a brief appearance in the late 1970s and early 1980s, only to (largely) disappear under the rigours of New Right policies. It has, he thinks, greater potential legitimacy than previously, because of Etzioni's (1995, 1998) work on communitarianism (discussed in the previous chapter) and the importance of focusing on and strengthening communities. Community social work is well designed to do this, since it 'seeks to tap into, support, enable and underpin the local networks of formal and informal relationships which constitute our basic definition of community' (NISW, 1982, para 23). It promotes, in other words, active citizenship, taking responsibility and acting together for collective well-being.

Lister (1998) suggests that self-help can assist to challenge and redraw the boundaries between the public and private, the political and non-political. Professionals can contribute to self-help groups by acting as catalysts and supporting the start of new groups. The social capital, not just of networks, as envisaged by Barclay, but of norms and trust that facilitate coordination and cooperation, can be facilitated by self-help group activity. Groups which improve services, for example, do so not just for themselves but for all who use those services. Participating in self-help groups encourages an active involvement which can enable greater influence in important developments and, just as important, the belief that one can exert such an influence. Active citizens, in short, can become more confident that they can direct their lives and influence their circumstances.

The second involves the associated area of *enhancing and developing service user identities and understanding*. Beresford and Wilson (1998) express concern about a debate which even suggests some people are 'not part of society'. Such a debate turns people into objects, with a label ('the excluded') rather than people. It reduces them to 'material on which to work'. Hence, an array of organisations and occupations are set up to ensure that these people are no longer 'the excluded'. Furthermore, they are very much passive, in the sense that they do not determine how they are defined, their voice is not heard. They are defined externally, by others who regard them as 'socially excluded'.

The first requirement, therefore, is to not to take some action, such as welfare to work, which some external authority determines will mean that they are included, but to include them in the debate about exclusion and inclusion itself. Such an involvement will allow them to define themselves and, from there, involve themselves in whatever action is required. Beresford and Wilson (1998) suggest three dimensions to this: ensuring all service user groups (the excluded) are able to present their perspectives, reflecting their different positions; incorporating the knowledge of those people regarded as excluded, knowledge which derives from their own experiences; and also incorporating their own analysis of their situation.

This is consistent with Giddens' (1994) observations about the potential for individuals as reflective citizens. These people are considerably more knowledgeable about their lives, and the institutions with which they interact than was the case in the past. This enables them to exercise greater autonomy and definition of their own identity.

Humphries (2000) makes a similar point. She considers it important to 'value subjugated knowledge', by which she means the knowledge and perspectives of those who are themselves excluded. McIvor likewise suggests that the emphasis on 'evidence-based' practice, with its restrictive view of what counts as evidence, can have the effect of excluding service user perceptions and knowledge.

This has implications, Humphries suggests, not just for social work actions, but for its intellectual base. It must go beyond, she thinks, technical and managerial values which predominate. This involves a reassessment of the status of knowledge, and including that of service users into the scientific discourse.

Ferguson (2003), however, has commented that the lives of the poor and marginalised are so embedded in disadvantage that it leaves little scope for service users to act to shape their lives and the nature of the services they receive. He suggests that social work can overcome its narrow regulatory functions, even in areas like child and family care, by facilitating reflexivity on the part of service users. Reflexivity, he defines (Ferguson, 2003, p. 199) as 'the ability to act in the world, and to critically reflect on our actions in a way that may reconstitute the way we act, and even reshape the very nature of self identity itself'.

This possibility, even in the realms of child protection, has been opened up, he thinks, by scepticism about expert discourses and their effectiveness in protecting children, prompted by child deaths. This has led to the 'demystifying' of professional expertise, enabling service users more effectively to challenge it. This may overstate the case, since the observation most frequently made is that agencies have responded to child deaths by increasing their regulatory and monitoring functions, and thus enhancing their managerialism.

However, Ferguson suggests that a 'space' has opened up, enabling the most vulnerable to seek to become active citizens by engaging with welfare agencies in ways which enable them to engage in life planning and long-term 'healing' and, in effect, to rewrite key aspects of their lives. As a part of social work practice, this is not an observation with which most would disagree.

Conclusion

While employment issues have been significant in relation to social exclusion – and some writers bemoan social work's own marginalisation in relation to enhancing people's employment prospects – most writers on social work regard their traditional 'client groups' as residing under the umbrella of social excluded groups. Indeed, employment, Barry (1998) thinks, is quite often not the most appropriate answer for problems encountered by marginalised groups, such as people who cannot work through, for example, ill health and disability. It is frequently, therefore, in areas outside those directly to do with unemployment and employment in which social work is able to make its contribution.

However, we get back to what Cheetham has referred to as the 'paradox' of social work and social exclusion (Drakeford, 2000). This paradox resides in the observation that, while social work ostensibly seeks to encourage social inclusion, it is at times, or in some quarters, seen as exclusionary. Part of the paradox, Cheetham thinks, lies in the contradictory and competing views about what constitutes inclusion amongst those most closely involved in many social work encounters – that is, when we go beyond the more abstract notion of exclusion to the more practical facets of what is actually done to encourage inclusion. Cheetham provides an example: from the perspective of providers, hospitalisation of mental health patients may be regarded as strongly excluding, while for relatives it may be the preferred option.

Another dimension, however, may lie with the regulatory functions carried out by social work. These are most apparent in child care and mental health work, often involving actions restricting liberty, or clients' and families' freedom of choice. Such actions almost inevitably invoke opposition from some quarters, especially where they deny the legitimacy of those actions (most obviously those designed to protect children). For those people social work actions, far from being inclusive, act to exclude those people who are affected.

A common feature underlying this paradox, however, lies in a generally accepted and enduring aspect of social work. Social workers work with marginalised groups, and are sited (socially speaking) between those marginalised groups and 'mainstream society'. It is this position which both enables social work to claim to be involved with social exclusion (and seek social inclusion) but also invokes the critical comments which contest this claim. It is this position, between the marginalised and the mainstream, that enables us to explore further the relationship between social work and social exclusion, through the enduring concerns, and facets, of social work. It is to these that we shall now turn.

Chapter four

The nature of social work

Social work and its concerns, it has often been observed, are 'socially constructed' (Parton, 1996; DoH, 1995; Payne, 1997, 1998; Dewees, 1999; Walker, 2001). In suggesting this, writers have argued that there is no fixed and objective state to social work, or to the problems with which it deals. What social workers do and the ways they do it, it is argued, have been subject to considerable alteration and change over time. With little fixed content, social work is seen to have been the consequence of changing social conditions, expectations and policy initiatives. Social work, it is suggested, is characterised, to a considerable degree, by ambiguity. Parton (1996, p. 6) has written of changing discourses:

> As the twentieth century proceeded, the growth of modern social work was increasingly dependent upon its interrelationships with the welfare state, which provided its primary rationale and legitimacy. As a result it mediated not only between the excluded and state agencies, but between other diverse state agencies and a wide range of philanthropic agencies and the diverse and overlapping discourses which informed and constituted them.

Parton (1996) and others (Howe, 1992), however, note the changes which have occurred in social work; as it has increasingly taken on regulatory functions, its claims to expertise have been increasingly challenged, or at least subjected to limitations. Social work has become more proceduralised and managed, with actions prescribed in relation to some of its more important functions (Howe, 1992). All of these were attempts to control both the actions of the social workers and the degree of risk arising in situations of potential serious harm to children.

Putting to one side, for the moment, the extent to which (for example) the growth of procedures and regulatory functions represent fundamental change in social work, or merely changes in emphasis, we need to distinguish between the *surface* characteristics of social work, at times subject to changes in context and emphasis, and its more *deep* and enduring elements. Social work, in other words, is subject both to change *and* continuity, and it is in the latter that its enduring and deeper-level characteristics, emerge. In focusing on enduring characteristics of social work, it is possible to recognise social work as being socially constructed, but in a rather different way from those authors who see it fundamentally defined in terms of, and subject to, flux and change. This follows a process, in which, as it transpires, the issue of social exclusion is at the heart.

Social work, marginalisation and social exclusion

One of the most enduring characteristics of social work is its central interest in those who have been socially excluded, long before the term social exclusion was used. Indeed, it emerged through an interest with, and focus on, this group. Thus, the 'space' occupied by social work is defined, to a considerable degree, by *its position in the interface between the mainstream and marginal in society*. It can be no surprise, therefore, that social work involves those who are poorest, most disadvantaged and marginalised. It is the nature of social work that this should be so.

The enduring nature of this theme is evident in the emergence of modern social work in the nineteenth century. Social work pioneers, generally middle-class, carried out their 'social work' by being involved, as Forsythe and Jordan (2002) comment, with 'society's outcasts', and in the process, seeking to treat them as moral beings. While the social philosophies of these Victorian philanthropists may have varied – and not always been attractive to the recipients of their help – their focus on 'society's outcasts' was a defining feature.

Philp (1979) has discussed how social work emerged between wealth and poverty in the nineteenth century. It operated through a mediating role, representing mainstream society to the marginalised, and the marginalised to mainstream society. These marginalised people included criminals, the insane and, most particularly, the poor. Social work was carried out through charitable and philanthropic work. In carrying out this work, they were able to present the values and beliefs of mainstream society (particularly those of self-discipline and thrift) to those who were poor and marginalised. Likewise, they were able to present the plight of the poor to mainstream society and elicit its support (including financial support) for their work.

In doing this, they were able to represent the 'good' poor to the rich, and the 'concerned' rich to the poor. It became important to distinguish between the deserving – those who were prepared to help themselves, and whose plight often could not easily be seen as their fault – and the undeserving – those whose fault it was they came to be in this marginalised position, and who could not be relied upon to help themselves (George and Wilding, 1994).

This required more than simple labels, however. It was necessary to get to know them and to be able to distinguish between them, through personal contact and understanding.

This points to a second dimension of social work: it is concerned with going beyond 'blanket' labels for those marginalised. Rather than simply refer to their 'objective' label – the poor, mentally ill or criminals – social work is concerned with identifying the person, or people, who are labelled this way. Rather than simply talk about a young offender, they are concerned with *this* young offender, called John, who has lived this life, had these experiences and feels these feelings. They are interested, in other words, with *creating subjectivity (the person) out of objective states (the label, such as offender)*.

With a young offender, for example, the social worker deals as much with the person as they do the offence. In writing a court report, the social worker is not simply presenting the objective facts of the case; they are seeking to paint a picture of the offender as a human being in his or her own right. The offences are put in the context of the life and social circumstances of the offence. The attitude of the young offender to the offence is identified (whether, for example, he/she is remorseful or not). Often, the impact of family background, peer group and disadvantage is alluded to. All these are designed to portray how it is to be an individual with these 'objective characteristics'. The report is written in such a way as to present the subject's essential humanity, and often their potential for change if this can be achieved. On the other hand, the work of the practitioner with the young offender also involves being clear about social (perhaps more precisely legal) expectations which are deemed to represent the values of mainstream society. Just as the Victorian charity workers sought, by personal contact, to distinguish the deserving from undeserving, and present the 'concerned rich' to the 'good poor' (and vice versa) so present-day workers, also through personal contact, seek to work with the subject of the client, while representing mainstream social values.

In working between the two, social workers are seeking to present the 'world' of the marginalised to mainstream society, and the values and perspectives (and frequently compassion and boundaries) of mainstream society to the marginalised. However, their capacity to create subjects out of their objective status can be limited where that objective status is overwhelming. It is not possible to 'speak for' the floridly psychotic, but only to understand their state externally. Their behaviour and utterances do not 'make sense' and cannot help us evoke the person. Where rationality is lacking, evoking the subject is not possible. Likewise, a mass child murderer will generally be 'beyond the pale'. It will not be possible to evoke any essential humanity in the face of acts widely perceived to be inhuman.

Public and private sphere

Underlying this central interest in, and involvement with, social exclusion, social work is placed between the 'public' and 'private' realms of social life in a way which reflects particular perceptions of rights and obligations, and dominant values within a society. Social work emerges from the interface of the public and the private spheres of social life – what Donzelot (1988) refers to as the 'social'. This interface relates to the rights and obligations of individuals and families on the one hand and society and the state on the other. It is, so to speak, a 'social space', one in which some aspects of the lives of citizens become the concerns of the state. The social space could relate to people's capacity to care for themselves, as with, for example, older people who have become physically frail. It can relate to the manner and quality with which parents are able to raise their children: how well are they able to protect them, or provide for their needs? It can relate to the extent to which people are able to 'make their way' in society, to look after their own interests and to ensure their needs are attended to. Such is the case with people suffering from mental health problems, or with young people who offend.

Social work has been employed where such people's capacity to manage their affairs is impaired. The circumstances in which this takes place are complex, and will become apparent as we go on. However, the principle – that society and the state has a legitimate interest in this personal sphere – is one which underlies the existence of social work.

Weber (1949) refers to it as the 'ethic of responsibility'. It is easy to envisage societies where the private spheres of individuals and families are considered the responsibility of no one but themselves. Indeed, while it may be doubtful that this was ever entirely the case, early Victorian British society, with its 'last resort' availability of the workhouse, may have come closest to this non-intrusive (and frankly uninterested) society and state.

The ethic of responsibility is a moral one – that it is right to intervene to help other society members where they are in difficulty, or in some sense in need. There are circumstances where, in the interests of the individuals themselves, the society or state claims the right to protect their interests. Where, for example (as we have seen) in the normally personal area of family life, children's needs are not being met, or they are subject to significant harm, their situation becomes of public concern. If parents cannot be trusted, then the state has a right to intervene to protect the child.

The third dimension of the ethic of responsibility is a widely held belief that human problems are responsive to intervention. Where support is given to families they can be helped to function better. Where guidance is given to a young offender, they may be persuaded to change their ways. Where someone subject to mental health problems is given help, they may resolve or ameliorate those problems, and function better in society. We could go on. However, the key here is that the greater the influence, and acceptance, of the ethic of responsibility, the greater will be the efforts on the part of that society to intervene and solve those problems.

The 'social' as social interactional

A further enduring element of social work is its interactional dimension: it works between the individual (or group) and society, or wider society. This is evident through its dominant form, over the years, of social casework. In essence this involves direct work by social workers with individuals and families, undertaken in the light of the social context in which they 'reside', also the psychological issues which emerge within this context and the individual's personal and family history (Hollis, 1972). Even where, as some might argue, the various elements of social casework were divided up, through care management, into assessing and intervening functions, often separately carried out, the central focus of practice – between the individual and family and wider society – remained the same.

We can likewise see the role of community social work working between the 'client' in the form of community groups and systems, and the wider social systems in which they operate (NISW, 1982). Community social work, of course, is far less a feature of social work than at points in the past but, as Holman (1998; cf. Smale, 1988; Delgado, 2000) observes, it is relevant to social exclusion and fits with the traditional interactional dimensions of social work. Where community social work seeks to identify and develop systems through which disadvantaged groups may begin to engage in mutual self-help, managing and mitigating facets of their disadvantage, they are operating at the interface, at the group and community level, between that group and wider society. To the extent that they seek to establish groups able to manage their own affairs, they seek to enable these groups to operate at that interface.

This interactional theme is also evident from early formulations. The central concern of social work at the Milford Conference of 1928 is as recognisable today as it was then. Social work, it was asserted, is always concerned to recognise that an individual's ability to care for themselves, plan their lives and operate in society – their 'capacity for self-maintenance' as it was put – can only be understood in the context of their environment or given social setting (Anderson, 1988). We see this emphasis at the heart of social work throughout its modern history, with writers such as Hamilton (1941), Younghusband (1951) and Towle (1969). Pincus and Minahan (1973, p. 9) wrote in the same vein, that 'social work is concerned with the interaction between people and their environment which affects the ability of people to accomplish their life tasks, alleviate their distress, and realise their aspirations and values'. The most recent formulation of the relationship between social work and social exclusion make explicit relationship to this interactional context (see, for example, Barry and Hallett, 1998; Pierson, 2002).

The extent to which this is at the heart of social work was made explicit some years ago by Webb, who drew attention to the way it transcended even the largest variations in practice orientation: 'Whether it is radical or traditional, social work can overlook neither the person nor society … both … are engaged in articulating the links and interdependencies between the individual and society' (Webb, 1981, p. 147). This common commitment to an interactional context nevertheless entails differing emphasis along what could be regarded as a continuum, with the individual at one end and social systems, or structures, at the other. Radical forms commonly concentrate on the latter (Bailey and Brake, 1975, 1980; Langan and Lee, 1989). While problems may be experienced by individuals or groups, they are in a context where social systems and structure are the prime focus, in the context of an unequal, exploitative and stress-inducing society. Social work needs, it is suggested, to be concerned with macro-level considerations in society as a whole. Whether, of course, such radical formulations can be undertaken while maintaining social work's form, is a question which we shall address later.

Behind this is another element: that this interaction, between individual or group and their social environment, is a dynamic one which operates in both directions – from the environment onto the individual and the individual onto the environment. The individual or group are both acting (taking action themselves in a way which influences the social environment) and acted upon (feeling, and responding to, the effects of the social environment on them). While this is most overt in systemic formulations of social work, it is evident also in all formulations of practice (Goldstein, 1973; Whittaker and Garbarino, 1983; Davies, 1994, 2002).

Individuals or groups are frequently understood in terms of the way the social environment has acted upon them. We can understand depression in terms of the anticipation or experience of unemployment, or poor parenting as a result of the pressures which disadvantage or poor life experiences have placed on an individual. More generally, we may make sense of the position of older people or disadvantaged parents in terms of social inequality, or of people with mental health problem in term of stigma and discrimination.

However, we also recognise that individuals and groups can and do act upon their social environment. When a practitioner works with an individual or family, they do not seek to 'change them' but to *enable them* to change and develop themselves, or at least maintain their situation by their own actions. When community social workers work with groups, it is to enable them to *act themselves*, to work on local social systems in order to achieve their ends.

Between role and person

Social workers' concern with subjects is at the core of their role (Perlman, 1968). This is something of a paradox, for 'role' and 'subject' have often been taken to be antithetical to each other, particularly by existentialists (Sartre, 1965; Cooper, 1999).

Formally, a role is generally regarded as a label for a particular set of rights and duties which relate to certain tasks. Take, for example, the role of the parent. A parent is expected to carry out adequately certain kinds of functions in relation to their children. They are expected to nurture them, to guide them and to protect them, at times from themselves. In more practical terms they are expected to feed them, to ensure minimum standards of hygiene and self-care, to enable their social education, and to ensure they attend school (amongst other things). When we talk, therefore, of 'a parent', it is the set of responsibilities, rights and duties which make up that role to which we are referring.

Just as a parent has certain rights and responsibilities, so does a social worker. It is implicit in the title or label of 'social worker'. When someone is said to be carrying out social work, it is because they are carrying out certain kinds of tasks. They may be helping to rehabilitate someone suffering a major illness or disability in the community. They may be listening to the distress of someone who has suffered bereavement. They may be asking questions of a parent, assessing the person's capability as a parent, in order to ensure the welfare of their children. The role itself is comprised of those myriad tasks which arise within the rights and responsibilities which define social work.

The notion of 'role', however, is one which is, in certain respects, denuded of the person who carries it out. It is, so to speak, a 'shell' into which an individual fits in carrying out certain socially defined or expected tasks. We can, for example, talk in the abstract about the role of the parent, without referring to any particular individual who carries it out. We can also understand this role in relation to other roles in a society and to social institutions. We can, for example, see the role of the parent in relation to the role of teacher. We know that a teacher is expected to educate children. We know that part of the parental role is to facilitate those educational processes, and in this we see the connection between the two roles, without once mentioning a specific person or, indeed, a particular child. Of course any particular parent (or teacher) could carry out their roles more or less effectively, but that simply serves to emphasise the 'content' of role. We not only know what it is, we have means to evaluate the performance of that role.

The role relationship is inherent in social worker–client interactions. If the social worker is there to 'do' social work, and the client is there to receive it, then they do so in their roles as social worker and client. Anderson (1988; also Schwartz, 1977; Shulman, 1999) identifies three sets of 'relational processes' which are present in any practice situation: the client, the environment resource systems that impact on the client and the social worker.

If we take, for example, a section 2 assessment under the Mental Health Act 1983, this involves an assessment of the need for compulsory hospital admission for assessment, or assessment followed by treatment. Where an Approved Social Worker undertakes this task, they are expected, where practicable, to consult with the 'nearest relative'. In carrying out these tasks, there are clear role relationships. If we assume the nearest relative is the spouse, we have a role relationship between the social worker, the spouse (as nearest relative, whom the social worker is expected to consult) and the client (or using more formal legal language, the patient). In the language of systems theory, we are talking of the client (the patient), the client's environmental resource system (or part of it) in the form of the nearest relative, and the social worker.

What we have here is what Merton (1968; Biddle, 1986) has called a 'role set' – that is, a set of interrelated rights and responsibilities which arise from three or more roles being in some formal relationship with each other. However, role relations are as much a part of practice with, for example, community groups, since the rights, responsibilities and tasks of social work are as much inherent in such work as that of compulsory admissions. If it were not, it would be difficult for each party to know what to expect of the other, let alone carry out tasks together.

However, it is widely understood that a core element of the social worker's role is the meeting of the person of the worker with the person of the client. Social workers, in other words, are not able simply to hide behind the label, rights and duties of practice, especially in some bureaucratised form. A key part of social work is its essential human nature – there needs to be a 'real' person there in order for social work to take place. How else, for example, could social work seek to achieve those key qualities of authenticity, empathy and concern, the striving for which are universally regarded as necessary (if not sufficient) conditions for the recognition of social work occurring?

Jordan (1978, 1979, 1987) and many others draw attention to this essentially humanistic aspect of social work. He emphasises the importance, as an aspect of practice, of the informality of social worker–client relations, of working in natural settings and of negotiating, rather than imposing, solutions. This may go too far – social workers do impose solutions sometimes, and their relationships have to have an element, sometimes an overwhelming element, of formality – but the meeting of two (or more) persons inevitably means that a degree of informality is often involved and desired. It is their human qualities which must lie at the heart of the social worker–client interaction. The social worker–client relationship is an intersubjective one.

Bartlett (1970) argues that an 'orientation to the person' is prime in social work. She suggests that the characteristic way with which social workers go about their business is to try to understand a situation from the viewpoint of the people who are in it. This does not, of course, always mean agreeing with their viewpoint. It is perfectly possible to listen to a parent's reasons for beating a child while neither approving of it, nor agreeing with the reasons put forward. Even, however, where this is the case, it is generally necessary for the practitioner to make sense of client reasoning if they are to have any hope of helping or doing anything about it.

It is necessary from the outset to engage with the client, and that is what is meant when it is suggested that social workers should 'start where the client is' (Haines, 1981; Compton and Galloway, 1989). This is encapsulated in what has been termed the 'search for meaning' as being at the heart of social work. Social workers consciously seek to make sense of the client's perceptions (England, 1986), and in this they are assuming their 'subject status', as beings who are conscious, have feelings, are able to make decisions and carry them out.

Being concerned about clients as subjects is not just a defining element of social work. It presupposes certain values which, too, are crucial to social work. That is, social work's very existence as a definable activity is dependent upon adherence to certain key values. The core value here – respect for persons – cannot be requisitioned by social work alone, but it does underlie the emphasis on personhood and on humans as conscious, sentient beings (Clark, 2002; Butrym, 1976; Horne 1987; Watson, 1978) . This principle underlies social work but is also morally basic – it is a presupposition for having any system of morality at all.

As subjects, humans have 'inherent worth', and it is this 'inherent worth' which means they demand (morally) respect. This does not come from some achievement or other, or from social status. Because someone is a doctor does not mean they are of greater moral worth than a cleaner. They have respect (in the moral sense) simply because of their inherent worth as a person. Furthermore, they cannot be treated as a means to some other end which might be valued. They must be treated as ends in themselves. This is a principle which may be illustrated by the ethics of medical research. The fact, for example, that we may, through some experimentation on a small number of people which may be damaging to them, achieve great benefit to a huge number of people does not provide justification for that experiment. It is treating people simply as 'means to some other end', and that is immoral.

Respect for persons is, I think, universally accepted as the fundamental principle for social work, and core to its practice. However, it is complicated in social work by some of the conditions with which social workers are expected to deal. The idea of personhood presupposes in the human being the capacity, or potential, for rational action. The issue here is: do all those involved in social work as clients have the capacity for rational action? Some people are defined by the fact that they have lost the capacity for rational action. What, for example, are we to think of those who have florid schizophrenia symptoms, or who are suffering psychotic depression? How are we to consider the position of young children, whose capacity to make decisions in their own long-term interest may be circumscribed by their stage of development?

One view (Budgen, 1982) is to consider children as 'potential persons', and mentally ill people as 'lapsed persons'. Such a view continues to emphasise their capacity for rationality, and hence for their status as persons. What, however, of those suffering senile dementia? Or whose learning disability is of such severity that their capacity for rational action is quite insufficient, in principle and practice, to qualify for personhood? Are they denuded of respect? Can social work legitimately use such people as a means to some end?

Well, clearly the answer is no. Social workers do not (and should not) treat people with severe learning difficulties or dementia as means to some other end. Their involvement with such people is designed to secure the latter's welfare, where they are unable to ensure it for themselves. Watson has suggested that a more encompassing idea would be 'respect for human beings'. While on the one hand, we might seek to secure their status as persons – as rational autonomous beings – this may not always be so. It is necessary, therefore, to value other aspects of our essential humanity, such as the capacity to be emotionally secure, the capacity to give and receive affection, and other distinctive aspects of human beings.

Social workers' responses to those without the capacity or potential for rational autonomy may be slightly different – for example securing their welfare, rather than encouraging their capacity for rational autonomy – but the moral basis for their concern remains. That concern, which involves seeking to act in their interest, does not prevent social workers from trying to get their (client's) views. The wishes and feelings of children, we all know, are a significant aspect of a social worker's assessment of a child's situation, even where ultimately decisions may be made which are not consistent with those wishes. Concern for welfare, in this case, means acting in their interests . This requires (at least) consideration of their views which, of course, means, in turn, treating them as subjects.

The socially defined concerns of social work

In dealing with social exclusion, then, social work operates between the client and the social environment, in the private sphere with public concerns, and in a role which requires intersubjective relations. This takes us some way, but it is not sufficient to make sense of social work. At a very pragmatic level, why should social work be concerned with some areas of social exclusion, but not others? What, for example, in Britain, is it about unemployment – and more particularly attempts to help people to return to work – which makes it such an important issue (if not the only one) in relation to social exclusion, and yet one which is not of direct concern of social work? Why is homelessness generally a peripheral issue when taken on its own – peripheral at least to state social work – when it is clearly a factor of considerable significance to social exclusion. There cannot, in other words, be a simple relationship between social exclusion and social work.

The issue here is that, in both social work and social exclusion, the terms being used, to a considerable degree, lead them to 'buy into' particular views of society and occupation. If social work is to be concerned with marginalised groups, as is the case if it is concerned with social exclusion, what does this mean for the nature of practice? How is it that some 'marginalised groups', and not others, are the focus for social work attention? And how is it that social work takes the form it does when dealing with these problems? The clue here is in the public/private dimension, and that of role and subject. For social work to be defined in those terms it needs to have some authority – social, legal, political or whatever – to claim a legitimate involvement with marginalised groups.

Socially constructing practice

Social work is concerned with marginalised groups or individuals, but not *all* marginalised groups and individuals. Such work is conducted with young offenders, abused children, people with mental health problems, children in need, and so on. However, these groups are social categories. They are not simply groups of people whose definition is self-evident. They involve areas of social life over which there is 'public concern', and hence we can talk of the sphere of the public with which social work is involved.

We can see how the areas of work with which social work is involved are 'socially defined by looking at the well-known example of child abuse (Pfohl, 1977; Parton, 1979, 1985). As we have commented earlier, child abuse was not always used to define certain parental actions. It was possible, in Victorian times, for parents to beat their children severely, and for this to be considered legitimate parental action. It could be defined as appropriate disciplining, and reflected assumptions about parent–child relations. Thus we can read for 'child abuse' in the twenty-first century, 'legitimate disciplining' or 'punishment' in the nineteenth.

During the twentieth century, there was increased interest in child welfare, but much of the more nefarious behaviour of parents remained behind closed doors, considered (as it was) an issue for the family. Indeed, where excessive violence by a parent against a child might be deplored, it was widely assumed that such acts were extremely rare. Those most frequently involved, such as health professionals, were reluctant to believe that parents could manifest such acts, and were unwilling to interfere in family affairs.

This all changed with the identification of the 'battered child syndrome'. The 'discovery' was augmented by powerful interest groups which were able both to get the issue into the public domain and had the social prestige to convince people of its significance. It was, in short, the involvement of the medical profession, and those allied to it, which brought the issue of child abuse most effectively into the public domain. Social work's huge, and leading, involvement with child abuse post-dates the advent of the battered child syndrome, even though it had been extensively involved in child welfare prior to that.

What the example of child abuse shows is the way in which social definitions emerge and exert an influence – that they are 'ways of seeing' certain kinds of social actions. What we have here is a certain class of actions which in one period was regarded as 'legitimate disciplining' and in another was regarded as 'child abuse'. These terms have hugely different implicit meanings. Legitimate disciplining conveys the impression of a dutiful parent, acting appropriately and within their rights, to ensure children are reared properly. Child abuse, on the other hand, conveys a picture of parent going well beyond legitimate behaviour, of actually damaging the child, and threatening their physical and emotional and other well-being.

The problems with which social work is concerned, like child abuse, are socially defined. They have a particular 'meaning content' and reflect a particular way of looking at social actions. However, it should also be said that this is not mere interpretation. Interpretation, as Woolgar and Pawlich (1985) note, must be the interpretation of *something*. The acts which were defined as 'legitimate disciplining' or 'child abuse' are real enough. Furthermore, these do not simply reflect changes in public attitudes, but changes in our understanding of what it takes to provide an appropriately nurturing environment to bring up children. This is no mere fad, but a growth of knowledge of the impact of different kinds of parenting on children. We only have to look at the huge impact of Bowlby's work to realise there is a 'real' dimension underlying changed views about parenting behaviour.

Social processes and objective status in practice

The example of child abuse tells us much about meaning, but also something about the processes by which certain marginalised groups come to be a focus for social work concern, but not others. Why is it that certain kinds of marginalised groups are identified but not others (in Britain at least)?

The answer to this has huge implications for the nature of social work. Social work is concerned with certain marginalised groups, where their marginal status, or the factors which contribute to their marginalisation, are considered to be 'social problems'. Commonly we may be concerned with levels of crime, mental or physical health, poverty, unemployment and so on.

We can understand 'widespread concern' more precisely through an awareness that an area of social life goes through a *process of emergence* in order to qualify as a social problem. During this process, social groups organise their activities, and these are designed to demonstrate the need to resolve, or at least ameliorate, the conditions to which they devote their attention. If a group is focusing on poverty, it will be carrying out activities which will focus attention, and seek to influence policy, on poverty. It is, as Spector and Kituse (1977, p. 76) comment, a form of claims making. The claim is made that this social issue should be seen in a certain way, that we should be concerned about it and that something should be done. This, of course, is what happened in relation to the 'battered child syndrome'.

However, claims making is not enough. It is the acceptance of those claims which becomes crucial. In what form can 'acceptance' be formulated? Its most pervasive, powerful and widespread form occurs when the key institutions of society adopt both the definition of the problem – for example child battering as abuse – and the need to act on that problem. In the case of Western industrialised societies, this is a process where political action is taken and responsibility is devolved down through state departments. It is no surprise, therefore, to see issues of child abuse and mental health subjected to legislation and made the responsibility of government, or government-funded, organisations.

The crucial point here is that it is *at the point of acceptance*, or following acceptance, of the legitimacy of the claims being made, that social work becomes involved. Social work become part of the response when the case has been won, the definition accepted and the need for action recognised. In addition, in relation to that particular problem, social work is considered the appropriate means with which to deal with it. It is with the *institutionalisation of particular social problems* that social work becomes involved.

The institutionalisation of these social problems, furthermore, defines for social work the nature of those problems. Social workers know this in a very practical way, as they consult legislation, or adhere to procedures arising from legislation or quasi-legislative edicts, in order to carry out their day-to-day work. Furthermore, as legislation changes, so does the focus for work and the approaches to practice. We can, for example, note the development of care management in Britain in the 1990s as one case in point, and of the greater proceduralisation of practice in relation to child protection as another (Fox Harding, 1997).

The notion of child abuse as being individualised acts often occurring in family settings is embedded within social work concerns. What was, perhaps, a perspective on certain acts, at one point even the subject of debate and argument, *becomes objective for social work itself*. Thus, for example, while the very idea of mental illness may be disputed in some quarters (Dain, 1989; Nasser, 1995; Crossley, 1998; Cox and Kelly, 2002), in social work, as an aspect of the work of practitioners, it is an objective reality. Mental illness exists. That this must be the case is evident in the close relationship between legislation and social work practice. In England, we have the Mental Health Act 1983, and in it there are references to mental disorder (and other states) which in no way indicate the term is contestable, but which treats it as unproblematic.

Thus we have another paradox about social work – that while processes of social construction occur in order for certain classes of social problems to emerge and become the concern of social work, their institutionalised acceptance as a social problem leads, for social work itself, to their objectification. They are, *for social work*, real, existing and objective areas of social life. Others, outside the discipline, may seek to contest these definitions, and consider it legitimate to do so. From the 'inside' however, they are objective.

Focus in social work – individualised consensus

Social work operates, overwhelmingly, through delegated authority, which arises after the case has been won and the claims and definitions made by social groups have been accepted. The political action, therefore, occurs *prior* to the involvement of social work. To the extent that we are able to consider social work to be political, it is in its adherence to the status quo. This cannot be otherwise, since it is overwhelmingly involved with institutionalised areas of social life.

This is widely understood in social policy texts, though many social work writers (rather, it must be said, than practitioners) uncomfortably seek to define social work in a more campaigning manner (Wagner, 1989; Wachholz and Mullaly, 2000). Social work involvement in areas of social life, however, it has been observed for some time, is a mark of its *de*politicisation (Gusfield, 1989; Wilding, 1982; Morgan 1980). Problems move from the political to the personal. Wilding (1982, p. 63) comments: 'The professions have contributed to a depoliticising of social problems, treating them rather as personal problems, susceptible to individual solutions by experts.' He comments further that the implicit message of this position is that problems may be dealt with within the existing pattern of economic and social relations. Such problems, it is implied, are marginal, technical and susceptible to expertise, or at last the collaboration of client and practitioner. In referring to 'marginal' problems, we find a language again identical to that used in relation to social exclusion.

This technical-individualised approach is further underlined by the bureau professional settings of most social workers, though which control may be exerted on practice (Howe, 1992; Harris, 1998). It is no coincidence that most social workers are sited in such settings, since they provide a framework which will enable them both to use their expertise, but to do so in a way in which practice is overseen by a variety of managerial mechanisms. These can vary from direct supervision to procedures with which social workers are expected to comply in carrying out their practice. The very hierarchy of these agencies is designed to ensure practice is overseen.

While, furthermore, voluntary agencies have become increasingly involved with social work practice, they are frequently funded by state agencies, which are thus able to exert considerable influence. The funding of these voluntary agencies is generally contingent upon their acceptance of institutional definitions, and processes of case management enable monitoring of practice in relation to particular cases. Much of the work, therefore, outside state agencies, involves sub-delegation.

Social work, then, is not concerned with the problem *per se*, but to *the individual (or at its most encompassing) group manifestation of that problem.* The logic of this position, however, means that its commitment is inevitably overwhelmingly to the former. More generally, such a position, focusing on groups defined as marginal (rather than mainstream) and on institutionally accepted definitions of problems (treating them as residual), commits them to an implicitly consensus model of society. This, it has been commented, is another feature social work shares with social exclusion (Levitas, 1999). Where practice is not entirely individualised, as it is in work with individuals and families, it remains constrained by its consensus assumptions. Social work, therefore, at the group level, is not in the business of challenging fundamental economic and social structures, but of ensuring, within those structures and through group processes, that people can gain greater control of their lives.

Social work's concern with the *individual manifestation of problems* involves practitioners acting as 'the definers of the individual instance' of general social problems, institutionally defined. This is particularly clear in relation to compulsory admission assessments under the Mental Health Act 1983. While the Mental Health Act identifies the *general class of person* about which concern is expressed – those suffering from a mental disorder, and for whom compulsory admission would be in the interests of their health and safety or the protection of others – it is for the social worker (with key others) to decide where this applies (Sheppard, 1990).

We can identify this individualisation further by returning to the way in which social problems confronted by social workers are socially constructed. Child abuse has been defined as a predominantly familial issue, or at least one which involves one or more adults and a specified child. The focus here is on acts of abuse, carried out by a perpetrator who is, in principle, identifiable. This is a profoundly individualistic way of viewing child abuse. As Gil (1975) commented long ago, this meaning is very restrictive. Many children can be harmed by social actions which do not occur in individualised contexts. Huge damage to the health and welfare of children can be caused at the level of social policy, by government action or inaction. The maintenance or widening of inequality, the increase in poverty, can have an impact on child morbidity and mortality, and significantly affect their life chances. However, this kind of information frequently operates at the level of statistics and simply does not have the 'shock' appeal' of individualised acts of violence and abuse perpetrated on children. Gil (1975), however, argues that the very individualised meaning of child abuse acts as a smokescreen, drawing attention away from the abuse perpetrated by the wider society and on a larger scale. We are again faced with an individualised approach which is implicit in the very meaning of the problems with which social work is concerned.

Conclusion

Social work, it is clear, has been centrally concerned with social exclusion long before the term was used. Indeed, the 'social space' occupied by social work is centrally defined in terms of its position between mainstream society and marginalised groups. However, this is not enough. What is needed for a proper definition of social work is the identification of facets which, on the one hand, *unify its various elements* and, on the other, *distinguish social work from other activities*.

For this we need to identify the *combination of facets* which together constitute its unique social space. In this we have been able to identify three key domains. The first relates to the interface between key social realms. These are the mainstream and marginalised, and the public and private. These are connected. The public concern in the realm of 'the private' is manifested in relation to marginal groups. We become concerned with older people, in realms of their life which would normally be their own concern (the private) where they are unable to manage them, or care for themselves, properly. The older person with dementia, unable properly to care for themselves, becomes a concern for social work in this way. That which was private becomes of public concern, and social work is the means by which that concern is expressed.

The second domain relates to the social construction of social work. This defines not only the subject matter of social work but the legitimacy with which it is carried out and the level at which it is conducted. Social work is social because it is socially constructed, while nevertheless treating the areas with which it is concerned as objective. It operates on social problems but specifically on individual instances. They are not so much concerned with mental health as a public issue, but with individuals who are mentally ill. Those who are socially problematic may be broadly and loosely divided into those who *are* problems – where problems of order arise, such as offending behaviour – and those who *have* problems – those in need over welfare considerations. They are, furthermore, tied in a very fundamental way to consensus assumptions and the status quo. This both provides a 'space' for social work and a limit to the nature of its practice.

Its third key domain relates to further pivotal features of the conduct of practice. Social work is interactional, involving a role, and role set, yet that role is (to a considerable degree) about person-to-person relations. Social work has an orientation to the person. It is about authenticity and intersubjectivity, recognising that social work involves a meeting of humans. At the same time social work characteristically operates between the individual or group and their social system. It enacts, in practice, the important insight that humans are socially situated, and uses that as a context to understand both client and social environment. At the same time, social work also enacts, in practice, a perspective that individuals and groups both act on their social environment and are acted upon by that social environment. In social work we find a dehumanised social category – that of role – defined in terms of the humanisation of its subjects.

It is in taking these facets together that we are able to identify the unique social space that is social work. It enables us to differentiate social work from other activities, from policing, nursing, medicine, counselling, teaching and other activities. This is because, while there may be some aspects of social work with which these other occupations are concerned (though it is doubtful that any are central definers of their own social space), it is the combination of these elements which uniquely defines and describes social work.

There is of course, some degree of permeability to these boundaries. Clearly there is some basis, for example, for development and change. This is obviously hugely the consequence of outside influences, such as legislation, but change may also emerge from within. I have argued elsewhere (Sheppard, 1997) that social work has some 'room for manoeuvre', and that this is evident in the emergence of feminist and anti-discriminatory practice forms. Where broad social trends make this viable, then the development of ideas from within social work and exerted (for example) through educational processes can influence the form of practice. The opportunity for experimentation may exist on the margins of social work practice – that farthest from its legislative influence, though, for example some voluntary agencies. However, they are limited by the consensus and order assumptions which permeate social work. While therefore, certain element of feminist ideas have received wide currency in social work, those of Marxism manifestly failed to influence forms of practice. Its structural orientation inevitably was in conflict with social work's consensus and order assumptions.

However, it is arguable (strongly in my view) that even more traditional notions of social work are profoundly radical, if in a different sense from that normally used. In a society which is characterised by competition, high levels of inequality and the frequent (negative) objectification of those most disadvantaged, social work is constructed in a form which challenges these dominant themes. Its central concern for the marginalised, the creation of people's subject status and the determination to place actions in a social context all betray an underlying humanitarianism. It is because of this, in my view, that (for example) anti-discrimination themes and some feminist influences have emerged, often from within social work, allowing development and change in practice without transcending the enduring characteristics of social work.

Chapter five

Knowledge and values, postmodernism and social work

The operation and analysis of social work would, on the surface, appear to reflect certain important assumptions or facets of social work. First, to analyse social work might be seen to imply that it is a single entity – that social work is a unified form of activity, as might be said, for example, of being a doctor, lawyer, teacher or soldier. Second, in so far as social work has a code of practice, reflecting its value base, we might reasonably assume that these values had some special status – that they distinguished between right and wrong conduct, and moral or immoral behaviour. Third, to the extent that social work is 'knowledge-based' we might consider that this provides social work with expertise, a way of viewing the world superior, in relevant areas, to that of people who do not have access to that knowledge base.

To assume that there was a consensus on these issues would be quite wrong. That is because postmodernism, which has gained increasing influence in social work writing, disputes every one of these assertions. Indeed, such assertions would, advocates of postmodernism would suggest, be associated with what they would call a 'modernist agenda'. What, however, is the validity of this position? Its analysis enables us to identify some profound aspects of social work.

Postmodernism has become very fashionable as a way of looking at social work (McBeath and Webb, 1991; Chambon and Irving, 1994; Parton, 1994a, 1994b, 1994c; Howe, 1994; Leonard, 1997; Meinert, 1998; Martinez-Brawley, 1999; Walker, 2001; Pease, 2002). The cynical might suggest that it is the latest in a long line of 'positions' (even fads) adopted by social work, or more precisely social work writers, from the emphasis on psychoanalysis, through Marxist models of practice, to the current interest in postmodernism itself. All these have a key element in common – that their origins lie outside social work. As intellectual positions, they emerged through psychology or psychiatry, sociology or politics, and they were seen as novel or interesting ways to view social work.

The apparent attraction of postmodernism is exemplified by Payne (1997). Viewing the proliferation of theories to guide social work practice, he suggested that a postmodern stance would enable practitioners the better to criticise, analyse and develop theories to meet client needs. This is because of the view held by postmodernists that there is no 'single truth', no knowledge which has a privileged status, better than any other perspectives. All perspectives have an equal claim to validity, to be treated seriously, and none can claim precedence over another. Thus we can expect to see a range of competing theories: it is entirely appropriate.

We can, however, distinguish two approaches. One seeks to analyse developments in social work from a postmodern position: how far, it is asked, are developments in social work a reflection of society having reached a stage of postmodernity? Social work here is the object of analysis. The other, reflected in Payne's approach, is to take a postmodern position in relation to the *conduct of social work* – that is, to see the practitioner (and occupation) *as* postmodernist, incorporating the assumptions and perspectives characteristic of postmodernism. In fact, to the extent that the former analysis leads writers to view social work as somehow 'postmodern', the boundaries between the first position (the external analysis of social work), and the second (the view of social workers as 'practising postmodernists') tends to be blurred.

What is it about postmodernism that attracts these writers? Postmodernism refers to an approach to the development of society, or societies or (indeed) cultures, which asserts that we have gone beyond the stage of modernism. Each of these two stages (modernism and postmodernism) involves clusters of characteristics by which societies or cultures may be recognised. Very broadly, postmodernism refers to the description of key facets of societal changes and development which have occurred on a global level. These changes involve fundamental developments, not only in significant aspects of our social lives, such as the organisation of work, but also in attitudes to such basic matters as the standing of knowledge and expertise, the status of values, and relationships between different cultures.

Changes in the organisation of work have occurred to a considerable degree, but not solely, as a result of developments in information technology. Increasingly work is characterised by flexibility and fragmentation, key notions in postmodernist analysis. In fast-changing work situations, it becomes necessary to create flexibility within organisations and, consequently, the capacity quickly to alter work patterns. Just as organisations require such flexibility, so workers need to manifest that flexibility. One of the key elements emerging is the growing importance of contractual arrangements, made between smaller-scale units, or between smaller units and larger organisations. The organisation of work, then, becomes characterised by contractual relations, a growing flexibility and a growth of fragmentation.

However, the 'fragmentation' goes further than this. Fragmentation can also refer to the ways in which different cultures become the focus for postmodernist analysis, and the locus around which knowledge and values form. Postmodernists argue that there has been a decline in confidence in the ideas of universal truths or values. These refer to truths or values which transcend cultures, time and geography. They are, postmodernists suggest, truths which are deemed to have some objective quality, a presentation of what we know about our world. It covers knowledge of science and of society.

Postmodernists, however, suggest that knowledge is dispersed and local – that is it resides within particular cultures and gains its validity from those cultures. Knowledge, then, is that which any particular culture regards as knowledge. It does not exist outside the belief, within that culture, that some piece of information constitutes knowledge. This can, of course, differ from one culture to another. However, assert postmodernists, there are no universal criteria by which we can establish that one form of knowledge is superior to another. One culture, for example, may assert that justice is to be manifested in terms of desert, and only desert. Those who work hardest should, on this principle (for example), be given the greatest rewards. Another culture may assert that need, and only need, provides the basis for the distribution of resources. In this case, those whose need is greatest, for example those in poverty or otherwise disadvantaged, would be those to whom priority would be given in the distribution of resources.

Behind this is a growth of doubt. If the modernist period, generally seen as lasting from the Renaissance until the mid-twentieth century, was characterised by a belief in the possibility of progress, the possibility that we can accrue knowledge about our world and society over time, that science could offer solutions to practical and natural problems while social science could help resolve societal problems, then the postmodern period is marked by a withdrawal from such confidence. Doubt exists about the possibility of transcendental 'objective' knowledge, about the capacity of science to identify and resolve problems in the natural world and (especially) of social science to resolve problems in the social world. Where in the past, for example, a belief may have existed that appropriate analysis of social problems (through social science) would identify the causes of those problems, the solutions to them and thence the means by which solutions could be implemented, such beliefs have been overtaken by doubt. We no longer suffer the naïve belief that programmes for offenders will eradicate criminality in society, any more than changing social circumstances will deal with mental health problems.

This knowledge relativism is mirrored in a value relativism. Just as there are no criteria by which any form of knowledge may be given a privileged position, so there is no system of values which may be privileged. There are no overarching criteria by which we can judge one value system to be superior to another, and in the absence of any such criteria, it is necessary to ascribe equal validity to different value systems. It is not possible, in other words, to criticise the set of values characteristic of one culture on the basis of values held in another. Each is valid in its own right. Such views in relation to social work, some might argue, would provide a bulwark against powerful groups (most often male and white) asserting the superiority of their value systems as against those of less powerful (often female and black) groups.

The absence of certainty, the development of doubt and the impossibility of appealing to some universal knowledge and values have left society (postmodernists suggest) in a position where risk is the key factor to consider. Contemporary society, it is suggested (Beck, 1992), is characterised by uncertainty and multiple choices. Lacking the sense of certainty which prevailed when order, progress and the possibility of objective knowledge were widely accepted, contemporary society becomes the 'risk society'. Alongside uncertainty and multiple choices goes a tendency to calculate the odds and to leave the mind open to possibilities for taking action.

The risk society is risk-aversive. Protection from harm is crucial. Knowledge does not produce stable possibilities, but rather is characterised by the chance of unintended consequences. Shorn of the opportunity to predict with any certainty, it is necessary to weigh up risks, and to calculate which, of a range of options, is the best to take.

Postmodern society, therefore, is characterised by fragmentation, by a pervasive sense of doubt, by an absence of any certain knowledge, objectivity or universal truths. Knowledge, or 'truths', are 'local', and relativism summarises the position of both knowledge and values. In the absence of certainty and the presence of doubt, society becomes the 'risk society', in which the calculation of risk is the basis for action.

Social work and postmodernism

Having (briefly) outlined some main themes in postmodernism, I want to look at them in relation to social work. My concern here is not to carry out a thoroughgoing critical appraisal of postmodernism, although such work is available and quite trenchant (for example, Smith and White, 1997; Atherton and Bolland, 2002a). Rather, I want to examine postmodernism in terms of the extent to which it can characterise social work. In other words, I want to answer the question: can social work be postmodernist? My answer is that it most definitely cannot, and that this becomes apparent when one examines key assumptions underlying postmodernism and puts these against key facets of social work, or *conditions necessary for its very existence. In order to be postmodernist, social work would cease to be social work.*

Attractive though these ideas may be, therefore, on the surface, they are dangerously antithetical to social work. Postmodernism becomes an important 'knowledge case study' which warns us of the limits to forms of knowledge with which social work can engage and yet remain social work.

In pursuit of this, I wish to examine three discrete, but crucial, areas. These are: fragmentation, knowledge and doubt, and values and relativism.

Fragmentation

The first, and shortest, of these areas is fragmentation. It is important to understand what fragmentation *cannot* mean. It is perfectly possible for there to be diverse elements, or ranges of activities, in social work, just as there are in other occupational areas. We can distinguish, for example, in medicine, between epidemiologists, surgeons, psychiatrists and paediatricians. Each is active in a separate segment of a unified whole that is medicine. Applied to social work, this would mean that there would be separate elements of social work, but they too would be part of a unified whole.

Fragmentation refers to a 'breaking apart' of some formerly unified object. In this case, fragmentation would refer to a breaking up of social work into separate parts. It is important to recognise this, for it is quite possible, otherwise, to mistake segmentation for fragmentation. Fragmentation would indicate just such a 'break up' of social work. How justifiable are such claims?

It is customary for those of a postmodern ilk to identify the 1970s as the 'high-water mark' of modernism in social work (Parton, 1994a, 1994b; Howe, 1994; McBeath and Webb, 1991; Walker, 2001). This, it is suggested, was reflected in two fundamental features. First, in Britain at least, aspects of social work which had been disparately organised came together in single social service departments. Prior to that we had child care officers, mental welfare officers and education welfare officers, all in different organisational contexts. Most of these came together under one organisation: the social services department. In these departments, although few social workers were at first qualified, social work represented the leading influence, and there was optimism (reflected in the Seebohm Report (Seebohm Report, 1968), which led to the establishment of social services departments) that this would lead to more coherent, unified service for clients. Personal social welfare would be provided through social services departments.

Secondly, much effort went into writing about a unified social work. A number of prominent authors sought to present a case for social work as a single unitary entity, whose disparate activities could be brought together under a single rubric. Thus we had terms like 'unitary' social work (Goldstein, 1973), or 'systems theory', in which authors sought to devise a guide on how to bring together the various 'levels' at which social work could be practised, including everything from intra-psychic elements to the macro level of society (Pincus and Minahan, 1973). Others tried to explain the structure of social work in terms of some single, unifying perspective. Thus, Bartlett (1970) suggested that while, for example, doctors were concerned with health and illness, social workers were concerned with social functioning.

These two features contrast dramatically with social work developments since the 1980s. This has been, it is suggested, a period of 'welfare pluralism' (Parton, 1994a). This has a number of facets. First, there is a greater emphasis on plural provision. Much of that formerly known as social work is now called social care. Much, also, is provided by voluntary agencies and private organisations, at times involving non-qualified workers. This contrasts with a previous situation, it is suggested, whereby services were largely provided by one organisation – the social services department. This has reflected fragmentation of services, which are now more dispersed.

The multiple sites for service provision have led to the growth of contractual, rather than hierarchical, accountability. Where in the past, individuals were responsible to those bureaucratically senior to them in an organisation, they now engage in inter-organisational relations which are specific, written and formal. This is particularly apparent in the split between purchaser and provider, characteristic of care management.

The social work role, it is suggested, has been split. Probation officers were required to have a qualification separate from social work, emphasising the difference of their roles. Care management provided for two separate roles – the purchaser, who carried out assessments, bought in services and reviewed the effectiveness of these services, and the provider, who actually carried out the interventions to maintain, alleviate or resolve problems and needs.

This, in effect, split the casework role, which was central to social work identity. Casework provided an internally coherent knowledge base, formulated on the 'psy complex' (the analysis of the individual in their immediate social environment), in which social workers not only carried out assessments, but followed up *themselves* with intervention (Parton, 1994a; Rose 1985). Alongside this, the *modus operandi* of social work changed. In the past social casework had sought to understand the individuals they worked with, seeking to explain their actions and, on the basis of this explanation, undertaking informed, knowledge-based intervention. Social workers have replaced these 'depth explanations' by the examination of surface performance. Social workers became concerned to control behaviour, rather than understand people, preventing the abusive act or criminal behaviour. The emphasis here was increasingly on procedures, contractual relations and so on, in an attempt to gain greater control over areas of social life (such as mental health, offending and child abuse) characterised by uncertainty and risk.

However, this (admittedly brief) summary of the postmodernist position suggests it is hugely overdrawn. First, it was never the case that these different elements of social work were as organisationally unified as is implied by postmodernists. Probation officers remained in probation departments (in England in any case), hospital social workers were often based in hospitals, mental health social workers were often in community mental health centres and education welfare officers were often in education departments. We may note the separate qualification of probation officers (in England), and even the dispersal of social workers in organisations, some of them (such as mental health authorities) hybrid. But social work never needed a single organisational base to be recognised as social work.

Second, there was no great unifying movement in social work literature, at least to the extent implied. Those that did formulate unitary conceptions of social work, such as the systems theorists, were arguably merely providing an overarching umbrella for the range of social work activities, rather than a deeper-level unifying conceptual analysis. Indeed, it remained the case that there was an ever-growing – some might say bewildering – range of 'theories' with which social workers might seek to deal with areas of their work. Indeed, these were so wide that some quite prominent academics (such as Sheldon, 1978) wrote disparagingly of the growth of social work theories with no criteria to choose which were most efficacious. If social work is fragmented by the range of forms of knowledge available to it (and it is arguable that this is segmentation rather than fragmentation), one may comment that 'twas ever thus'.

This reflects, furthermore, a salutary dose of modesty in social work in relation to its knowledge. There was no time during which social work was able to claim that it had the formula to resolve consistently the deep-seated problems of those with whom it operated. If workers held such thoughts, reviews of effectiveness would soon have disabused them of such confidence (Fischer, 1976), although subsequent reviews have painted much more optimistic scenarios (Sheldon, 1986; Macdonald and Sheldon, 1992). Indeed, if the 1970s were the 'high-water mark' of modernism in social work, they began with their most famous child death tragedy (in Britain), that of Maria Colwell, which hugely shook confidence in social work, both within and outside the occupation. Social workers themselves have long held certain reservations about the easy applicability of social science knowledge to social work practice (Marsh and Triselliotis,1996).

It is, in short, difficult to identify the time when social work had the kind of confidence in its efficacy which is implied by postmodernists, and from which, according to their tale, social work has had to withdraw in the face of evidence that such confidence is unsustainable.

We may recognise developments in nomenclature, particularly in the advent of the term 'social care'. However, it would be a mistake to see all aspects of what is now social care to have been part of what was formerly termed social work. There have always been non-qualified workers (many of them in Britain working as social workers in the early 1970s), amongst whom could be included residential care workers, home helps and family support workers. Much of this work, although often engaged in the first place by social workers, was not carried out by social workers, and only termed social work to the extent that social workers engaged such people to help in their work.

Indeed, this reflects a further aspect of social work, including social casework. Although previously there had been no formal divide between assessment and intervention, purchaser and provider, the use of others in carrying out their intervention was commonplace in social work. Social workers did not 'do' everything, but engaged home helps, day care centres, family centres and the like to carry out caring tasks.

Finally, we may comment that care management is no longer (if it ever was) the all-pervasive influence it appeared (to some) to be during the 1990s. There has been a considerable retreat, in Britain, from the excesses of care management, and social workers (for example in child care) do, in fact, carry out both assessments and interventions on a large scale, much as they ever did. The analysts of postmodernism who called care management to their aid now seem peculiarly imprisoned in a very narrow time frame indeed – an imprisonment not really necessary, even at the time, provided continuities, as well as change, had been properly observed (Sheppard, 1995).

Knowledge

Postmodernists are unavoidably interpretivists. Pardeck and his colleagues (1994a, 1994b; Pardeck and Murphy, 1993) comment to that effect in their generally positive stance about a relationship between postmodernism and social work. Of course this might appear to replace one piece of jargon with another, but it does give us important insights.

The first thing to note about this approach is that knowledge is socially generated – it arises within a particular context. Thus if one is asking the question: 'how is it that some information is counted by humans in any particular culture as knowledge?', we would be drawn to an answer which suggests that we should look to the cultural context. The kind of thing we would be looking to are the norms and expectations present in that society or culture. We could look also to those processes by which that which the society views to be knowledge comes to be viewed as knowledge. Indeed, we could even ask further questions: 'what do they mean by knowledge?' or 'do they have a concept of knowledge?' Thus, what counts as knowledge will be likely to differ as between different cultures.

In this context, 'culture' is a realm of 'shared meaning'. That is, those people in the society which has any particular culture subscribe to the same sorts (or system) of views and beliefs about the world. These beliefs relate to all aspects of social life, human beings as well as what we know as a society. These, in turn, involve interpretations of the world. When we look at the world, we make sense of it by making interpretations.

While the point is made in a postmodern context, it applies as much to historical as to contemporary cultures. So, for example, ancient Egyptians used to rely absolutely on the flooding of the Nile from one year to the next. If it did not flood, the consequences for them were catastrophic, being deprived of both water and fertile soil to grow their crops. They were in constant fear that chaos would overtake their world, and that they were therefore permanently at risk of catastrophes, like the failure of the Nile to flood, occurring.

The concept of Maat, in which balance could be created out of this potential chaos, was important to them. To ensure order was maintained in their world (Maat) it was necessary to ensure the god Amun looked benignly upon them. This was achieved in a number of ways, one of which was through the Pharaoh. The Egyptians believed that it was necessary to communicate with the gods through the Pharaoh who was himself a god and upon whom, therefore, great responsibility was placed to ensure the welfare of his people. He would annually privately attend the temple at Thebes, during which he communed with the god Amun, to ensure that Maat was created, and the people's welfare was assured. This included (it particularly included) the flooding of the Nile. When the Nile flooded, this was seen to be because of the benign work of Amun, the intercession on their behalf by the Pharaoh, and evidence that Maat was observed.

For the Egyptians, therefore, their interpretation of the origins of the annual flooding of the Nile rested on deep religious beliefs, which served to maintain the civil order of society, with the key position attributed to the Pharaoh. The flooding of the Nile was not simply a natural occurrence (although it was that), it was one to be understood in relation to the acts of their gods and the position of the Pharaohs. Their 'knowledge' related to their religion, gods and Pharaohs.

Just as we can look to past culture for interpretations, so we can look to different cultures characterised by differing interpretations today. For West African societies, sexual mutilation of women is part of a process defining womanhood. In mainstream Europe it is seen as abuse. For many Israelis, the building of a wall between Israeli and Palestinian communities is seen as a necessary defensive act. For many Palestinians it is an act of aggression, highly provocative. The acts of the IRA, defensive and political in the eyes of many Irish Catholics, were seen as simple murder by Irish Protestants. I cite here extreme examples, simply to highlight the significance of interpretation.

All knowledge unavoidably involves interpretation (that is the position of postmodernists). When this is allied to the importance of culture and shared meaning we find two highly significant points. The first is that knowledge is 'local' – that is, that which is considered knowledge is embedded within a culture, and this may vary between cultures. So what is knowledge in one culture is not deemed knowledge in another. The second is that no one form of knowledge, or knowledge claim, is superior to another. It is not possible to suggest knowledge existent within one culture is superior or inferior to that within another. This is because there are no criteria (it is believed) by which one form of knowledge my be judged superior to another, and all observations on the world, including the social world, are necessarily interpretations. There are, as postmodernists are fond of saying, no universal truths. What we have, therefore, are culturally based interpretations (or 'local knowledge').

Some (apparent) consequences for social work

For social work, it is suggested that one of the key consequences of this position is that communicative competence is placed at the heart of practice. The various interpretations of the social world are expressed, it is thought, through language (Barthes, 1985). Thus, language becomes central to this communicative competence. Such competence enables the social worker both to express themselves in a way understood by the client, and also to find a way to understand what the client wants to convey. Since we are all in the business of interpreting, we are seeking accurately to interpret others' interpretations, and to enable them to interpret accurately our interpretations. Such, it is thought, is the nature of reflexivity (Pardeck et al., 1994a).

Thus, social work is in the business of understanding and conveying meaning accurately. Social workers are not, it is thought, legitimately involved in the assessment of facts, objectively undertaken, diagnosing the clients' problems, and identifying means to resolve those problems (a curiously detached relationship with the imperatives of the real world).

A rather different view is taken by Walker (2001), arising from similar assumptions, however. Without universal truths, there is a decline in confidence in the efficacy and progress of knowledge in solving human problems. Social work suffers from a similar process, in which uncertainty becomes the key to understanding practice. If social workers cannot claim they can resolve problems using the methods at their disposal (and in this respect they were seriously undermined by the child death scandals, which periodically occurred), then some other means needed to be found to deal with these problems. Instead of resolving problems, therefore, they are in the business of managing uncertainty. Risk becomes the key term which underlies much of social work practice.

The consequence is that monitoring, assessment and analysis of risk become central to social work (Lupton, 1999). Social workers are expected to have competencies in the assessment of, and response to, risk. These competencies are behaviourally based and, in some form or another, measurable (at least in the assessment of student social workers). Alongside this, procedures become highly significant. It is the capacity to follow these, rather than the possession of some esoteric knowledge, which becomes most significant for practice. Likewise, an emphasis on management and monitoring of the social worker's own practice comes to the fore.

A third feature, it is argued, emerges in the relationship between worker and client (Pocock, 1995). If knowledge is tenuous and 'local', then how can we sustain the position of the expert? The position of the expert is grounded on the idea that he or she has particular knowledge – expertise – in certain facets of social life. In its clearest form, the client approaches the expert for help, which the latter is able to give on the basis of their knowledge, and (ideally) the client goes away happy with their problems dealt with. However, this position requires us to have some meaningful notion of both expert and knowledge, which breaks down in the face of knowledge uncertainty. This is further damaged by the (apparent) very public failure of social workers to protect children, with highly visible child deaths. Indeed, why cannot the client themselves be seen as the expert (Smale et al., 1993)? This neatly reverses the hierarchical relationship between worker and client. The social worker–client relationship becomes equal: potentially, with the client given 'expertise', the latter can become the expert in his or her own life.

Social work assumptions and the marginalising of postmodernism

Assuming for the moment that these postmodern consequences for social work are accurately portrayed, how suitable can we consider such an analysis for social work? An important problem here is that one question ('how is it that some information is counted by humans in any particular culture as knowledge?') is insidiously replaced by another ('what counts as knowledge?' or 'what can we know'?). The former requires us to look at the ways cultures operate, and to make some empirical observations about societal behaviour perceptions and actions in relation to what people consider 'real', or things that they can 'know'. Thus, some societies may contain a wide belief in magic and witchcraft, while others may not, placing greater faith in science.

The latter question, however, requires us to look at the logic by which knowledge is gained, providing (on grounds of reason) a way of identifying what may count as knowledge as compared with prejudice or faith. By what process, for example, should we find out whether the earth goes round the sun, or the sun round the earth? We can recognise that different societies have different views about the relationship between the sun and earth. Thus, the mediaeval church was adamant the sun went round the earth, while twenty-first-century European society generally regards the reverse to be the case. Which, though, is correct? Even the church today would accede that the earth goes round the sun.

The key here is that interpretivists – and hence postmodernists – obscure the difference between the two types of question . The first ('how is it that some information is counted by humans in any particular culture as knowledge?') is properly a sociological question. The latter ('what counts as knowledge?' or 'what can we know?') is properly one of epistemology – that is, the philosophy of knowledge. The consequences are serious. It means that knowledge is no more nor less than what any one culture says it is. Thus, to take our example further, the view that the earth goes round the sun has no greater credence than that which states that the sun goes round the earth. Each position is equally valid. The fact that no self-respecting astronomer – indeed any reasonably informed and educated human being – would give equal credence to these two statements is of no consequence. This situation is clearly absurd, and arises because of the confusion of two completely different kinds of question, and because postmodernists refuse to accede to the idea that different kinds of information have greater or less claim to legitimacy as forms of knowledge, depending on the process by which that information is gained.

However, we can go further than this, because (in this respect) the 'assumptive world' of social work coincides with this rather (common-sense) epistemological position. We can draw attention here to terms like 'child abuse' or 'mental health'. There are those that suggest that both are contested concepts. For example, we have already seen how parental actions which were widely considered to be legitimate in Victorian times, and which involved beating, are now considered to be abusive. Terms like 'spare the rod and spoil the child' and 'children should be seen and not heard' were widely prevalent. Child abuse, it is suggested therefore (DoH, 1995), should be understood as an essentially relative concept, one which changes in time and place.

Underlying this is an idea that this is a matter of a changed value base. Formerly desirable behaviours, deserving approbation, have become undesirable behaviours, deserving disapprobation. That this is the case there can be no doubt. Clearly the ways children are regarded, as well as what are considered desirable and undesirable parental behaviours, have changed over time.

It may be, therefore, that a change in values has created a change in 'label', and that these involve changes in time and place, but does that mean that it is not in some sense 'real'? We now have far better access to information about the consequence of abuse on children. From Bowlby onwards (Rutter, 1981, 1999), we have become ever more aware of the effect of maltreatment, both in the short and long term, on children. Actions, therefore, which might have been considered conducive to the creation of a well-balanced individual or good citizen in the nineteenth century, we now know, are more likely to be psychologically and, at times, physically damaging. Thus, forms of parenting now regarded as abusive are not simply regarded to be wrong, but to cause pain and suffering to the child.

Not 'sparing the rod' today, however, would be considered as a case of child abuse within social work (and indeed widely outside it). Furthermore, legislation which requires that the 'wishes and feelings of the child' should be considered whenever making decisions about them could hardly be further than the Victorian adage about being 'seen and not heard'. The point is, as we have noted earlier, that social work moves between the objective status of a person (as a child abuser) and their subject (as a person in their own right).

There is an unavoidable 'core of objectivity' in social work. Some statuses are implicitly and explicitly assumed *within* social work to be objective. The assumption that mental illness (and more broadly mental disorder) exists is evident in compulsory admissions assessments. Approved Social Workers are involved in a process, part of which is to determine whether or not the person is mentally ill. There is no process whereby they are expected to determine whether mental illness or disorder as a concept is, or is not, legitimate. Its legitimacy – its objective status in other words – is already assumed. The same goes for the concept of 'significant harm', which in child care legislation is associated with child abuse. That significant harm can occur is not a matter for debate when the social worker is carrying out an assessment of risk. It is only whether or not significant harm has occurred *in this particular case*.

None of this suggests that, as an *individual in their own right*, a person whose job is social work cannot have reservations about concepts like mental illness or child abuse, or even deny their legitimacy (though the practical effect of this might well be to make it difficult for them personally to carry out social work tasks). However *qua* social worker – that is, in their role as social worker – statuses like child abuse and mental illness are objective. Indeed it is part, as we have seen, of the way in which social work is conceptualised or defined.

We may take this still further. The very ideas of child abuse and significant harm to the child arise in a context in which the fact that significant harm to a child *can* occur as a result of certain parental actions is accepted. Where does this come from? It comes from 'the evidence'. There has been an accumulation of evidence to show this relationship between parental actions and harm to children, and this has had an impact on the legislation which both underwrites and defines social work.

Imagine if the opposite were the case. Suppose that research had shown that severe beatings did have good short-term and long-term effects on children. Children were immediately happy following a severe beating, they were better adjusted personally, happier and better citizens. No serious physical consequences arose. It is difficult to imagine, in that context, that legislation effectively banning severe beatings would have been put in place.

The point here is that social work is also tied thereby to a notion that knowledge may be created though the accumulation of evidence. Social work operates in a situation in which the assumption is not that the position in relation to parenting in Victorian Britain has equivalent legitimacy to that in contemporary society. Underlying social work is an assumption that evidence shows this not to be the case. Not all positions are regarded as equal in relation to knowledge. We now know that child abuse exits, and that it can cause significant harm to the child – that is an assumption within social work, because that underlies the legislation by which the very nature of social work is determined. The point here is that social work is built on a process which accepts that not all positions are equal, by virtue of their being accepted within any one culture, but that evidence which counts as knowledge can inform the way in which we understand the world.

This, it should be noted, predates notions of evidence-based knowledge, although it is not inconsistent with that approach. Social work, therefore, has an assumptive world in which some areas of social life (not necessarily all, nor necessarily all that social workers deal with) may be regarded as objective. Furthermore, social work is built on the assumption that some forms of evidence count as knowledge. In both respects, social work is entirely inconsistent with postmodernism. A coherent notion of social work and its realm, therefore, means that it, and its practitioners (in their capacity as social workers), cannot be postmodernists. If we analyse postmodernism from the vantage of social work, rather than vice versa (which is characteristically the way those who favour a postmodernist conception of social work operate), we find that the former is found severely wanting, and quite inappropriate as a way of 'seeing the world', or, indeed, practice.

Values

If there are, according to postmodernists, no universal truths and all 'truths' are 'local', then it is equally the case that there are no universal values. Just as there are no criteria by which we can plausibly assert one truth to be superior to another – to be more objective – so there are no criteria by which we are able to assert one set of values to be superior to another. Why is this? It is because, if we are to assert the superiority of one set of values over another, then we would need to have a set of criteria which stood outside, and above, the various systems of morality which already exist. So argue the postmodernists.

We are here again presented with a confusion of questions. There is, on the one hand, the sociological question: 'what are the values characteristic of particular cultures, and how do they differ from those of other cultures?' On the other hand, there is the question, appropriate to moral philosophy: 'what should we do?' or 'how should we act?' The first question requires empirical analysis. What are the various cultures? What are the values characteristic of those cultures? What is the relationship between culture and values or moral standards? When diverse cultures nevertheless have similar moralities, what are the reasons for this?

The second question is rather different. It is an exercise in reasoning. It requires us to argue a case which, while it may draw upon empirical evidence, does not necessarily link us to one particular culture or other. One way of looking at this may be in terms of some profound principle, such as 'the greatest happiness for the greatest number' – a utilitarian principle. If we are to answer the question 'what should I do?' or 'how should I act?', the answer would be 'in accordance with a set of moral principles which ensures the greatest happiness for the greatest number'.

Another principle may, however, be one which refers to self-realisation. This refers to a position where humans reach a state of 'rational autonomy' – that is, in which their actions are guided by a combination of reason and clear moral principles. Again, in answer to the question 'what should I do?' or 'how should I act?', it would be according to a principle which emphasises decision making as both rational and moral. We could argue that the morality of acts is determined by their outcome, or that morality is invested in the acts themselves, for example, what a person does or the intentions when they are carried out. The key to all this, however, is that such consideration is not the prisoner of culture. It is not limited to, or presented in terms of, one culture or another. It is a reasoning process, by which thinkers seek to identify ethical principles.

Indeed, some writers have sought to emphasise the bankruptcy of relying on what they call 'social morality' (Milne, 1968). This is a level of ethical awareness and of actions which tie in with the established morality of a particular society. This, it is argued, however, is surely not the highest principle upon which ethics can be based. What of the limits to any established morality? If we define ourselves in terms of the established morality, we are tied to the status quo. It is profoundly conservative. It is also profoundly limiting. Should not the rational moral person be able to reflect upon the established morality of the time? Should they not critically appraise it, and act according to their own judgements? If they do not, they are not fully autonomous – they are not properly making decisions for themselves. Their acts are prescribed (by the prevailing social morality) rather than based on reason.

Interestingly, such thinking does not prevent one examining values prevalent in culture other than one's own. Indeed, such examination may actually help the process of reasoning about the ethical basis for actions to be taken. However, this in no way assumes that cultures have equal claims to moral excellence, and that there are no criteria to choose between them. We are not reduced to what is termed a 'cultural relativism'.

The position of postmodernists is one that should be profoundly uncomfortable for social workers. There are clear problems with this moral relativism, problems which could be argued with no reference to social work at all. However, that is not the primary point of the argument presented here. The discomfort arises from something else: that social work, by its very nature cannot be morally relativistic in this way.

As with its stance on truth, postmodernism offers, on the surface, a seductive route for social work. By suggesting that values are local, that no one set can be proclaimed to be superior to another, it appears to appeal to a sense of fairness and equality, even of anti-racism. By what right, it would assert, can you, as a white social worker, proclaim the superiority of your principles, over the values of some other culture? Indeed, this is an approach which characterised colonial attitudes and imperialism – the superiority of the white man (sic) over the less advanced indigenous population which made up parts of the empire. In (quite rightly) reacting against such smug superiority, it might be argued, do we not justifiably treat values characteristic of all cultures equally?

The central problem resides with the assumptions underlying this position. If no one system of values can be proclaimed superior to another, by what right can social work itself have a code of ethics? What, indeed, is the point of this code? It is no better than any other code. First, there is no reason to adhere to it, other than it may represent the personal preference of a particular individual or group. It reduces adherence to ethics to an answer which justifies actions in terms of the statement 'because I like it', or 'because that's what I want to do'. One might also adhere to a code of ethics because if one did not, one might be professionally 'struck off'. If you broke the code of ethics you may no longer be able to practise as a social worker. But again, that reduces morality to a profoundly self-serving exercise – following the code simply because it preserves your job.

Take the anti-racist position outlined above. What are the consequences of the moral relativism underlying postmodernism? Well, it is actually to undermine your own anti-racist position. If no moral stance should take precedence over any other moral stances, then what are the grounds for asserting one's anti-racist stance over that, say, of the Ku Klux Klan? Theirs is, historically, the tradition of the lynch mob, of the assertion of the superiority of the white race (sic) over black people, of the systematic exploitation and exclusion from power of all who are not seen to be white.

Is this the way social work should be conducted? If not, on what grounds should we exclude such conduct? We could argue that it is against the social work code of ethics. But we are immediately presented with the riposte: on what grounds may you assert the superiority of your code of ethics over that of the Ku Klux Klan? If you are morally relativistic, then there are no grounds.

The position, which is inherent in social work itself, however, necessarily precludes the moral relativism of postmodernism. It does so because of its inherent commitment to the subject and its associated moral stance of respecting persons or human beings. This is not simply some 'add on' extra to social work, something which social workers decided they should commit themselves to. It is part of the necessary conditions for actions to be recognised as social work actions, and as modern social work emerged, so these facets emerged as integral aspects. If a social worker were to be asked 'why should you not adopt the values of the Ku Klux Klan?', the answer is fairly straightforward: because in doing so we do violence to people as human beings, because (at the very least) we are not respecting them as persons or human beings, because in doing so we are denying their subject status, as people who are worthy of innate value. *It is because, in short, it would not be social work.* The hate-filled prescriptions of the Ku Klux Klan are excluded from social work precisely because social work is inherently not morally relativistic, and cannot be so.

Atherton and Bolland (2002a) have drawn attention to the attraction of postmodernism to some feminists – of some importance given the influence feminism has had on social work over the past two decades. One can see how the emphasis on pluralism of ideas might be attractive to a feminism which was seeking to establish itself against a more mainstream – 'malestream' – dominant ideas. Pluralism of ideas would provide a means, it might be thought, to open up a space for feminist thought. However, as Atherton and Bolland (2002a) note, this is problematic, because feminism is a principled argument for the recognition of a set of preferred values, whilst postmodernism denies that there are any such constructs (values) that have any meaning. There are no criteria by which 'preferred values' may be identified. Brown (1994) suggests postmodernism puts feminism in a bind. Women, Brown thinks, have a distinct spot from which to view the world, but postmodernism argues that it does not matter in the end.

To the extent that social work is feminist, therefore, it follows that postmodernism represents an inappropriate – contradictory in fact – set of ideas. However, we need to ask ourselves what it is about (some) feminist ideas which make them appropriate for social work, while postmodernism is not. It is not a matter of whether postmodernism is consistent with a set of ideas like feminism, but whether it is consistent with social work itself. At the heart of feminism is a commitment to the innate value of humans which is apparent in social work. The problem for feminists (at a very basic level) is that society is constituted in such a way as to deprive women of the respect and opportunities which would flow from women being recognised as having innate value.

It is not enough, therefore, for Atherton and Bolland (2002a) to argue that postmodernism and feminism are inconsistent with each other. This would be of no concern to social work if it were not for the *appropriateness* of the relationship of feminism to social work. It is in their commitment to the innate value and worth of humans that, at the level of values, social work and feminism achieve some harmony. Of course, the legitimacy of this symmetry of positions depends on the legitimacy of the case feminists put forward. Again, though, postmodernists can give no positions any special status, because there are no universal truths, no positions which can claim to have precedence over any others. The very idea of a 'legitimate case' put forward by feminists is alien to postmodernism.

Postmodernists, then, cannot commit themselves even to the concept of innate worth and value of human beings, because such ideas are simply discourse, preferences which have no right to precedence over other positions which may be diametrically opposing.

Hugman (2001) and Crimeen and Wilson (1997) have argued that social work has a distinct and definable value base, and that the value base should be used to 'get a bearing' on the way in which the profession should respond to postmodernist ideas and developments. Social work should not, they suggest, operate from a full-blown pluralism, because such a position contradicts the value base. The paedophile, the landlord unlawfully trying to evict tenants, those who engage in domestic violence – all have their own 'truths', but in the everyday world of practice, social workers make decisions and take actions based on the view that these 'truths' are less plausible than others (Leonard, 1997). It follows, Hugman suggests, that, notwithstanding any influence of postmodernism, or plurality of ethics, the social work education processes should equip students to make their own informed choices with respect to professional values.

With this, I think, we can agree. Clearly if social workers are to be moral agents – and in the sense meant in moral philosophy this is exactly what they must be – then they need to be clear about their actions, the moral base for them and the reasoning which links the moral base to these actions. However, I would suggest, Hugman (2001) does not – explicitly at least – go far enough. It is not enough to 'follow' a code of ethics or even to make personal judgements, laudable though both may be. One is still left with the argument – why should you choose to follow this code of ethics, if it can claim no moral superiority over any other morality?

The answer lies in the very nature of social work. To 'do' social work, certain values need be inherent in the actions of social workers. An inherent position of social work is that all value positions are not equal in status, and this is reflected in the code of ethics adopted. Social workers are not in the business of suggesting that it is a matter of opinion whether a woman is beaten up by her partner or a four-year-old is sexually abused by an adult. *It is inherent in their position that they cannot be morally neutral in the face of such social, and personal, issues.*

Conclusion

I have argued here that postmodern tenets are profoundly at odds with social work. There can be no such thing as 'postmodernist social work' because the key positions of postmodernism are flagrantly antithetical to social work itself.

Perhaps a key problem lies with the expanse of the intellectual terrain which postmodernists purport to examine. It may be, for example, that a concern for tolerance, which is manifested by postmodernists – specifically warning us against the dangers of totalitarianism inherent in commitments to universal truths – is a particular area which may be examined. Likewise, we might look to the public perception of science and social science. How far, we might ask, is there confidence in the ideas of social science as a means for improvement and progress in society? We may also examine society in terms of cultures, identifying areas of difference and fragmentation. However, postmodernists seek to bring these, and other features, together in an all-embracing examination of the postmodern condition. Furthermore, those that profess to be postmodernists are committed to particular intellectual positions. They do this while asserting the 'death' of general theory.

It may be too much to suggest that postmodernism presents itself a general theory, partly because it does not have the detail which might properly be its characteristic. However, postmodernists, with their emphasis on culture, and the local, on relativism of both knowledge and morals, and the breadth of their undertaking, come close to having a general theory which denies the validity of general theory.

This tendency to bring disparate areas together, as if a single statement were made, is evident in Parton's (1994a, p. 93) comment on social work. He writes: 'The notion of the generic social worker working in the unified agency and drawing upon casework informed by particular forms of psychology and displaying particular skills in human relationships seems outmoded.' In this, Parton brings together generic social work(er) *and* the unified agency *and* casework *and* particular forms of psychology *and* particular skills in human relationships, in one statement 'of being outmoded'. I do not wish to be over-critical of Parton, who is a distinguished scholar and who shows some care in his writing about postmodernism, as well as awareness of the dangers of nihilism. However, this does demonstrate – and in relation only to social work – the tendency to cluster a range of areas together, presenting it as a single creed or analysis. This is a tendency evident in postmodernism as a whole.

However, postmodernism suffers also from the erection of a 'straw position'. It insists that we either accept 'universal truths' or the impossibility of truths other than those local and socially constructed (indeed, these are metaphorical truths). That is, that we can only accept perspectives, none more valid than the other. In this it does a major disservice to our understanding of knowledge. Realists have long recognised that truths may be provisional, based on the capacity of theories to provide the best explanation of any particular phenomena. The best explanation for any particular thing is that which explains it most accurately and comprehensively.

In science, Newtonian physics seemed to provide the best explanation of the workings of the universe until relativity theory emerged. The latter provided a more all-embracing explanation of the universe, and was able to account for certain aspects which Newtonian physics could not. Each was true in its own way. Relativity theory, though, was 'better'. However, postmodernism deliberately refuses to accept that any knowledge may be superior because it explains more or is supported better by evidence. All have equal validity, and this must always be the case. If so, we are left with the position, as shown earlier, that it is as legitimate to suggest the sun goes round the earth as that the earth goes round the sun.

This leaves us with a more sophisticated position than postmodernism is prepared to consider. We can accept that knowledge can be both objective and provisional. We can also accept the possibility that some areas of knowledge are contested (for example, by rival explanations). It may even be possible to accept that, in some cases, these contested areas of knowledge have different but equally valid explanations (that is, one theory or explanation is as good as another). This, however, does not lead us to the wholesale rejection of the possibility of objective knowledge, nor of the possibility of truth, even if provisional. This attunes much more closely with the way social work operates than with postmodernism, and we will be exploring this further in subsequent chapters.

Chapter six

Need

Some writers have suggested that, in recent years, there has been a shift from an emphasis on a 'response to need' to a 'response to risk' orientation in social work (Parton, 1994a; Walker, 2001). In fact, need still provides a focal point for policy documents concerning social work intervention. Indeed, as we shall see later, there is a strong link between the concepts of need and of risk, in the form of 'harm to the individual'. It is, therefore, quite appropriate to place the issue of need at the heart of social work practice. However, the significance of social exclusion to social work indicates that this, too, should be considered in relation to need. In what sense is need relevant to social work? And how does it relate to social work's concern with social exclusion?

One way of looking at this is to consider the position of those socially excluded, relative to others in society. The implication of notions of social exclusion is that those excluded are deprived, when compared with others in society. They may, for example, be unable to participate fully in that society because of that deprivation. Those who are unemployed are (obviously) excluded from employment, an area in which most working-age adults are involved. However, as we have seen, there is considerable concern that the absence of employment becomes associated with other factors which serve to exclude in other areas of social life.

Individual areas, such as poverty, obviously place some at a disadvantage. To the extent that the basics of human life – an adequate diet, clothing and so on – are absent because of that poverty, such people may be seen to be in need. Likewise, others may be excluded on health grounds. Those with disability may be disadvantaged not just by the impact of the disability itself but by inadequate societal responses which restrict rather than enable them. Such people may be said to be 'in need'. The same goes for those with mental health problems, older people and others, who are part of a concern for social exclusion and who are also central to both the project and the idea of social work.

Social exclusion, then, and social work are concerned with those who are marginalised through some disadvantage. That disadvantage and the notion of social exclusion are consistent with the idea that they are, in some respect, in need. Need is therefore an appropriate and central facet of our analysis. However, this is not straightforward. In what sense is need an aspect of social work? How does this fit with social work's central concern with social exclusion? How are the three brought together? These are issues which require exploration.

Need and relativism

Rather as we discussed in the last chapter on postmodernism, there is a fundamental issue in relation to need, as to whether it can be considered an objective or relativist concept. In the previous chapter, we rejected, as inconsistent with the very idea of social work, the notion that objectivism could be completely removed from our understanding of social work issues. This leaves us with an 'objective core' to social work but also some room for manoeuvre beyond that core. This is something we will continue to explore, but what does this mean for our treatment of need?

One way of looking at need – in official documents – is that it is 'a dynamic concept, the definitions of which will change with national legislation, changes in local policy, the availability of resources, the patterns of local demand' (DoH, 1991a, p. 12). This relativistic approach indicates strongly that there is no 'objective content' to need: it simply refers to states which at one time or another, or one place or another, we define as need states. Indeed, this policy document goes further (DoH, 1991a, p. 12), suggesting that it is even a personal concept, changing according to the views of individuals who believe they are, or are not, in need. One person's state of need might be another's state of normality.

Smith's study (1980), although presented some time ago, is relevant here. He was interested in the relationship between the concept of need and the professionals, like social workers, who used it. Need, he argued, was an expression of particular preferences, expectations and definitions which occur in particular cultures. However, while being, in essence, the representation of subjective preferences (that is, the perspectives of individuals and groups), it is presented by key welfare groups *as if it were* objective. Need becomes seen as objective, because it is defined as such by people in positions of power.

At the legislative level, those powerful people would be legislators. At the practice level, when decisions are made about individual cases ('are these people in need?'), they are made by professionals. The objectification of need, in routine day-to-day practice, occurs through the successive judgements and actions of welfare practitioners. What are, in essence judgements of (say) child care, parenting or the quality of life of an older person, based on the standards of a particular culture, are presented as objective states. The family, or parent, is 'in need' because child care is not adequate. The older person is 'in need' because their quality of life is not good enough. Their objective status of 'being in need' is ascribed by professionals in positions of power to make such definitions. In reality, however, all such judgements, thinks Smith, are subjective and culture-dependent.

This position makes clear what a relativistic notion of need entails. There is no inherent content to need, no definition which can be applied across cultures and time periods. What is defined as need in one culture or time period would not be so defined in another. Need is what a culture, or person, defines it to be, nothing more, nothing less. We may define a family without a washing machine, at the beginning of the twenty-first century, as a family 'in need'. This would not be so at the beginning of the twentieth century, for the obvious reason that there were no washing machines! Need, in short can be given no plausible cross-cultural content (Winch, 1958, 1964).

This is, according to Runciman (1972), because the ways people view the world, the ways they view *their* world – their hopes, fears and expectations – are dependent upon the frame of reference that people use. In this he is alluding to reference groups – those groups against whom individuals assess their own position and aspirations. They are those groups to whom they *refer*, to judge their position. Any society may contain any number of groups. We might, for example, take as our frame of reference groups with a similar socio-economic status. A social worker may, for example, want similar wages and working conditions to those of teachers and nurses. A plumber may be more concerned with the working conditions and pay of electricians. Doctors, however, may not look to unskilled workers as the reference for their own aspirations.

Runciman's interest was with the relative nature of the sense of deprivation, to which we have referred earlier. The sense of deprivation (and hence of being 'in need') emerges relative to those others in relation to whom people refer themselves. An individual or group compares himself, herself or themselves against others whom they regard to be comparable to themselves. Thus, for example, when considering the issue of the level at which the poverty line should be 'marked' in twenty-first-century Britain, it is not nineteenth-century standards or third world countries to which reference is made in relation to standards or expectations. Such a comparison would lead to a profoundly lower poverty line than that which is currently officially presented. Rather, it is the standards of British society in the twenty-first century.

Of course, even here, there are differences in perspective, but the historical and cross-cultural comparisons serve to make the point.

Other areas of social life are relevant both for social work and the concept of need. Social and historical context, according to many studies, particularly those which employ cross-cultural analysis, social psychology and anthropology, play a major part in definitions, standards and expectations of personal and family life which are of interest to social work. If we take parenting – indeed mothering – we find quite important differences in expectations across different cultures. There are, for example, profound influences on parenting practice according to such factors as ethnicity, socio-economic status of the family, and neighbourhood and community (Kotchnick and Forehand, 2002). Likewise, during the twentieth century there have been major changes in familial expectations in relation to child rearing. These include the emergence of new parenting approaches and structures, such as cohabiting and non-marital co-parenting (Pinsoff, 2002). Even the way in which children are 'talked to' can vary across cultures (Johnston and Wong, 2002).

The family is another area where cultural and historical changes are important (Gadlin and Tizard, 1984). In addition to parenting, families can, however, reflect marital status, relations within the community and moral expectations (Halstead, 1999). Such differences can have considerable significance in multicultural contexts. Thus in circumstances of diversity, the home or family values picked up by children can contradict and even be in serious conflict with those in important institutions of socialisation, such as community schools. Likewise, even one's sense of 'self' and identity may be affected by culture and context. Thus, the concept of 'self', the idea of the extent to which the self is malleable and changeable, the relationship with and impact of the external world, and the relationship of self to others are all facets related to culture (Heine, 2001). Indeed, self-identity may be closely related to cultural identity, affected by collective perceptions of those in that culture and affecting those collective perceptions (Nagel, 1994).

These divergences, it is suggested, are so considerable that we can only regard need in its cultural context. If we are to consider the need of families, children, parenting or identity, then we can only do so by reference to the culture and norms within which these people live. On this analysis, social work (it would seem) is culture-dependent. Indeed, to see things differently might actually be oppressive (it could be argued). Where standards and expectations are imported from one culture to another, they can be a thinly disguised method of acting discriminatively against those in the culture upon which the standards are imposed.

Of course, once we move towards the level of culture as the arbiter of standards of needs, it is a small step to go to the level of the individual, as outlined in the policy documents noted earlier. If need perceptions are entirely relativistic, then why stop at standards expected in a particular culture? Why not extend that to the perceptions of individuals? In the more individualistic of disciplines, this is exactly what happens. Orthodox welfare economics maintains that individuals are the only authority on their interests and wants. They also have a right to decide and act autonomously. It is their preferences through which what is consumed (or produced) should be determined (Penz, 1986). Need, on this view, is tightly associated with individual preference.

However, from the point of view of social work, this can create difficulties. Are we, for example, to accept that the expectations and standards of child care in any particular family are valid in their own right, regardless of what they are? What if these involve violence against the children or emotional deprivation? On what grounds might a social worker claim the right to intervene? There would be no grounds, if individuals or families were considered to be the determinants of standards. Clearly, while the individual may, at times, be the 'expert in their own needs' (Smale et al., 1993), there are limits to the extent to which such a position can be pursued, while remaining consistent with the nature of social work.

Objective needs

An undiluted relativistic notion of need is, therefore, not sufficient on intellectual grounds, and not sufficient in relation to the nature of social work. We may additionally remind ourselves of the problems of relativism outlined earlier:

- Relativism claims, as a universal truth, that there is no such thing as a universal truth.
- Relativism enables no criteria for the judgement of any particular culture or set of actions, no matter how abhorrent. It would, therefore, provide no firm basis on which to pursue, for example, anti-racism (since an anti-racist position would have no greater validity than a racist position) or to condemn the Holocaust.

An objective concept of need provides an alternative. Such an approach would present need, not as the prisoner of culture or individual preference, but as something that can be defined in relation to enduring human characteristics and interests. In its most 'certain' form, need definition is relatively unproblematic. It is something which the expert, with objective information, can identify in any particular instant. Where there is a heart problem, the heart specialist is able to define someone as being in need. Indeed, it is so objective that we are able to use instruments with which to identify heart conditions. Much of modern medicine is based on such technical methods to objectively identify ill health.

While social work is not able to call upon instruments of the sort used by doctors (although of course the work of doctors in areas such as child abuse or ill health often requires the use of such instruments, which are then relevant for social work), there is considerable implicit commitment to an objectivist notion of need, even in policy documents. This is evident in relation to social work in areas where care management is most influential. The assessment of need is central to care management (and one should say enduring social work) practice. The advent of care management in the early 1990s led to a drive for a more explicit and clear set of need 'identifiers'. If social workers were to assess need, they had to know how to recognise it. They should also seek to be looking at the same areas. Social worker A should be looking at the same set of needs as social worker B, otherwise how could they be regarded as acting fairly and consistently (or as consistently as possible)?

The problems which can occur in practice, without such clarity and (implicit) objectivity, were apparent in empirical studies on need measurement. Aldgate and Tunstill (1995), for example, suggested that need was identified by local authorities in only the most general of terms. 'Need groups', at best, were (inadequately) defined in terms of arbitrary social and demographic criteria. Colton et al. (1995) also found that social workers were defining needs in a wide variety of ways in the conduct of their practice, with little agreement as to how a child in need (they were focusing on child care practice) should be defined. Thus, there was an arbitrariness both at the more general (local policy) level and the more specific (individual practice) level.

Official documents, however, had already recognised this requirement for both explicit definitions of need and the setting of priorities (DoH, 1991b). Not only was this required through policy statements but it needed to be operationalised through guidance and criteria. These criteria needed to be comprehensive – covering all areas of need – and particular – able to identify and focus upon each individual area of need. In effect, this required need to be operationalised and classified in a manner which enabled a detailed identification of the types and ranges of need. The documents started with six broad classifications which should be covered in a comprehensive assessment: personal/social care, health care, accommodation, finance, education/employment/leisure and transport/ access. These were general areas, but they too could be classified in terms of more detailed criteria.

This interest in identification and classification – very much technical aspects of need assessment – has been maintained, and is evident through more recent (and current) policy documents, such as the *Assessment Framework for Children in Need and their Families* (DoH, 2000). This, too, identified general need areas: child development needs, parenting capacity, and family and environmental factors.

In those areas, furthermore, a range of more specific needs were classified. In the area of the child's needs, for example, the following areas were identified: health, education, emotional and behavioural development, identity, family and social relationships, social presentation and self-care skills. Indeed, the Department of Health have more recently gone a great deal further, developing instruments which enable detailed areas of need to be classified and identified according to quite narrow age groups (DoH, 2002). These involve, furthermore, the ticking of boxes, so that quite specific needs can be identified by individual social workers in relations to each particular child.

This is interesting because the specificity and box ticking give a clear aura of objective technical judgements being made. However, as important is the relationship between the framework and instruments developed and the evidence upon which it is based. Much of the basis for this is specifically evidence drawn from decades of psychological study of child development and parenting in the context of family and wider social environment (DoH, 2000). Many of these studies themselves were characterised by an objectivist commitment – that they were examining real aspects of child development in context – with the consequent implications that practice was, by incorporating that evidence, also incorporating that same commitment. Likewise, the manner in which this was done – by creating classifications, and even lists with boxes to tick – further emphasised an objectivism inherent in need assessment. Needs could, in advance, be classified, boxes ticked, a technical assessment made.

In taking an objective approach two key dimensions are, according to Miller (1976), important. First, it is necessary to distinguish between, on the one hand, wants and, on the other, needs. Second, we must have a differentiated concept of need – we must know, in other words, in relation to *what* the need is felt.

We may look first to the difference between wants and needs. Need is a condition, according to Miller, which is ascribed to a person objectively. It is something of which both the individual and someone else might be aware. Indeed, it could also be something about which both could be *unaware*. Take a heart condition. An individual may have serious problem with the arteries leading to and from their heart. This may be a condition which, if not dealt with, could lead to cardiac arrest. The person may or may not be aware of this. They may or may not have visited a doctor about it. Regardless of those facts, and of whether it has been identified, they clearly have a heart condition. It exists outside our, and others', awareness of it.

A want, according to Miller, is a psychological state ascribed on the basis of a person's avowal or declaration. We may, for example, state that we 'want' another bar of chocolate, or a new washing machine (even while our current one is working). The first thing is that, with a want, a person is subjectively aware of that want. If I want sweets, I am the one who can say. You do not know I want more sweets until I tell you. Unlike the heart condition, furthermore, I can hardly want sweets without the subjective awareness that I want them.

However, there is a further difference between a want and need. This relates to consequences. According to Barry (1965), need statements must conform to the structure, 'A needs X *in order to* Y'. If we take our example of need above, we could state that a person needs a heart bypass operation *in order to* prevent a heart attack. The need, here, is for a heart bypass operation. The consequence is that a heart attack is prevented.

We can intuitively see the difference between the want (for sweets) and the need (for a heart bypass operation). However, this intuition becomes manifestly clear when we look to consequences. If the person wanting the sweets is deprived of them, the consequences are trivial, compared with the person whose need is for a heart bypass operation. If a person were to say that they needed some more sweets, we would give that statement a rather different status from one by a heart specialist who said that a person needed a heart bypass operation.

Part of the problem arises because we generally leave the notion of consequences out of need statements. Thus, we could state that a person 'needs a new washing machine' or that they 'need a heart bypass operation'. However, the absence of a new washing machine might be a few dirty clothes, or a noisier wash if you already have an old washing machine that works. The absence of heart bypass surgery could mean death.

It is, then, a focus on consequences which help us to understand need. But is there any criterion we can use which will help make this clearer? The distinction between wants and needs emerges through the concept of *harm* (Feinberg, 1973, p. 111). This is particularly interesting because harm is at the heart of child care legislation. The concept of 'children in need' (section 17, Children Act 1989) makes reference to a reasonable standard of health or development in which this is likely not to be achieved, or would be impaired, without the provision of services. It also refers to disability as a criterion for being 'in need'. More interestingly, however, is the reference to the need for a response to children who are 'suffering, or likely to suffer, significant harm' (section 31.2). The distinction between the section 17 and 31 criteria is one that is reflected in the difference between being 'in need' and 'at risk' (DoH, 1995). Indeed, it has been emphasised that those 'at risk' should also be considered to be 'in need' (Parton, 1997). If those 'at risk' are suffering 'significant harm', it is consistent to see those with health and development impairment, and disability, as suffering harm. Indeed, as we shall see, such a statement would conform to notions of basic need.

Harm, then, an objectivist concept relating directly to a notion of need which involves negative consequences, is at the heart of legislation governing social work practice. The implication of this is that harm will be the consequence of not responding to need. Since harm is related (according to Feinberg, 1973) to a person's interests, harm follows a set of circumstances which interferes with or thwarts their interests. This is obvious in the case of the person with a heart condition. The failure to have heart bypass surgery could place the person's life at risk, leading to death. Hence the absence of surgery has a *consequence*, and that consequence is *harm* to the person. Can the same be said of the person who wants a few more sweets? Fairly obviously, not really. Indeed, not having sweets may *prevent* harm, in the form of tooth decay.

How then, can we look at general areas, such as health development and disability, the focus of legislation? We should first recognise these are in fact *general* areas. However, if we look at health, as one of these criteria, our example of heart surgery is relevant. It may be rarer for a child to need heart surgery, but some children do need such intervention. Hence, we can see harm – indeed significant harm – accruing to a child without surgery. This is a dramatic example, but harm can be identified through more routine, if also very debilitating conditions, such as cystic fibrosis, where some of the more dangerous symptoms include impairment of the respiratory system. Here, everyday care and support for the child may also require support for parents, designed to reduce the harmful effects of the disease on the child.

Once one refers to need in this kind of way – that it relates to consequences and to harm – then there is an implicit commitment to universal standards (Thompson, 1987). This is because we have criteria by which need may be identified and that these criteria, therefore, apply to everyone. If someone will suffer significant harm if no action is taken, then they are 'in need' (of that action). Harm is, so to speak, a 'qualification' for being in need, regardless of those to whom it applies.

The contrast with wants, then, is not just an intuitive matter, nor a matter of individual preference or culture. That, anyway, is the argument of the objectivists, an argument which we need to take seriously in view of the objectivist core to social work we outlined earlier. But is it enough? The argument around the issue of heart bypass surgery would seem to be clear-cut. But is even *this* 'life and death' issue one to which we can all subscribe? For an older person, who has a number of physical ailments, and who may have seen many of their erstwhile friends die, the fear of death may not be very great. Indeed, it might be welcomed. In what sense could such a person be considered to suffer harm, then, even if they died? One answer might be that the issue of heart bypass surgery requires closer examination, and that particular conditions might render the notion of harm to the individual redundant in particular cases. It might also be argued that the notion of universalism might be slightly amended, to include the overwhelming majority of people rather than absolutely everyone. That would fit with ideas of an instinct for survival amongst human. While, then, we look to an overwhelming majority, *for all practical purposes*, the issue of harm in relation to the absence of heart bypass surgery would, in fact, be universal. However, we can return later to this issue.

What about less obvious examples? What about standards which seem to relate to particular societies in particular time periods? Are we, for example, to accept that levels of state income support present in the early to mid-twentieth century are an appropriate means to distinguish those 'in need' from those not 'in need' in the twenty-first century? Or should we respond to the greater wealth in society by raising expectations and examining the higher minimum levels of state support necessary to distinguish between those in need and not in need, compared with fifty or one hundred years ago? This, of course, is the argument of those who subscribe to the notion of relative deprivation discussed earlier. Such a position might suggest that harm would follow from an income which was below that required for income support.

Of course, we could simply argue that we should have a universal notion of harm which applies to all societies in all time periods. But that would seem to disregard clear variations in notions of need which have occurred in different times and places. To disregard these, it might be suggested, could leave the notion of need out of contact with the real world, a distant, abstract concept which has little relevance to the very people to whom it is supposed to apply. There would be little point to such a metaphysical discussion with such limited application.

This, of course, raises again the whole issue of relativistic notions of need. We might argue that the objectivists have greater depth and insight in their analysis, and that it reflects an objectivist core to social work, which makes it meaningful. But it remains insufficient, on its own, either to be universally applicable or applicable to the nuances of social work.

Basic and social need

Our analysis, therefore, while showing the necessity for an objectivist core to need, to make it meaningful for and consistent with social work, nevertheless leaves it inadequate to fully explain need as a concept for social work. This may help to explain why it is that we see both objectivist and relativistic notions of need within legislation, policy and practice guidelines for social work. Need, then, as a practical concept, and as used by social work, is one which has two elements, one which reflects standards which may be regarded to be universal, and the other which may be influenced by time, place, and even personal preference.

Basic needs

Objectivist notions of need have been associated with the idea that humans have fundamental drives which are part of an enduring nature. If humans are to suffer harm, it is suggested, they do so in relation to drives which they are, so to speak, programmed to pursue. Hull's (1943) drive theory relates primarily to fundamental physiological states. Thus there is a need for food (hunger), water (thirst), air, the avoidance of injury (pain), the need for rest and for sleep. Maslow's (1954) well-known taxonomy of needs goes further than the merely physiological. He added the concerns of personal growth, motivation and self-realisation. He developed a hierarchy of need, in which the more basic needs had more urgency and priority and, as these were satisfied, so other needs came into focus. Maslow classified five forms of need: safety, psychological, love, esteem and actualisation. When the more basic needs, such as the avoidance of hunger, were satisfied, so higher-order needs would emerge, and the individual would be driven to satisfy those needs.

The problem with these drive notions of need is that they rather take humans as people who can make decisions of their own accord out of the equation. To be 'driven' in this way is to have, it would appear, little conscious control over what it is you are being driven to achieve. To the extent that conscious will is involved, it merely seeks to find a way to satisfy those needs. Humans are at the beck and call of their drives. This hardly reflects humans as the subject beings we know them to be, able to choose and make decisions for themselves.

Furthermore, as Midgely (1984) pointed out, this hardly covers situations where choice is unavoidable. There may, for example, be circumstances in which mutually exclusive goals (or drives) need to be considered – that is, the pursuit of one necessarily implies the abandonment or curtailment of the other. This might be the case with a single parent who, on the one hand, may need to gain employment to pay the bills while, on the other, have a strong drive to nurture. That person has to make a choice about which they are to pursue.

Simple drive notions of need, therefore, are insufficient, and inconsistent with the idea of social work. Having stated that, it would be foolish indeed to dislocate the notion of need from some perception of human nature. Taylor (1973) has suggested that values would be unintelligible if not, in some sense, related to human nature, and this applies equally well to need. *What we need,* in other words, is inevitably going to be associated in some way with *who we are*. This takes our analysis to a more fundamental level than that of societies, historical epochs or cultures. It suggests, in fact, that we are, first and foremost, human beings, and that need should be anchored on an understanding of us as humans.

In focusing on this level, more fundamental than that which relativists, by the very nature of their analysis, are prepared to consider, we are able to look at what has been called basic needs. Two central features of human need, it has been argued by a number of scholars, are survival and autonomy (Plant et al., 1982; Thompson, 1987; Braybrooke, 1987; Doyal and Gough, 1991). Survival, clearly, is a precondition for being able to do anything at all, regardless of culture. One can hardly talk coherently about the notion of need in relation to those who are dead. This, though, relates also to our self-directing nature – humans' capacity to make decisions and to act on them, to direct their own lives. Again, rather obviously, survival is a prerequisite for any human to make self-directing decisions and actions. It follows, therefore, that anything which threatens survival is either the cause or the potential cause of harm to the individual.

Doyal and Gough (1991) go rather further than this, however, suggesting that survival is too narrow a criterion for the consideration of need. They argue that health is central to the capacity of an individual to direct their own lives and carry out their own decisions. Here again, they are appealing to a notion of what it is to be human – human nature if you will – which relates to the capacity for conscious, self-directing decision making. Even to undertake routine tasks of a sort which we would perform on a day-to-day basis, we require certain minimum standards of physical health. Major disability, for example, can interfere with an individual's capabilities in just such a way and, in the light of this, it is not surprising, as we found earlier, to discover disability to be one of the key criteria for identifying need in the UK's Children Act 1989. The harm accruing here relates (at least) to the interference with a person's capacity to carry out their own lives, but of course can relate to the effects of the ill health or disability on the person, both in their physical and mental well-being.

Some might suggest that this reflects a biomedical approach to health, one characteristic of Western medicine. Relativists would question whether this could be transferred across cultures (Morgan et al., 1985).There is, of course, a danger of descent into absurdity here, in the attempt to undermine the principle of universality and assert the primacy of culture and social construction. However, Doyal and Gough (1991) nevertheless confront this argument through the example of tuberculosis. They suggest that individuals with TB, however defined, will have a subjective awareness of illness. They also point out that our best medical understanding provides both the most complete explanation of TB and its most effective treatment. If someone has TB, in short, it will be no respecter of cultural relativism. It will not change as a result of an altered definition. No amount of social construction will turn it from a damaging disease, even a killer, into a benign condition.

Autonomy is the second dimension of basic need, one that is (perhaps) less obviously relevant. However, it again applies through our understanding of humans as subjects with a capacity for self-direction, acting upon the decisions they make. This, as we have seen, is a central element of social work, an underlying feature of humans which is at the heart of the idea of social work. As such, therefore, the notion of autonomy as central to our understanding of need is consistent with assumptions about humans inherent within social work.

Autonomy is necessary in order for people to be self-directing. One aspect of autonomy is freedom from hindrance or constraint. Most obviously this can involve the actions of one person on another, or a group on an individual. Clearly you are unable to act autonomously – under your own direction – if you are constrained. Doyal and Gough suggest that, in order to avoid this, a framework of social rules – laws and the like – are necessary. Such rules can give freedom from arbitrary constraint. (Of course there are circumstances where constraints operate for other purposes, such as imprisonment, but these have particular purposes and operate in relation to certain conditions.)

A second aspect involves the inherent capacities within an individual him or herself actually to make decisions and act autonomously. This is quite a complex idea, and we will deal with it in more detail later. Presented in technical terms, it is about the ability to formulate rules and to follow them in the conduct of one's life. In less daunting terms we can perhaps use the example of mental illness. Where a person is suffering a severe mental illness, they may be suffering delusions or hallucinations which influence the conduct of their life (quite apart from the unpleasantness of these experiences). They may hear voices telling them they are useless or evil, or believe others are out to entrap and hurt them. Such experiences interfere hugely with the person's capacity to conduct their own life according to their wishes, their social functioning often deteriorates, and it is difficult to say that they are self-directing or autonomous people.

Autonomy and survival, or health, then, are key dimensions to a universal and objective notion of human need. While, however, it may be possible to identify basic human needs, the capacity to satisfy those needs can vary across different cultures. That is because their technical capabilities, social organisation and financial resources will also vary. Nevertheless, some authors (Sen, 1984; Doyal and Gough, 1991) suggest it is possible to identify resources which could satisfy needs which have transcultural relevance – that is, they apply, in principle, to all cultures and are therefore universal.

Social needs

Not all states to which the ascription 'need' is made could be called basic needs. They are not, in other words, about survival, health (at least in the sense of major ill health) or autonomy. Where today we might suggest that a person 'needs' a washing machine, this would not in past time or, indeed, currently in many countries be defined as a need. Of course, the possession of a washing machine may make life easier and improve the impulse towards good hygiene, but it would be difficult to maintain that, in general, the possession of one was a basic need.

We could simply regard the possession of a washing machine as a want. This may, indeed, be more accurate, although many would define the absence of a washing machine as a 'need' state. A family on low income, say, headed by a single parent and with three or more children, might well be widely considered to be 'in need' of a washing machine. Welfare professionals such as social workers, who may be concerned, at the same time, with issues of child care more generally, would also be likely to see the absence of a washing machine as a need which should be rectified.

Therefore, once we move away from basic needs, while we begin to enter rather more hazy areas, it remains the case that the term 'need' is used to denote circumstances which would not qualify as basic needs. What, then, are we looking at here? First, we should recognise that there is no 'hard and fast' distinction between states of need and states where there is no need. A family with child care and parenting problems may have a multiplicity of difficulties, and the absence of a washing machine could be thrown into the equation. It is contextualised (although many may still regard the absence of a washing machine as a need state, even for a family without many other problems).

However, beyond this we should consider the expectations and values which underlie this area of 'social need': societal expectations have changed as society itself has changed. Where the wealth of a society has increased, goods which were formerly considered luxuries become perceived as necessities. These standards reflect, broadly, a consensus about minimum expectations which should exist in a society. Of course, a 100 per cent consensus is unlikely in any culture, and there may be some differences. However, for practical purposes (and such purposes are particularly relevant to a practical activity like social work), a consensus could be said to exist where there is a sufficiently large majority who subscribe to a particular position. As such, they are society-specific or culture-specific. They are not standards which may be universally applied in time and place, but expectations which apply to this society at this particular time. Interestingly, such a statement is closer to the position of relativists than objectivists.

It is, indeed, a position reflected in social work. What is important here is not that a consensus in fact exists (although it may well exist), but that *social work, by its very nature, assumes a consensus to exist.* This is, as we have seen, a necessary consequence of social work becoming involved in problems, and indeed social work being defined, at the point where the argument has been won. In practical terms, it is about particular issues being enshrined in legislation, policy and procedure, and their being dealt with, on an individual basis, by social work.

Social work, then, in its very nature, enshrines elements of societal standards which encapsulate social need. What is found to be acceptable (for example, in relation to the living conditions of older people, the care of those with learning disabilities or children's educational performance and attendance at school) reflects, at least in part, some of these social needs.

However, we can go further than this. The possibility of different perceptions of need, based on individual judgements, has emerged as professional power has been challenged. Instead of being passive consumers of professional judgements of need, which was more prevalently the case in the past, clients have had an increasing say in determining the nature of their needs (Evans and Harris, 2004). Notions like service users being experts in their own circumstances and needs (Smale et al., 1993) imply not only the possibility of different judgements about the nature and extent of need, but also that the right to make such judgements is not vested in social workers alone.

This position has been adopted as one of those in which empowerment is pursued, an issue to which we will be turning later. It reflects, furthermore, definitions of need which were identified long ago by Bradshaw (1972). *Felt need*, Bradshaw thought (p. 641), reflected the perception of need held by the individual him or herself. What I think are my needs *are* my needs, in the sense that I feel them to be such. In social work this would be the needs the client or service user him or herself considered themselves to have. Hence, if I felt I needed day care for my children, that would represent a felt need, regardless of what the social worker thought.

Needs, alternatively, can be *ascribed*. These would be those needs which others would ascribe to the person concerned, whether or not they themselves felt they had such needs. The sense of ascription used here is different from that used by objectivists. They would use the term 'ascribe' to describe circumstance where an independent objective definition and identification of needs could take place. 'Ascribe' in the sense being used here refers merely to a perception, a particular view of whether or not a person has any needs. The only critical point about this is that it is someone other than the person him or herself who is making the judgment of need.

In social work such ascription would be made by the practitioner. Thus, a parent might, in the light of child care problems, consider they needed more support, such as a family support worker or day care. A practitioner, on the other hand, might consider this was not enough on its own, and that the risk to the child was such that what was needed was for the child to be accommodated. The point here is that that felt needs are those identified by the client, and the ascribed needs are those identified by the practitioner.

Conclusion

Social work encapsulates a concept, or perhaps concepts, of need which have both objective and subjective dimensions. It is absolutely necessary for social work to have a concept of need that is consistent with the idea of social work itself. That idea incorporates the notion of humans as subject beings, but also that an undiluted relativism is quite inconsistent with social work and inadequate as an understanding of the human condition. Hence the need for a core of objectivism in need, just as there is in social work.

They also are both universalist (applicable in all cultural and historical circumstances) and also reflective, to some degree, of standards and expectations in individual cultures. There is even some room for individualised definitions of need, which the client is able to judge.

To a considerable degree, the consensus assumptions underlying social work play a part. Basic needs may be seen to be universalist in principle (and hence objective), but social needs are also seen to have a high degree of consensus underlying them. However, the 'grey' edges occur where social need merges into individualised judgements of felt need. There is a spectrum, moving between the objective and the (apparently) entirely subjective. In this, while holding to an objectivist core, social work (metaphorically) refuses to be limited by debates about need which are unnecessarily polarised. Social work subscribes to two concepts of need (basic and social) and possibly a third (that these can be individually defined).

That there is an objectivist core is of major significance because, as we have seen, social work would lose its meaning if it were to descend into an undiluted relativism. Nevertheless, objectivism is not the only way in which need is considered. We are left with the dilemma: which concept of need is appropriate to which set of circumstances? Is it merely an arbitrary decision? Do social

Chapter seven

Authority and choice

Social work has long been associated with two apparently contradictory themes: those of care and control. On the one hand social work is widely viewed, both from within and without, as an activity which is centrally involved with helping. Its focus on people as subjects, with their innate value, the concern for empathising with their plight, all point to a profession whose focus is on the welfare of others.

On the other hand, social work has also had a sustained concern with control, admittedly on a micro-social level. Social work has been concerned, in different ways, with standards of behaviour. When involved with young offenders, they work with 'rule breakers', young people who have transgressed the bounds of behaviour set by the law. When involved in child protection, social workers are empowered to take actions which can contradict the wishes of parents and, through the courts, enforce those actions. Children in local authority care can be placed there precisely because they are suffering or likely to suffer significant harm While the child is cared for, controls are often being placed on the parents. Likewise, in the arena of mental health, compulsory admission is precisely that: an action which is compulsory. In all these respects social workers are taking on a role which involves the use of authority.

The use of such authority sits uneasily, it would appear, with the notion of 'choice', one which has been strongly pursued in recent years. Choice would appear to be inherent in certain approaches to need, which we have outlined. This is most evident in individualised conceptions of need, where the individual is the judge of their own needs, and such judgements reflect their own values and standards. To the extent that social work is responsive to such need judgements – and many would say that this is a matter of available funding as much as value commitment – they are responding to client choice.

Care management, such a force in Britain until relatively recently (Sheppard, 1995) strongly prosecuted the idea of client choice (or, in care management terminology, consumer or user choice). The principles of care management – if not, frequently, its policy and financially derived practice – relied strongly on the rhetoric of choice, the client deciding what particular services they needed. Packages of care were to be the response to these choices, and a market in social care was to provide an environment to facilitate the exercise of choice. Predictably, perhaps, the practice never lived up to these ideals, but we should not underestimate the impact of the rhetoric of choice on the 'frame of thinking' about practice.

This would seem to have strong moral justification, in so far as social work is concerned with those who are socially excluded. Such people are, as we have seen, by definition, disadvantaged and marginalised, with their capacity to exercise choice restricted by their exclusion. Choice, in effect, enhances their capacity to determine the direction of their lives, in their immediate environment. Allied to a response to need, choice would seem to provide, through social work, an appropriate micro-level (in societal terms) response to social exclusion. People who are socially excluded are specifically more able to determine the direction of their lives in relation to those needs which arise as a result of social exclusion.

How, then, is this choice reconciled with an authority role which involves such a clear exercise of control over the lives of some individuals and families? Are there particular circumstances in which control, rather than choice, is on the agenda, and how are we to recognise these? What, indeed, is the relationship between choice, authority and control, response to need and social exclusion? The answer to this lies in our understanding of the notion of self-determination and the centrality of rationality to the social work understanding of what it is to be human. *Rationality and self-determination*, in other words, *are key elements of the idea of social work*.

Encouraging rationality as a response to need

Self-determination occurs where, according to McDermott (1976, p. 3), the behaviour of an individual emanates from his or her own wishes, choices and decisions. One way of looking at this relates to the capacity of an individual to exercise choice, to make and carry out decisions. The idea here is that not everyone is able to exercise choice, to determine what they want. There are, it is thought, *internal constraints*, related to their mental capacities, that prevent them from making choices and carrying out decisions.

There is an intuitive dimension to this. If we were to take a very young child, we do not generally regard it as desirable to give them unrestricted capability to decide what they should do or have, or how they should behave. This is because we do not regard them as having the capacity to make such decisions. Left to themselves, for instance, they may well choose to eat sweets, cakes and crisps in preference to food which would constitute a more healthy diet. Allowing them full rein on their desires could lead, in the relatively short term, to serious health problems. Limits, then, are generally placed on the child's ability to decide its diet. The task of a parent is to look out for the interests of the child, to guide them and enable them to develop and grow. It is the parent who is generally regarded as the arbiter of what a child should or should not do, even if they do so while paying heed to the overt wishes of the child. This, in everyday terms, is what is meant by carrying out parental responsibility.

Without stating this overtly, we implicitly judge the child to have internal constraints on their capacity to determine what they can or should do. They have not reached a state of maturity where they are able to make such decisions. As an issue for self-determination, this has been referred to in the literature as 'positive freedom'. Positive freedom refers to the capacity of the individual actually to exercise choice, unimpeded by internal constraints (Berlin, 1969). It is about being free to choose, because you are able to make a choice. The child mentioned earlier is driven by immediate desires, unable properly to make decisions based on what is best for their health. Their immediate desires and their mental capacities make it difficult for them to understand the nature of the choices and decisions to be made. Because of this, they are not properly free to choose.

Taylor (1991) considered this to be an 'exercise concept' – that is, we are self-determining to the extent that our mental capacities allow us, in a very real sense, to exercise choice. The example above shows the restrictions which apply to a child's capacity to choose and, at a fundamental level, some of the justification for parental responsibility. We can, interestingly, frame this concept of self-determination, in terms of need. In this we draw on Barry's objectivist formula, mentioned in the previous chapter, of 'A needs X in order to Y': here, 'the child needs parental guidance in relation to their diet to prevent them falling into ill health'. We can immediately, then, see the connection between need and self-determination. There is a clear concept of harm (ill health) which will occur if no response to need occurs. The capacity for self-determination is central to the creation of need: because of the 'internal constraints' (arising from the child's immaturity) and their incapacity to understand properly the consequences of their behaviour and integrate such understanding into their actions) a state of need arises. The need is for parental guidance (and, of course, an appropriate diet).

We do not have to confine ourselves to children in this respect. Much of the work of social work practitioners involves those for whom internal constraint on their capacity for self-determination is a significant issue. This includes adults. Take, for example, someone suffering from agoraphobia. This is a mental health issue which is well within the realms of social work. Agoraphobics are people whose fear of open spaces restricts their movements. The term 'restriction' makes clear that they are not able to do what they would otherwise wish. The restriction, however, is not some external constraint, being imprisoned or in some other way being prevented from movement. The restriction exists within the mind – it is an internal constraint.

The restriction, furthermore, is in relation to what would widely be considered normal activities. They may not be able to shop, to visit friends, go to the cinema or attend sporting events. The reason is that to do so – to step outside their front door – fills them with anxiety. Such people frequently appreciate that their actions are not rational. This realisation, however, does not enable them to overcome their phobia, with its consequent restriction on movement. Likewise a parent may not be able to behave in the ways they might wish. Parents may aspire to bring their children up calmly, wisely, in the child's best interest. However, they may fly into rages from time to time. These could have a variety of influencing factors. They may, for example be under considerable stress, say from a continuously low income, the behaviour of a child with attention deficit hyperactivity disorder, or their own past life experiences which have left them psychologically vulnerable to particular facets of parenting. A mother, already depressed, aware that her parenting is not as good as she would like, may well react to a child's demands with anger, an anger fuelled by her own guilt that she cannot provide the care to which she would aspire. In all these cases, the standards to which the woman is aspiring are not achieved because of factors which seem to be beyond her control.

These are serious themes within the practice of social work (Sheppard, 2001). Social work responses are often designed to seek to eliminate these internal constraints or at least to reduce their impact. Direct, face-to-face counselling may be designed to enable women to focus on situations where they lose their temper, and then to control their anger. It might explore past life experiences – the woman may have been abused as a child – which are having an effect on her capacity to parent right now. They may refer the woman for help from a psychologist or a group, for the same purpose. Their more significant aspiration – to parent the child well, or at least adequately – are being undermined by the more immediate impulse to express their anger, and this puts them in a state of need. We can again express this in a 'need statement': 'the woman needs social work counselling in order to prevent periodic rages which can damage the child's psychological development and physical health'.

There is a central element of rationality involved in this notion of self-determination. The mother wishes to parent the child well, and for both of them this should exclude flying into rages, yet she nonetheless flies into rages. Her immediate impulse is not subject to the control of her longer-term aims (Edwards, 1982). She is actually doing what she does not want to do. The rationality referred to here involves the relationship between means and end. If her end or aiming point is to parent in a certain way (which she believes will lead to a well-balanced child and adult, able themselves to formulate life plans in their best interests and carry them out), then, according to her (and no doubt the social worker), she is not going the best way about achieving this. There is a gap between the end or aim and the methods pursued to achieve that aim. When you wish to achieve an outcome, it makes sense (it is rational) to choose methods which are likely to led to that outcome, rather than methods which are very likely not to lead to that outcome.

One way of formulating this situation, in term of rationality, is that the outcome to be pursued is rational behaviour on the part of the parent. The woman herself wishes to act more rationally and, as a response to need, social work actions would be designed to enhance her capacity for rational behaviour, or at the very least mitigate the worst consequences of the irrational behaviour. Rational behaviour, as a minimum (it can involve more), involves being able to formulate life plans and execute strategies which will enhance the capacity to achieve these life plans. Part of the life plans for this woman involves being a good parent, and more specific goals in relation to the conduct of parenting arise from this.

Just as there is an explicit connection, in British legislation, between need, harm and adequate child care, so there is also a direct connection with the notion of rationality. Indeed, there is a direct connection between all three and social work intervention. The standards of behaviour which social workers are expected to maintain and support, in the legislation, are those of the 'reasonable parent' – reasonable being derivative from rational. This is apparent from the Children Act section 13, under which a care or supervision order may be granted if the child is suffering, or is likely to suffer, significant harm, and if the care provided by the parent is 'not what it would be reasonable to expect parent to give him' (DoH, 1989, p. 25).

This is highly significant because we are now able to link the authority role of the social worker with the rationality of the parent. This, in turn, relates to their 'internal constraints' which prevent them from acting rationally. Rational behaviour, for a person in the role of parent, involves adhering to certain minimum standards. Those minimum standards are directly, in turn, related to the concept of harm – the harm that would be done if those minimum standards were not achieved. An objectivist notion of need is, in this case, directly tied to the capacity of social workers to act, even if the parent does not wish (for example) for the child to be taken into care.

We have, then, a clear indication that social work does not simply continue to have an objectivist core, in the form of its formulation of need, but that this objectivist core is related to the authority role of the social worker. In this respect, practitioners derive their authority from an assumption that lies within the very heart of the idea of social work: that they are looking at need objectively. There is, here, not the simple equivalence of view which characterises a relativist position. There is no assumption that the view of the parent has equal validity to that of the social worker. The assumption, indeed, is that the view of the parent, if differing from that of the social worker (or more specifically the court to which the social worker would apply), *does not have equal validity to that of the social worker*, with very practical consequence for the actions which social workers are empowered to carry out.

In either case that we have described – that of social work support to enable the parent to parent better, or social work action to remove the child from a parent where, if this were not done, significant harm would occur – social work is centrally involved with the issue of rationality. To support the parent is to encourage rationality. To remove the child will be to prevent the harm which would otherwise be done by unreasonable parenting. Where the social worker is seeking to rehabilitate the child home, he or she is looking to see the manifestation of reasonable parenting in order for that to take place.

Where, therefore, social workers are confronted with internal constraints to self-determination, they are seeking to encourage rationality – they are, in abstract terms, *seeking to encourage rationality in the irrational*.

Encouraging choice as a response to need

Self-determination has another, widely understood meaning, probably more frequently used than that which we have discussed so far. In general use, this kind of self-determination occurs when there are no *external constraints* on an individual from carrying out his or her wishes. A person is free to determine what they do, or what happens to them, because there is no one, or nothing, stopping them from being able to do so. This is most obvious in relation to circumstances where these conditions do not exist. A person in prison, for example, is not free to walk around in society and, because of this, is not able to determine where he or she goes or what they do. They are constrained by their imprisonment. Likewise, someone who has a gun trained upon them may feel equally constrained to behave in a way which does not lead to the person with the gun pulling the trigger.

This concept of self-determination is concerned with the problem of coercion and its avoidance. A person is not self-determining to the extent that their actions are the subject of some form of coercion. Coercion involves a deliberate interference with the actions, or scope for actions, of one human being, by one or more other humans. We can, for example, identify both the presence of a gun and imprisonment, as we have already outlined, as being coercive. These are obstacles in the way of a person determining for themselves what their actions will be. Self-determination occurs to the extent that coercion is removed from a situation (Berlin, 1969, p. 122).

Furthermore, the presence of self-determination is, on a value basis, a good thing. Coercion is seen as evil because it prevents humans from being able to act upon their own life plans. It undermines him or her as a thinking and valuing person, able to make plans and execute decisions (Hayek, 1960). This is an absolutely central part (as we have seen) of the human condition. Thus, depriving a person of their capacity for self-determination, by applying external constraints, is morally not defensible (this, of course, applies to those who, for example, are not being punished for some law-breaking behaviour – in effect those who are fully members of civil society). Interestingly, as with our discussion of need, there is direct reference to what it is to be human to decide what is, in moral terms, good.

This is a very different conception of self-determination from that which focuses on internal constraints. With its focus on external constraints, for example, the person who is agoraphobic, while not leaving the confines of their own home, is nevertheless self-determining. There are no other humans preventing him or her from going out. It is, in effect, their decision not to leave the house, even though it may be a decision reached reluctantly. The agoraphobic is not self-determining, then, when the concept is based on internal constraints, but is self-determining when it is based on external constraints. Hence it is clear, through this further conceptualisation, that social workers' actions in relation, for example, to agoraphobia, in which they seek to help a person to overcome their condition, are based firmly on a notion of internal constraints in relation to self-determination.

Where does this leave us in relation to any link between self-determination and the authority role of social work? In relation to the external constraints argument, social work is, at a certain point, involved in the removal of the capacity for self-determination. The parent whose parenting falls below that which is considered to be reasonable will have to face consequences. In this case, the consequences are, in terms of the external constraints argument, a form of coercion. Social workers, in undertaking their authority role, will, at times, have to act coercively towards the client. The parent may have their child received into care, or accommodated, or they may change their behaviour to prevent that from happening but, in either case, they are acting under duress – they are being coerced (so the argument would go). This position would suggest that social workers may, in some circumstances, enable a client to be self-determining, while in others act coercively towards their clients: care and control.

In this apparently coercive action, two themes emerge. On the one hand there are cases where social work is overtly (on the external constraints perspective) acting coercively. This is where a child protection assessment is undertaken: court proceedings occur; the child is, indeed, received into care. They are empowered to act in this way through the legislation. This we may refer to as '*overt coercion*'.

However, there is another, more insidious form of (external constraints) coercion present. In these cases, social work may be an intervention designed to support what the parent is trying to do. The parent may be concerned with the quality of their parenting, and be working with the social worker to improve it (or at least to maintain it). Both legislation (through the Children Act) and policy guidance (on family support) strongly encourage family support in child care practice, retaining the use of statutory (coercive) power as a last resort.

The problem, however, is that these supportive functions do not exist in some vacuum, insulated from the more authority-based coercive powers. Indeed, even where social workers are carrying out their tasks to support the family, with every intention of maintaining the child with their family, their authority role remains. The potential for (external constraint) coercive action can hang like a sword of Damocles over the conduct of their practice. This, furthermore, is no mere academic speculation. There is clear evidence that parents are well aware of the (external constraints) coercive powers of social workers, and that this has a major impact on the way many of them behave. Knowing that you are being helped by someone who has powers to seek for a child to be received into care, regardless of the fact that they may genuinely be trying to maintain the child within the family, is often a spectre which hangs over parents. Indeed, there is evidence that some mothers find it difficult to recognise that social workers are carrying out supportive functions in seeking to maintain the child within the family, because they are so overwhelmed by the more coercive powers which are held by social workers, should things not go right (Sheppard, 2001; Thoburn, 1995). The emotional stakes are so high and the potential powers so great that they practically define the nature of social work intervention. Thus, in contrast to our earlier concept of overt coercion, we have here the concept of *latent coercion*.

Hobbes' paradox asserts that, since all decisions are made in a context in which people are affected by their surrounding circumstances, they can therefore be regarded as always being self-determining. However, this is clearly absurd, and is particularly highlighted in relation to our concept of latent coercion. Indeed, evidence suggests that parents can be totally overwhelmed by the spectre of the authority powers held by social work in child care, and that this can overwhelm the conduct of practice. Its effects seep into all aspects of the parents' interactions with the social worker, can lead to aggressive behaviour and even be associated with a heightened likelihood of depression (Sheppard, 2001).

There can, therefore, be no doubt that some clients *experience* the actions, and even the involvement, of social work as coercive. Does this, however, undermine the notion that social work, when carrying out its actions on the basis of the authority role, is acting to enhance self-determination? It does not, and the reason is that the acts are not (in principle) arbitrary. They are undertaken when harm is assessed as occurring, or likely to occur, and hence the issue of need is central. Alongside this are the clearly stated conditions for that need.

First, the legislation which gives both content and meaning to social work is very clear about the concept of the 'reasonable' parent. It subscribes to a notion of rationality, at the same time as referring directly to the objectivist notion of harm. There is a clear commitment to the 'internal constraints' notion of self-determination, and this is directly related to need (both in theory and in the legislation). Second, the fact that the parents may differ in their view of need, it follows from the objectivist position, does not mean that their position has a validity equal to that of the social worker. Indeed, by their demurring from the position of the social worker (when agreed by the courts), they are demonstrating that their position does not have equal validity.

Hence, it is quite possible for social work actions to be perceived as coercive by parents, who are implicitly committed to an external constraints notion of self-determination while, within the framework of social work, it is about rationality and the *capacity* for self-determination (which is absent in the parent). However, we can go further than this. Other controlling actions of social work are directly linked to rationality. This is the case with compulsory admissions under the Mental Health Act, 1983. The very notion of mental illness is closely associated with rationality. This is clear both intuitively – with symptoms such as delusions and hallucinations being central features of some more severe mental illness – and in philosophical discussion, which links mental illness with circumstances in which an individual is unable to exercise rational autonomy (Edwards, 1982). Their very condition, in other words, suggests that, on an internal constraints model, they are not self-determining.

However, legislation goes further than this, requiring harm to be the result if action is not undertaken. This is the purpose of the additional requirement that compulsory admission should be in the interests of the health or safety of the person (patient, in legal terminology) or the protection of other persons.

The conditions, therefore, which prevent social work's controlling actions, in principle, from being arbitrary is that an overt link is made between need and self-determination. In both child care and mental health law, it is the presence of an 'internal constraints' notion of self-determination which acts as the trigger for controlling actions, hence ensuring they are not arbitrary. Indeed, we can go further than that. While seeking to prevent harm occurring, these controlling actions provide circumstances where self-determination (in an internal constraints sense) may return or emerge. To the extent that rehabilitation of a child is to take place to his or her family, this entails that parenting should become reasonable. In seeking to resolve a mental illness, or reduce or eliminate the symptoms, the professionals involved are seeking to return the individual to a state of rational autonomy.

Internal constraints and external help

We have shown so far that there are particular conditions in place when controlling actions – those which on an internal constraints notion of self-determination would be considered coercive – are taken up in social work. Those particular conditions require a link between the rationality of behaviour of clients and the presence of harm, which directly links need with self-determination. Indeed, to the extent that the capacity to exercise choice requires the removal of internal constraints, authority-based actions – those regarded as the controlling actions of social work – may be said to promote self-determination and, hence, the capacity for choice. How can you genuinely choose if those choices are not determined by you?

A further area related to the authority role of social workers involves also carers. This is the case, for example, where Guardianship is pursued under the Mental Health Act, 1983. In these cases, the authority role of the social worker is invoked when a person is placed under Guardianship. This occurs when they have a mental disorder of a nature or degree which warrants reception into Guardianship, and such action is on the interests of the welfare of the patient (client) or for the protection of others. In these circumstances a carer may well act as Guardian, and hence be a consequence of the authority role of the social worker.

In these circumstances, carers can be involved in decision making, as well as those about whom the decisions are being made. Both are, in a sense, clients, but they are often distinguished by their status as client (or user) and carer. The importance of the role of carer in the decision-making process is frequently alluded to in legislation and policy documents (for example, DoH, 1991a,

1991b). This emerges, furthermore, without any necessary reference to the authority role of the social worker. Does the role of the carer, in any way, limit the capacity of the client to exercise choice? Can their influence limit the client's room to choose?

The position of the carer is an interesting, one, especially in relation to self-determination and choice. It is best approached in relation to those where an internal constraints notion of self-determination is employed. This would be the case, for example, with an adult with severe learning difficulties or suffering dementia – such people would not be seen to be self-determining because of the internal constraints presented by their mental status. In these cases they are not capable of exercising self-determination, or at least their capacity to do so is limited.

The position here again involves a link between needs and 'internal constraints' self-determination. What is needed is a form of action which is in the interests of the client. How is this determined? Feinberg (1973, 1977) identifies two forms of interests. Ulterior interests are stable and long-term – those that promote and contribute to the avoidance of harm. Welfare interests are those which are indispensable to achieve their long-term, ulterior interests. Our ulterior interests, derived, for example, from a need to nurture and the drive to reproduce, may be the establishment and raising of a family. They may be to avoid major ill health, which is inimical to basic needs. Our welfare interests, which contribute to the achievement, say, of the avoidance of major ill health, may be sufficient income, proper housing, sufficient supervision – the danger of wandering amongst traffic or of forgetting a boiling chip pan to, say, someone suffering dementia should not be underestimated – and so on. In short, the promotion of our welfare, under these circumstances, is in the interests of the individual because the absence of such promotion could result in harm.

What is required here is a close relationship between the interests of the client and those of the carer. The first circumstance in which this is to be achieved is when the carer has a strong personal stake in the interests of the client. This is not some brief stake, but one which is very long-term. This personal stake involves a very close identification with the client on the part of the carer. In these circumstances, what is good for the client is also good for the carer. Likewise, what is harmful to the client also entails harm to the carer. This condition is most obviously fulfilled in the case of a loving parent.

The second circumstance is where the client's interests are promoted by the enhancement or promotion of the carer's interests. Likewise, harm to the carer would entail harm to the client. Take the case of a person whose physical or learning disability is such that they are wholly reliant on the carer. The capacity of the carer to care would be closely associated with the welfare of the client – the extent to which their needs are fulfilled. However, the act of caring for the client may itself exert huge strains on the carer. They may find that there is considerable physical exertion, that their social circle becomes more limited (engendering feelings of loneliness), that the demands of the client exert an emotional toll, and so on. The stress experienced might undermine their capacity to care. In such circumstances the interests of the carer – for a reduction of the levels of stress – are identical to those of the client. It may be, therefore, that a period of respite care, giving the carer a break, would be in both their interests, since it would reduce stress in the carer and renew their commitment and capability to care for the client.

These conditions, where there is a close identity between the interests of the client and carer, provide a justification for the involvement of a carer in decision making for the client. Where complete identity is achieved, we might suggest that, should the client briefly possess the capacity for self-determination (the removal of internal constraints), the decisions made by the carer would have been the decision made by the client him or herself. (We are here imagining this state for the purpose of the logic of the argument.) Of course, the extent to which there is a symmetry of the client's and carer's interests can vary. We might suggest that the capacity fully to act on behalf of the client will depend on the extent to which there is an identity of interest, as outlined above.

The client's capacity for self-determination, furthermore, will vary according to their capabilities. Few people have, for instance, such severe learning disabilities or dementia that decision making is justifiably completely taken over by others, although this can happen. The capacity for limited self-determination seems to be one implicitly invested in children. A young child may not, as we have seen, have the capacity and maturity to make all long-term decisions for themselves, to take responsibility for and govern their own lives. They may well, however, have a view, and that view can contribute significantly to an understanding of their needs and interests. It is this limited capacity for self-determination which helps us to understand the importance in the legislation (Children Act, 1989) for paying regard to the wishes and feelings of the child.

None of this, of course can prevent mistakes being made, in the real world. For example, a person who genuinely has the interests of the client at heart may nevertheless take actions which are not in their interests. A carer may, for example, be so committed to taking responsibility for the care of a client that they do not seek, or take advantage of the availability of, respite care. This can lead to a breakdown of their capacity to care, which is in neither the client's nor the carer's interests. We may also find that the carer does not genuinely have the interests of the client at heart. They may take income from state benefits, designed to meet the minimum need requirements of the client, and use it for their own purposes. Not all carers' actions, in other words, will be benign.

However, we are here discussing the principles. These practical examples show circumstances where those principles are, for one reason or another, not being observed in the real world. The principles provide guidance for recognising where this occurs.

Conclusion

We have shown, in this chapter, a close and important relationship between the notion of needs, the authority role of the social workers and the issue of self-determination in the client. If it is the case that much of practice should be about promoting client choice – a position accepted in policy and legislative guidance, as well as social work values – then what are the implications for the employment of the authority role in social work? How is it that social workers can both be in the business of promoting choice and yet have this authority role, carrying out 'controlling' functions?

The answer lies in the capacity of the client actually to exercise choice. Social workers operate with an authority role where the capacity to exercise choice, on the part of the client, is deemed to be impaired. The mentally ill person, the parent who is unable to reach the minimum standards of reasonable (rational) parenting, the person with severe learning difficulties or dementia, are all subject to 'internal constraints' on their capacity for self-determination, and hence for the exercise of choice.

How do we determine these internal constraints on the capacity for self-determination? Much of this is closely associated with an objectivist notion of need. Social workers are engaged, when carrying out their authority roles, in a process of recognition of harm, a position closely associated with an objectivist notion of need. Furthermore, their powers – and hence behaviour – in such circumstances betray a position in which they are assumed (within the framework of social work assumptions already outlined) to have 'superior' or more objective knowledge.

This is quite clear from their powers. The mentally ill person who is compulsorily admitted may proclaim their mental health but if, on the professional judgement of doctors and social workers (assuming the Approved Social Worker is making the application), they are suffering from a mental illness and the other criteria are fulfilled, they will be compulsorily admitted. The assumption is that the professionals, rather than the patient/client, are correct, because action may be taken against the wishes of the patient/client as expressed by them.

Likewise, social workers can be engaged in a process of receiving a child into care, against the wishes of the parents. The protestations of the parents may amount, in principle, to a claim that their parenting is reasonable but, where received into care, this is not a position that is accepted. The position of the parents in this case, and of the mentally ill person in the case of someone compulsorily admitted, *is not, in other words, being considered to have equal validity to that presented by the social worker.* Since the notion of 'equal validity' is at the heart of the claims of relativists, we can see again that there is an objectivist core to social work.

We should note with interest that in both cases, social workers do not make the decisions alone, nor are they the final decision makers. In the case of compulsory admissions, they make the decisions with doctors. In the case of reception into care (compulsory), this is a decision made finally by the court. In both cases, however, it is demonstrable that the principle of equal validity is not being adhered to, and hence they are not adopting a relativist position.

It is therefore possible to argue, on the one hand, that the promotion of choice is, indeed, a central part of social work but that the authority role of the social worker is invoked, to a considerable degree, where the capacity on the part of the client to exercise choice is impaired. One cannot choose if one's capacity to choose is impaired.

The exercise of authority can be further related to client choice in two ways. In some circumstances the capacity to choose – the capacity for self-determination, on the internal constraints model – is permanently impaired. This would be the case, for example, where someone has severe learning disabilities or dementia. Under these circumstances, the social workers are engaged in a function in which the continued promotion of welfare by others – those, in other words, monitoring their position, choosing what should be done for them and so on – remains all that may be aspired to by social workers and others involved in their care.

However, in other cases, the social worker is engaged in a process in which they may be actively promoting the capacity of the client for self-determination. They are promoting, or attempting to engender in the client, the capacity to choose. If we take the person compulsorily admitted to mental hospital, social workers are often (if not always, because of the limits to our knowledge) involved in a process in which the client (patient) is to have their mental health restored. To the extent that mental illness is involved with the capacity to reason (Edwards, 1982), the restoration of mental health involves also the restoration of the capacity for rational thought. The internal constraints on their capacity for self-determination are removed, and they are able again to choose.

What, however, of circumstances where clients are deemed not to have any internal constraints – where they are deemed, in their mental capacities at least, to be capable of self-determination? This is the case in all areas of social work practice where the authority role is not involved. These people are deemed to have the capacity to choose. Working with older people or adults with physical disability, social workers are generally involved with people whose mental capacities, whose abilities to choose, are not in question. What if there is a disagreement between worker and client about their assessment of the situation, or what should be done about it? There may well be no 'authority powers' for the social worker to act against the client's wishes.

The point is here that both social workers and clients are deemed, implicitly, to be capable of choice. A difference of opinion is one expressed by two rational agents (or people). There are no criteria, in law, for asserting some objective superiority on the part of the social worker. In this case, the position of the client and worker are indeed implicitly deemed to have equal validity. It indicates strongly, therefore, that while social work does possess an objectivist core, this is not the whole story.

It is possible for rational beings to disagree. Social life is such that there is not always one objective position in relation to particular situations. People can hold perspectives on those situations which, in principle, have equal validity. There is no perfect correspondence – one might not expect this in the complex reality of the lived world rather than the elegant abstractions of the social scientist – but it would appear that this position relates most closely to individualised notions of need and social need. Basic need, on the other hand. is a more objectivist concept.

In taking this position, social work is showing an epistemological sophistication (epistemology, you will remember, refers to the philosophy of knowledge – what we can know) which is often lacking in social scientists, who adhere exclusively to an objectivist *or* relativist position. Faced with the realities of social life, social work recognises (implicitly) that some issues afford greater certainty – more objectivity – than others. Furthermore, there is a set of criteria in which it is possible to discern circumstances in which objective knowledge is possible and where, on the other hand, we can only present a case, one which has only equal validity to others. The heart of objectivity in social work lies with the idea which links human need to key aspects of what it is to be human, which we examined in the previous chapter.

All this is possible to identify because the meaning – the content of social work, if you like – is, to a considerable degree, the result of legislation. We outlined this in chapter four.

So what does this say about the social work role? It tells us of three fundamental characteristics of social work:

- It tells us that in some circumstances they are involved in the care of those for whom achieving a state of rationality is not possible.
- They are involved in a process of promoting rationality amongst the irrational.
- In principle, they are involved in encouraging choice – in the external constraints sense – amongst the rational.

This third area is of further interest and leads us, unerringly, towards the consideration of a major issue in contemporary social work – that of empowerment.

Chapter eight

Empowerment

The idea of empowerment has become embedded within social work in recent years. There is a huge range of texts on the subject, from more theoretical tomes to very practical 'how to do' texts (Brown, 1995; Servian, 1996; Busch and Valentine, 2000; Lee, 2001; Pease 2002; Adams, 2003; Hurdle and Stromall, 2003). In relation to the latter, in particular, empowerment is seen as a rather unproblematic concept. The concern is on how one can 'practise' empowerment – thus turning it practically into a technique for social workers. It is as much a key issue for education and training. In the UK Higher Education Funding Council's *Benchmarking Document*, one of the five key areas of study involves understanding the nature of social work services in contemporary society, with particular reference to empowerment (QAA, 2000, para 3.1.1).

One of the problems with empowerment is that it is a bit like the US idea of motherhood and apple pie – everyone thinks it is an absolutely fine idea and is quite committed to it. However, it is not really straightforward. A central problem lies at its heart: in that it has a diverse range of meanings, some of these not at all consistent with each other. Can we consider ourselves to have empowered someone when we have listened to what they say, and done what they want? Or when we have helped their general functioning, so they can perform their life tasks better? Are they empowered when they understand themselves better? Or when that understanding is rooted in understanding of gender? Or, indeed, of disadvantage?

So we then follow this up with other questions. Under what particular notion of empowerment are you operating? Indeed, the absence of consistence can mean that adopting one form of empowerment involves contradicting another form. What then? Are you empowering or not empowering?

Empowerment actually rests, to a considerable degree, on the social philosophy of its proponents. This will form part of our exploration in this chapter. However, commonly, it contains within it the idea that clients are in some sense disadvantaged or (relatively) powerless. Empowerment involves the accretion of power (Lukes, 1974; Gould, 1994). This power involves the power to exercise choice as to how one should direct one's life. We can see this in notions as diverse as the involvement of clients in partnership (White and Harris, 2001) and in collective involvement and participation which enable groups to influence the direction of events within a community (Craig and Mayo, 1995).

There are two ways in which we can see choice as at the heart of empowerment:

- Individuals or groups are empowered when those factors are overcome which limit or prevent them having equal opportunity to exercise and act upon choice.
- Individuals or groups are empowered when they gain a greater understanding of their 'true' interests and are able to act upon them.

The first – which we may call the 'empirical self' – assumes that people are able to make their own judgements and decisions and that, in making them, they are self-determining. The task of empowerment is to enable them to be self-determining by removing, or not placing in their way, external constraints. The second is a 'potential self' formula. Here, people can only be self-determining where they have a proper understanding of their situation and, therefore, of the choices they can make. Empowerment involves helping them reach a proper understanding, as a result of which they can be self-determining.

If this seems reminiscent of our discussions in the previous chapter, it is no coincidence. These two notions draw upon the idea that someone is self-determining (and therefore able to exercise choice) when either external constraints are removed or internal (mental) constraints are removed. These are exactly the issues which emerge in any proper understanding of the use of authority in social work. Yet, this surely places us in a very direct dilemma: if there is such a close underlying relationship with the exercise of authority, how on earth can social work claim to be empowering?

This is an important question – one largely avoided in the literature on empowerment – one to which we shall return later. However, we should first explicate the ways in which empowerment is used. We can identify four different uses of the term empowerment, and we shall look at each in turn.

Active willing choice

One key concern for social work in recent years has been to enable the client to decide what should happen to him or her. However, this power also requires that he or she determine both their needs and what should be done about them (obviously within financial constraints). This approach has an implicit agenda: a limitation on professional power to make these decisions. Social workers, as professionals, are no longer arbiters of need, definers of what the problem is and what should be done about it. Instead, the social worker becomes the facilitator of the client's own decision-making process. They help the client to come to a decision, but the decision is most definitely that of the client (Smale et al., 1993). The client is empowered here in two respects:

- by restricting the power of the practitioners and turning them into facilitators;
- by recognising that the clients themselves know best what they need and what should be done for them.

This is the client as rational individual able to make his or her own decisions. What is required here is simply the provision of a context in which that process can take place in an informed way. This is most akin to the 'rational client' model discussed in the previous chapter, and to the 'empirical self' outlined earlier.

One of the central concerns of social work involves the nature of the relationship between worker and client. In recent years there has been a move towards – where clients are rational in the sense discussed in the last chapter – a democratisation of the relationship. Indeed, the notion of client sovereignty – of their having the right to make decisions for themselves, rather than have those decisions made for them – has become an increasing aspect of practice (Howe, 1996; Evetts, 2002).

One of the issues which has gone under the heading of 'empowerment', therefore, relates to this democratisation of the client–worker relationship. What are the conditions under which democratisation, or even client sovereignty, can be achieved?

Let us take a relatively straightforward example. In this example, the social worker is seeking to be non-directive. They are seeking to facilitate 'active willing choice' on the part of the client. An older person, fully capable of making her own decisions, has become physically frail and wishes to decide which residential home, of those in the area, it would be best for her to choose. Indeed, we could go further, since she may decide whether she wants residential care or some other package of care, including respite and day care.

We may expect a process to be undertaken in which the social worker discusses with the older person what she might be looking for, helps her clarify her ideas, and does so by acquainting her better with the alternatives available. The client may well be taken to visit various residential establishments, day care facilities and so on, and, in the light of these, be helped to consider exactly what she wants. It is a process, it would appear, of information provision, based on the social worker's awareness of local resources, combined with discussion and deliberation, through which the client is ultimately able to make up her mind. In this model the social worker, using his or her expertise, is nevertheless the servant of the client, whose interests are achieved through the decisions she makes.

However, even this apparently simple situation is not that straightforward. Very often, such older people have lived in their homes for decades. They hold memories and emotions for the place which are not lightly cast aside. They may have lived many years with a spouse, who may have died there. It may be the place where they raised their children, where their grandchildren were first brought to them. The decision to move, in other words, is likely not just to be an instrumental one, based on some calculation about 'best interests', given their physical condition. It will often be profoundly emotional, and at times extremely difficult.

Nevertheless, social workers are still in the business of helping the client make up his or her mind. Writers such as Ragg (1977), Keith Lucas (1972) and Jordan (1979) refer to this as encouraging 'active willing choice'. While, then, much of the task of the social worker is to inform, considerable importance is placed on the client's presentation – their active description. This involves informing the social worker, as clearly and accurately as possible, how they feel about their options. The social worker, in turn, needs to create an environment in which the client feels able to inform on matters that might be, for them, rather sensitive. Keith Lucas (1972) suggests the key elements, for the practitioner, are the capacity for honesty and the engendering of trust, and (through appropriate questioning) to draw out as accurate a picture as possible of the client's situation and aspirations.

The description involves a focus not just on the practical alternatives available to the client, but the emotional implications of choosing one or other of these alternatives. An active willing choice is made when, having worked through both practical and emotional implications, the client is able genuinely to decide what they want. It is a role for the social worker which may, in some respects, be therapeutic as well as facilitative.

Such anyway, is the picture of the benign social worker in a democratised relationship, operating on the basis of equality, or even client sovereignty, where active willing choice is achieved. This is one notion of empowerment. However, there are a number of conditions which would serve to undermine this client equality and sovereignty. Three may be identified here.

Some clients may be *susceptible to suggestions* by others, particularly those whom they may see as 'knowledgeable' in the area. They are 'suggestible'. However, this suggestibility can become insidious, paradoxically, where non-directive approaches are adopted. For some considerable time, there has been an awareness that non-directive approaches can be subtly directive. Certain kinds of verbal and particularly non-verbal communication – nods, grunts and 'mms' – can encourage certain directions and disclosures of information in interviews, while closing off others.

One problem here is that, no matter how non-directive a practitioner seeks to be, their own perceptions and focus are likely to appear, but covertly rather than overtly. In concentrating on some matters but not others, they subtly direct the client in certain directions, and it takes an effort of resistance for redirection to occur. This is all the more difficult because of the covert nature of the direction. The client may feel uncomfortable but be unaware of what is happening.

It is interesting, in this light, that some evidence suggests clients prefer some degree of advice and guidance to none at all (Sheppard, 1992, 1993). One obvious aspect of this may be that the client could feel they are tapping into the social worker's expertise. However, it may be that, by making suggestions and giving advice, the social worker is presenting the client with options with which the latter may agree or disagree in an open manner. It also provides a context in which the client can make their own suggestions. Such work could actually facilitate democratisation of the relationship.

A second element involves *persuasion*. It might seem surprising, but persuasion does not have to be antithetical to equality. Persuasion is fine, as long as it is the client who is able to make the decision. Their capacity to be able to make that decision, however, requires that they are able to deliberate properly on the matter (in our example the choices available between forms of residential care and supported living in the community). Persuasion needs to be rational; it needs to be an argument put forward for or against a position, in which evidence is presented in support of each position. It also involves being open to counter-arguments.

In order for persuasion to be rational there actually needs to be a core element of equality. It is a dialogue between equals. The assumption of equality, Benn (1967) suggests, arises because the openness to counter-arguments assumes and requires that you regard the other person as having equal status. If you are not open to counter-argument, you are not engaging in persuasion, but hectoring – to the extent that you are being open about what you are doing.

However, other features can undermine the legitimacy of persuasion by harming the capacity of the individual to make their own choice. One is the authority of the person seeking to persuade. As we have seen, social workers do have a significant authority role. However, they frequently deal with vulnerable people, and social workers may, to those people, appear to have an authority or power which they do not necessarily possess. A physically frail older person may assume that social workers have greater powers to decide where he or she resides than they, in reality, have. Where such assumptions exist, it may be relatively easy to persuade a client to a certain course of action – say, choosing one particular residential home – because they do not realise that they actually have a choice.

Another facet undermining active willing choice is where persuasion is characterised by deception. *Deception* is the deliberate provision of information designed to mislead. It is significant, in this case (apart from the value issues involved) because deception undermines the relationship between persuasion and active willing choice. In order to make a choice, one needs to be sure that the range of information provided is accurate. If it is not accurate, then clearly the client cannot be making a 'choice' – they do not have an accurate presentation of the real alternatives before them. If, for example, an older person were told that his neighbours were not particularly enthusiastic about providing needed support if he were to remain at home, when in fact those neighbours did not mind so doing, then he may well veer towards entering residential care, even if he would have preferred to remain at home. This, indeed can be quite subtle. Being 'not enthusiastic' does not mean 'not prepared if asked', particularly if such neighbours were aware that otherwise the older person might have to enter residential care, with an accompanying sense of loss and distress.

Persuasion, therefore, can be a part of the social worker's interaction with the client, provided it is rational and encourages choice. The interesting point here, of course, is that this notion of empowerment – active willing choice – involves a meeting of rational client with rational social worker. Much of what is involved is merely information giving, in that the client is assumed to know what is best for them. It is not just that there is an equality between client and worker, or even 'client sovereignty', it is that the client is in the best position to decide what is in their best interests. There is no particular 'personal growth' development or deeper understanding required. It is just a rational conversation between rational agents, through which the client can make their decisions.

Self-realisation

Another sense in which the term empowerment is used is that of self-realisation. This goes beyond the 'democratic relationship' outlined in the previous section, in which the worker is there to facilitate client decision making; the client is empowered to the extent that previous notions of 'professionals know best' are broken down and replaced by client sovereignty. Where self-realisation is involved, we are talking about personal growth.

'Personal growth' generally refers to the process by which an individual gains a deeper understanding of themselves than had previously been the case. It is often the focus for counselling. Personal growth might be the aim where someone subject to depression seeks to understand better the nature and origins of their depression, and why it is that they are susceptible to it. The idea is that where they have greater understanding they have the potential for greater control. If you know what it is about *you* that helps generate and maintain depression, then you may be able to deal with those facets of your personality, and interactions with others, which cause depression.

However, it can be more than that. To 'self-realise' is to become what you have the potential to become. It is this that denotes 'personal growth'. The individual, through a helping process, is able to 'grow as a person', to become more than they have been before, to be more at ease with themselves and their world.

A woman may, for example, be the subject of domestic violence in a marriage which is profoundly unsatisfying for her and yet find that, despite her experience of domestic violence, she remains with her partner. She may do so even though she is worried that living in that environment may be emotionally damaging to her children. She may have quite ambivalent feelings towards her partner. He may be quite inconsistent, generally behaving reasonably and, at times, quite caring. At others he may become threatening and even violent.

Nevertheless, she is uncertain what to do. Should she remain with him? Or should she go? What would the effects be on the children if she left? Would they be worse if she stayed? Underneath all this, however, may be the need to understand herself better, in order to know what to do in this situation. How is it that she has become involved with this man? Why is it that she has not left him? What is it that she gets out of the relationship? What is it about *her* that is important in this situation? Understanding herself can lead to personal growth, enabling her to appraise the situation better, or even reappraise it entirely. It enables her to address her own needs and interests rather better. That, at least, is the idea.

Underlying this is again an issue of choice, and the capacity to choose, in the senses we discussed in the previous chapter. Reaching a state of 'self-realisation' means reaching a stage of self-knowledge – of understanding oneself. The emphasis is on humans as autonomous, or potentially autonomous – that is, able to be self-directing based on an understanding of themselves. In the case we have mentioned, it is a more profound understanding on the part of the woman of herself which will enable her to make decisions – about staying or going, or the circumstances under which she may be prepared to stay.

If the person has the potential capacity to take responsibility for their lives, then it is, in turn, the social worker's responsibility to help them to do so. The social worker acts as a catalyst, probing and observing, enabling the person to develop insight into themselves and their situation through these probes and observations. The social worker is the 'helper' or facilitator of a process through which the client achieves a state (or a state greater than previously) of self-determination.

Keith Lucas (1972) is one of a number of writers who makes a great deal of self-fulfilment on the part of the client as a major objective of practice (Ragg, 1977; Jordan 1979; Wilkes, 1981). He contrasts this with notions like social functioning. For him social functioning merely means enabling the client to perform roles better than previously, to be a better father or mother, worker, colleague, and so on (or to be at least minimally competent in performing them). Performing a social role adequately is, he feels, rather close to conformity. When promoting social functioning, therefore, social workers are getting dangerously close to forcing – or at least encouraging – social conformity on an individual (Keith Lucas, 1972, p. 13). It tends towards social policing of the morals and behaviours of people, rather than promoting them as valuable persons in their own right.

There is something of 'the gift' in all this. Keith Lucas (1972) and Ragg (1977) both emphasise that a key aspect of this is 'helping', and that this involves 'giving' (of oneself). Help is something given by one person (the social worker) to another (the client). The other side of this is the capacity of the client to make use of this help. The woman who sought help (in our example, in relation to her violent relationship with her partner) has to be able to make use of the help in order to grow as a person. If, for example, there are aspects of her as a person (for example, low self-esteem and contempt for herself) which contribute to her preparedness to stay with the violent partner, then this is something which she has to face. If not, there can be no room for personal growth. That is not to suggest that this is an easy process.

However, this is also about the person of the helper. As Jordan (1979) points out, it may not always be clear to the client exactly what these qualities are, but 'somehow, without knowing why, I shall feel better after having talked to him [or her] because I shall not have escaped from anything or twisted anything … but I shall have been recognised, treated as real by a fellow human being' (Jordan, 1979, p. 26). Those qualities, generally recognised as empathy, warmth and genuineness, may also contribute to the attractiveness, for the social worker, of this sort of work. It is subject to subject (clearly a central aspect of social work) and essentially a very 'human' relationship.

This notion of self-realisation, of personal growth, is related to the idea of the self-determining individual as being free of internal constraints, as outlined in the previous chapter. It is a process of achieving self-determination, of being able to make choices and reach decisions which, without personal growth, could not have occurred in such an enlightened manner. It is, however, one in which the worker and client come together through mutual agreement, in which the decision, on the part of the client, is unencumbered by any external constraints, such as those of the authority role of the social worker. In some respects, therefore, this notion of self-realisation has something in common with that given in relation to social work's authority role, in which self-determination is what needs to be achieved, and requires some degree of insight and enlightenment on the part of the client.

However, this is also a profoundly individualised notion of social work. It really has more in common with counselling. The implicit picture here is that of two individuals coming together to work on the problems of one of them, without the encumbrance of the state or the social responsibilities which permeate social work practice. The whole point of social workers working in the realm of the social (why they are *social* workers) is that the very construction of social work excludes this individualised, purely privatised, notion of a relationship between worker and client. This much is clearly evident from previous chapters. Social workers have a role, and that role means that they are 'agents of society'. It also entails that the very meaning of the social worker–client relationship cannot simply be created in the client–worker situation or meetings. In the case of the woman subject to domestic violence, a woman with children, the social worker involved cannot escape his or her responsibilities to the children and any threats to them (emotional or physical) which may occur as a result of the domestic violence. Indeed, it is quite likely that social workers would not be involved in the first place if it were not for child care issues.

Indeed, what happens if this involves a clash with social work responsibilities? Suppose the woman, even having experienced some personal growth, wishes to remain with her partner, despite periods of violence. Is this something which the social worker can tolerate, in view of the potential threat to the children? It may not be. This points to another aspect of this individualised, personalised notion of the relationship; that is, that there is an assumption that, ultimately, there is some kind of agreement between worker and client as to what is best and, indeed, that this is ultimately to be determined by the client. However, it may not be ultimately determined by the client, particularly where the authority role of the social worker is involved.

We cannot get away from the fact that, although personal growth may be a part of what takes place, at times, in social work intervention, it is quite limited as a description of purpose in social work practice.

Gender

Feminist ideas have had a huge impact on social work in the past two decades. This reflects a wider influence in the social sciences and society at large. In relation to social work, feminist ideas have been closely associated with the empowerment agenda, although reflecting the specifics of feminist theory. From this perspective (or set of perspectives), empowerment, for women, is closely linked to gender; that is, the social construction of 'womanhood' and the position of women in society.

While recognising this underlying theme, it is also important to recognise that different positions are adopted *within* the broad church of feminist thought, and these have been related to the practice of social work. Dominelli (2002), for example, identifies four intellectual groupings: liberal, radical, Marxist and socialist, and black feminism. These differ in value systems and the forms of politicisation they pursue. Liberal feminists, for example, are characterised by underlying beliefs in independence, equal opportunities and individualism. They have, however, in their more individualistic focus, been criticised for an inability to critique the overall structure of society. Radical feminists focus on the system of patriarchy, the social organisation, they argue, which systematically favours men, leaving them dominant and privileged at the expense of women. These, in turn, have been criticised for failing to look at structural issues *other* than patriarchy. Marxists and socialists place the economic system under scrutiny, focusing in particular on the ways in which this system produces inequality and disadvantage, and how it operates to the detriment of women. Black feminists have taken racism as their starting point (including that of white feminists), seeking to link the dynamics of racism to that of patriarchy in society.

In turn, these analyses have differing implications for social work. Those who, for example, are attracted by a Marxist feminism are drawn towards a form of social work which inevitably must seek to operate on the wider social structure and social policy, since it is at this level that the disadvantage of women originates. Social work influenced by liberal feminists, whose analysis pays less attention to these structural issues, will focus more at the individual and familial level. This, of course, serves to emphasise the potential diversity within feminist intellectual traditions. However – and we shall consider some of the reasons later in relation to Marxist/structural social work – the undeniably significant impact of feminist thought on the *practice* of social work (as opposed to its academic writing) has been greatest where it tends towards the liberal tradition and in relation to race.

Despite the intellectual diversity of feminist thought, there is a common link in the concern with the position and social construction of women, encapsulated in the term 'gender'. Just as those in social work who are concerned with self-realisation focus on personal growth, so feminist theorists are also interested in the capacity in women for personal growth and development. However, for them, those who focus on self-realisation, as outlined above, have an overemphasis on psychology, where instead true personal growth is to be achieved by an additional understanding of the social and political position of women (Summerson Carr, 2003). Personal growth, through a feminist lens, requires the synthesis of a psychological understanding with social understanding.

The personal development aim, then, in feminist practice, is for a changed consciousness, a changed appreciation on the part of individual women of their own situation, derived from an understanding of the position of women in society. It is one which recognises the individual woman's own position as one of oppression, but that it arises because of a common oppression experienced by *all* women. A fundamental change in women's consciousness, where they are disempowered, is necessary for empowerment to take place. There is a process of *praxis* – the bringing together of feminist theory, the practical experience of the woman and the conduct of practice – which enables feminist practitioners to act in an empowering way and for women, in turn, to be empowered (GlenMaye, 1998).

There are, therefore, two dimensions which are the concern of feminists. It is important that women free themselves from both inner *and* outer hindrances to their personal growth and development. The inner hindrances lie in their self-image, self-understanding and self-esteem. The outer hindrances, closely related to the inner ones, are the features of a society which consistently disadvantage and oppress women.

A criticism of traditional (pre-feminist) social work is that the voice of women clients is lost in the conduct of practice. Many social work techniques, it is suggested, perceived and assessed women in ways which had little bearing on their own perceptions of their situation. There should, instead, be a focus on the subjective shared experience of oppression, and feminist social work should develop its understanding from the day-to-day experiences of women clients and workers (Hudson, 1985). Feminist practice involves helping women reframe and reconstruct their experiences in a manner which will help give them greater control over their own lives.

Our example of the woman subject to domestic violence illustrates this point. While an approach seeking to achieve self-realisation concentrates on enabling the woman to understand herself and her actions, the better able to decide what to do, feminist approaches consider this to be insufficient. Instead, it is important to understand domestic violence as an *issue*, particularly one of gender. It is one commonly suffered by women, and an appropriate appreciation by the woman of her own position requires her also to appreciate the position of the many women suffering domestic violence. Domestic violence, in other words, is not just about her partner, her and their relationship, it is about men and women more generally, and about sets of values and behaviours which enable domestic violence to be widespread.

To overcome her oppression, which can have severe psychological as well as other consequences, the woman needs (according to this approach) to develop a 'higher understanding' of her position. If a changed consciousness is required, as Sibeon (1990) points out, there is a false consciousness to start with, and many feminist writers implicitly or explicitly subscribe to this position. This is an idea that the individual is mistaken because he or she does not have a full understanding of their true situation and interests.

The implication of this is that some women (those of a feminist persuasion) have a higher understanding (than those who do not). What, though, of women who assert their own commitment to a traditional role for women, such as mother, homemaker, housewife and so on? Can they be right, in view of feminist theory? It would appear difficult to sustain such a position. This, however, would appear to undermine the very validity of women's experiences which have been championed by writers such as Hudson (1985).

Some writers (see Dominelli 2002) have sought to square this circle by recourse to a postmodernist position. There is, they suggest, no one truth, but many truths located in different 'places'. Thus the 'feminist truth' can coexist with the 'traditional truth', with each accepting the validity of the other. However, this rather undermines the feminist position, since it is precisely in its *opposition* to the more traditional perspectives that it seeks to claim validity. One cannot set oneself up in opposition to a position, only to agree that it is, nevertheless, as valid and true as one's own (McInnes-Miller and Weiling, 2002). Indeed, it undermines the very moral force for the feminist case (or cases).

It is in attempting to accept the unacceptable that feminism may be caught in this fix. But it is also about two quite different perceptions of self-determination, which we outlined earlier. Using an 'external constraints' notion, the woman committed to traditional perspectives of womanhood is, indeed, making decisions for herself. She is choosing, of her own volition, a traditional role. However, an 'internal constraints' notion suggests that she is not self-determining, She is, in her commitment to traditional values, necessarily not self-determining, because she is in a state of false consciousness. She does not fully understand her situation, so she is not able to make fully informed self-determining actions.

Dominelli and Macleod (1989, pp. 80–81) in fact reject evidence that some women may be happy with their lives, referring to a mistaken sense of 'contentment'. They argue that 'revelations from feminist work questions whether the contentment of an unknown number of women is being bought at a morally unacceptable price in terms of reinforcing a set of social relations that are fundamentally detrimental to women's emotional welfare'. This insight is achieved through the higher understanding of the position of women gained from feminism.

Feminist empowerment, therefore, is committed to a notion of self-determination which focuses, in examining women's understanding of their position, on 'internal constraints'. Women are able to choose properly only when they understand fully. The task of the practitioner is to help them reach a higher understanding than may previously have been the case. Women are empowered through this higher understanding which enables them to act more fully in their own interests.

Structural and Marxist practice

Feminism and Marxism have a common interest in the way the workings of society impact on those most disadvantaged. Both are concerned with ideology, and how ideas dominant in a society can distort people's perceptions of their true interests. Feminists may be concerned by, for example, dominant models of the 'traditional housewife' which, they may argue, limit women's capacity to reach their true potential. Marxists may be concerned that a commitment to the current economic and social system undermines people's capacity to see how this limits them, particularly those most disadvantaged. In the case of feminism, the concern with societal functioning focuses on gender. In the case of Marxism the focus is on economic disadvantage, inequality and the ideology and power dimensions associated with them.

This has been the theme of a number of writers (Corrigan and Leonard, 1978; Jones, 1983; Rojek et al., 1988; Mullaly, 1998). Like feminists, Marxist writers have criticised the focus on the individual in their immediate environment, characteristic of traditional social work. Traditional social work makes a great deal about values of client care, empathy, respect for persons and so on. However, for Leonard (1975) these claims are fraudulent because they are impossible to achieve within a capitalist society. Capitalist society has a system with inequality at its heart and some social groups in dominant economic and social positions at the expense of others. Inequality of this sort inevitably means there are losers as well as winners in the competitive environment of capitalism, and traditional social work does nothing to alter these basic facets of society.

These very individualised values in traditional social work, Leonard thought, served a mystifying function. Those committed to such values would see social work as an outlet for their own efforts, consistent with their own beliefs. Goals such as self-fulfilment and self-realisation are simply not possible in a capitalist society. For such goals to be achieved, it is necessary to transcend capitalism and to create a social system in which the achievement of human needs is widely possible. There is, in other words, a necessary focus on society as a whole, rather than on the individual or family in their immediate social environment.

The analysis and understanding of society and its structures, therefore, are necessary if the resolution of fundamental human needs, including achievement of self-realisation, are to be achieved. The most extensive statement of Marxism as an empowering form of social work practice was made by Corrigan and Leonard (1978). There are two key elements to this: class and class conflict, and the examination of the role of the state. Corrigan and Leonard (1978) identified some of those elements widely perceived to be significant by Marxist writers. The dominant mode of production – capitalism – provides the base for society. On this basis the social and political institutions of society, as well as its dominant ideology, emerge.

Capitalism's economic base throws up classes of owners (bourgeoisie) and workers (proletariat). The former own the means of production, distribution and exchange, while the latter are forced to sell their labour in order to obtain wages. The relationship between former and latter is one of exploitation, particularly economic. The inequalities which emerge in a capitalist society are not accidental. They are the determined result of the economic and social system. They occur alongside the highly competitive characteristics of capitalist society, helping to produce a strong emphasis on individualism. The result of this and other facets of capitalism is that a whole range of social problems emerge, many of which are directly the concern of social work. It is no coincidence that many of the clients of social workers are amongst the most economically deprived in society.

The classes – proletariat and bourgeoisie – have fundamentally different and conflicting interests. However, the exploited group, the working class, is the progressive force in society. It is through working-class actions that social and economic change may occur to create a fairer society, more in tune with human needs. There is, then, a struggle between classes.

The state, however, propounds the long-term interests of the ruling class (the bourgeoisie). This is because, while it may appear to be a neutral site for governance, it is actually an instrument for the most powerful groups in society. However, the long-term interests of the ruling class do not involve an unrelenting attack on the working class. An enlightened view of the interests of the ruling class recognises that inequalities which are too great are liable to foment a political reaction amongst the exploited and disadvantaged. The welfare state, therefore, comes into being as a means to ameliorate the worst effects of capitalism (Miller and Neusess, 1978).

However, its concern is not merely with the economic, but the associated social. Through the welfare state, institutions emerge to deal with many of the problems whose origins lie with the nature of society itself and with its structure and inequalities. One such institution is that of social work. At the same time, however, according to this view, there is an emphasis on social pathology as a means of analysing these problems amongst the clients of social work. This social pathology involves explaining the problems and needs of individuals, such as those who abuse children or break the law, at the level of the individual. Offending behaviour may occur because an individual has not been sufficiently socialised to observe standards of behaviour. Child abuse may emerge because of past life experiences which damage the psychological capacities of a parent to carry out their parental functions properly. However, the real origin of these problems ultimately lies with a society which operates in a way which inevitably produces a whole range of social problems. It is in concentrating on the individual, on the emphasis on social pathology, that welfare state professionals are involved in a mystifying process, where the true explanation is to be found at the level of society.

The embracing of this analysis involves the adoption of profoundly different modes of practice from that characteristic of traditional social work. At one level, there is a commitment to gaining more resources for the disadvantaged and exploited groups in society. However, this is one of the more immediate goals of radical practitioners, and it is insufficient on its own to tackle the real problems. Social workers should, Corrigan and Leonard (1978) suggested, be allied to the main progressive forces in society. Within the working class, trade unions have a critical position in this respect. Trade unions, given their political ideology, can contribute to the defence of the welfare state and to the protection of social workers engaged in more radical practice. They can also contribute to the development of a wider political consciousness which would be a force for progress. In addition there is an emphasis on collective action on the part of social workers. With clients, this means facilitating their linkage with organisations of oppressed community groups, or groups such as the

Child Poverty Action Group, acting on their behalf or representing them. For social workers themselves, and within their organisations, this requires working collectively with colleagues.

The final dimension (one shared in some respects with feminism) is the raising of consciousness, or conscientisation (Friere, 1972). This is the process of uncovering the political roots of people's individual experiences of powerlessness and oppression (Gutterez and Lewis, 1999). It is about developing a deeper understanding on the part of the individual of the origins of their difficulties and their common interest, in this respect, with others. It involves a process of praxis: bringing together the experiences of the oppressed with a critical analysis of the society in which these experiences are produced. It involves also a process by which the growing understanding is linked to action designed to deal with the real causes of their oppression. Thus, individuals develop a consciousness of oppression and of their ability, with others, to challenge that oppression.

Empowerment, on this formulation, therefore, is necessarily a profoundly political process, whose ultimate aim is the transcendence of the capitalist system itself. The personal problems of the individuals with whom social workers work are also public issues. Empowering social work practice necessarily involves tackling these public issues.

There are profound problems, however, to this notion of empowerment as a form of social work practice (as opposed to political activity). Halmos (1978) challenged this conflation of the 'personal' and 'political', suggesting they were separate areas of social life. The solution, likewise, rests in different realms. We cannot achieve social change by a 'personal' involvement with troubled individuals. Likewise, we cannot hope to achieve change in troubled individuals, or those with difficult relations, through political action. Personalising the political, or politicising the personal, therefore, must fail. In any case, not all troubles which are the concern of social work can be traced to an economic or political origin. It would be preposterous to suggest, for example, that the origins of the problems of people who have physical or learning disability lies in the social or economic structure or the political system.

The emphasis on structure and issues, furthermore, sits uneasily with a social work whose social construction involves a focus on individuals in their immediate social environment. We have seen earlier how social work operates between the public and the private, role and person, subject and object, on concerns which have been socially constructed and legitimised before its involvement. Social work is less *about* political agitation than its long-term *consequence*.

Social work operates with a generally individualised – never social structural – focus on issues whose nature and definition have already been set. Marxism may provide a challenge to individualised practice and give social workers considerable pause for thought. It cannot, however, provide a form of social work, because its very theory prescribes a realm of operation, the level of social structure, which is 'out of bounds' for practice. It is no coincidence that Marxist practice has never even gained a toehold on practice.

Conclusion

With social work so identified with the notion of empowerment, one might expect it to be a coherent and clear concept. However, empowerment would also appear to be loosely connected to the ideas of social exclusion and inclusion which, as we have seen, go to the heart of social work. To the extent that social exclusion is associated with the absence of power and participation in society, the idea of empowering would seem to fit neatly with social work's core business.

This, however, underestimates the diversity of its use. We have, in fact, a number of mutually incompatible notions. First, we have the problem: is empowerment about the empirical self or the potential self? Is it about enabling the person in their overt and stated desires, in relation to their need? Or is it about helping them to reframe their existing ideas – which can involve false consciousness – in order that they gain a deeper understanding of their condition, and can act on that deeper understanding? This is important, because if the second is the case, it implies that it would not be empowering to act upon the existing stated wishes of the person. Yet the 'empirical self' formulation *requires* that this be the case (acting on their existing wishes) for empowerment to take place. It means that some actions (which with one approach would be considered empowering) would (with another) be regarded as not empowering, and even potentially coercive.

Beyond this, the division between empirical and potential self is one also underlying the authority role in social work. This creates the rather problematic position for those espousing the cause of empowerment: that the lack of understanding underlying the 'potential self' formulation of empowerment reflects closely that situation characterising circumstances in which the authority role is legitimised. This creates the rather alarming position that 'control' in social work is difficult to distinguish, in its underlying assumptions, from some formulations of 'empowerment'. This, I am sure, is not the intention of those, like feminists, who espouse the cause of empowerment but, in certain key respects, it is an unavoidable consequence of their assumptions.

A further problem lies in the societal assumptions underlying these different formulations. There is the world of difference between formulations which focus solely on the developmental psychology of self-realisation and others which require wholesale social change. The former concentrates largely on the individual in his or her immediate circumstances; the latter requires action at a more societal level as part of intervention. Each position, furthermore, denies the validity of the other. While Leonard (1975) regarded the developmental psychology position of self-realisation to be a process of mystification and social pathology, Halmos (1978) considered it entirely invalid to focus on the political as part of the personal, which he considered quite separate domains.

Beyond this, certain formulations are simply inconsistent with the idea of social work, as we have noted. The very nature and meaning of social work requires that structural-level interventions are not really 'social work'. It can be no surprise, therefore, that Marxist social work ideas have never really had any influence on the conduct of practice interventions. This, it should be emphasised, is not a personal comment on my part about the validity of Marxism as a system of analysis or a recipe for action in modern industrial society. Indeed, at a personal level, there are aspects of Marxism which I consider to have penetrative insight into modern industrial society. That, however, is different from suggesting that Marxism is consistent with the idea of social work. It is not, and cannot be.

This is the advantage of feminist ideas. For while some radical and Marxist feminists would have the same problem incorporating their ideas into a practice of social work, other feminist formulations would not. Not only are they consistent with the appropriate 'societal level' of intervention for social work, some adopt forms of knowledge which are also consistent with social work (Sheppard, 1997, 1998). The requirement, therefore, that a core of objectivity be at the heart of social work is one with which many feminist could sympathise. Just as this is an essential for the values (and practice) of social work to have any real meaning, so it also gives a moral coherence and power to the position of feminists who take a similar position in relation to knowledge and our understanding of social life. Once we understand these points, it can be of little surprise to see the influence of feminist ideas on practice (as opposed to writings) on social work in recent years, compared with the absence of influence of Marxism.

Summerson Carr's comment on empowerment, therefore, has huge resonance for social work. 'There has been a virtual chorus of discontent regarding the haziness with which empowerment has been defined in the literature' (Summerson Carr, 2003, p. 10). If there is a problem with the term intellectually, how much greater is that problem going to be when we try to adopt it (if 'it' is what it can be said to be) for practice? Yet that appears to have been exactly what has been attempted. Students are expected to demonstrate their capacity 'to empower' as if it were simply a technical act of the skilled practitioner. However, it is not even a coherent concept. It cannot possibly lead to a coherent practice.

It seems, therefore, that 'empowerment' provides a very poor basis on which to found the aims, and even processes, of social work. It may be that the term is more significant because of its emotive content than anything else: it makes those who propound it feel good about the nature of their work. That might certainly help explain its huge influence on social work, alongside its contradictions and problematic coherence.

It is not, however, the only concept which has been put forward in recent years. The others may lack the emotive appeal of a term like empowerment, but perhaps provide for the better understanding of what social work is about. We shall turn to these relatively neglected concepts next.

Chapter nine

Maintenance, social functioning and coping

Nearly a quarter of a century ago, Howe (1980) warned against social work – and particularly social work academics – seeking to aggrandise the occupation by making claims that it could not possibly achieve. He was thinking of the ideas of the time, especially some aspects of radical practice, in particular Marxism. Social work, on these formulations, claimed to be involved in processes that even established and demonstrably effective professions, such as medicine, did not assert. In its Marxist form, social work was supposed to be involved in processes leading to change in the very form of society. Even more modest assertions of the capacity to create positive change, which did not involve societal change, made claims which, in reality, social work found hard to fulfil. Social work was in danger of being its own worst enemy.

It is not unreasonable to suggest that this tendency exists today. Some of the notions of empowerment present social workers with the same aggrandised notions of a sort which Howe earlier detected. Social work writing, a part of which has always looked to sociology for guidance, now looks to postmodernism, where in the past it was Marxism. As the 'centre of gravity' in sociology has changed, so major elements of social work writing find themselves reflecting this. We may, I think, expect the same sort of thing to happen in the future, not necessarily to the benefit or illumination of social work practice.

Not all writing has, however, sought to make such grand claims. There is a stream of ideas which make more modest claims for social work, a modesty which makes the claims potentially more sustainable. These do not seek to present social work as engendering greater power in its clients, or of changing the very fabric of society or even of too great a level of expectations of individual change. They are characterised by a perception of social work's position in society which is more easily congruent with the position it actually occupies.

However, the language of choice does not paint the picture of the social worker as heroic professional, as is the case with notions like empowerment, the formulae for Marxist practice or a focus on structure for practice. It may be for this reason that these ideas have attracted rather less attention.

While, for example, empowerment is written into the expectations for competent practice in social work qualifying courses (how does one 'empower' competently, when it is conceptually so elusive?) and the term 'postmodernism' appears in one publication after another, we see no such focus on terms such as maintenance, social functioning or coping. And yet, in the messy, chronic and ever-changing situations with which practitioners are so frequently confronted, the capacity (for example) of the social worker to help the client to cope, or to maintain a family as a viable unit, is often a far more realistic objective. One is, frankly, far more likely to ask of the practitioner in everyday situations, 'how is Mrs. Jones coping lately?' than 'has Mrs. Jones been empowered in the last week?'

Maintenance theory

Maintenance theory is a concept developed by Martin Davies over various editions of the *Essential Social Worker*. Davies felt that social work had been damaged by perceptions that it could be some kind of left-wing activity working for social change (on the one hand) or some form of psychotherapeutic activity engendering psychological improvement (on the other).

Davies's ideas, at heart, have the merit of simplicity. His view is that social work is fundamentally in the business of maintenance – the maintenance of the individual or family on one hand, and the maintenance of the society on the other. The term used here, it should be noted, is important for Davies. It is maintaining, rather than changing, which dominates a proper conception of social work. The social worker is involved, in his or her own humble way, with seeking to ensure that the society as it is and the individual both remain viable. He uses the metaphor of social workers being the 'maintenance mechanics' of society, oiling its wheels to ensure its smooth functioning.

The assumptions he adopts about humans and societies point specifically to a residual role for social work. Social workers cannot be the shock troops in the achievement of social change. They operate at the margins. He suggests that in all (modern) societies, and within the framework of the wider social and economic community, individuals and families will maintain themselves, exist in relative self-sufficiency and derive personal satisfaction from the way they make use of opportunities that are presumed to exist. He points to the 'underlying assumption about the ultimate primacy of the human unit [presumably human being] living his or her own life to the best of his or her ability' (Davies, 1994, p. 57). Indeed, it reflects a fundamental belief in the capacity of 'man'[sic] to improve his circumstances without doing so at the expense of others.

He also adopts a consensus model of society. Social work, he suggests, reflects the values widely shared in society, in relation to particular welfare problems. Society, it is recognised, has imperfections, and social work is concerned with ameliorating the effects of these imperfections. Indeed, he suggests that one can recognise the importance of social policy and structural change but, in relation to these imperfections, the individualist approach of social work is justified and legitimised. He suggests that if social workers were not around to perform the tasks they carry out, then it would be necessary to rectify this by creating some group of workers who carried out these functions.

In working with these 'casualties' of societies, social workers express care: they see the anguish of the poor, share the pain of the mother coping with the Down's syndrome child, experience at close range the degradation of the dole queue, realise that offenders are never all bad. In the process, they recognise the naivety of ideological attempts to change human affairs wholly at arm's length and only in accordance with general theories.

What, then, is the terrain of social workers? They work at the end of a spectrum where dysfunctioning has either reached chronic or epidemic proportions, or where its effects are spilling over into the lives of vulnerable people. They seek to maintain society. They are employed by the state to curb some of the excesses of deviant behaviour. Thus they have a role in the protection of children, in working with young offenders and in compulsory admissions to psychiatric hospitals. These actions are intended to contribute to the smooth running of society, to *maintain* it.

Social workers are also concerned with ameliorating the living conditions of those who are finding it difficult to cope without help. They focus, through agency objectives, on improving the quality of life of various people. Social workers seek to maintain the independence of adults, to protect the short- and long-term interests of children and to contribute to the creation of a climate in which citizens can maximise their potential for personal development.

Maintenance is manifested in two fundamental ways. Social workers first strive to 'hold the line', to prevent deterioration in performance, to combat the client's feelings that life can only get worse. They also seek to do such work on the environment that will reverse any strong running momentum that will make decline inevitable.

However, following on from this, they hope to reach the point where the client's own capacity for self-help begins to re-emerge and where growth and improvement – and therefore change – become feasible. Interestingly, while Davies argues that social work is about maintenance rather than change, he does see change as a potential aspect of maintenance. It is not, however, the social worker who changes the client. Rather, by helping the latter to maintain themselves, they help the conditions to emerge where the client will be able, through their own efforts, to create change.

It is the focus on the individual and society that is the dual concern of social work. In pursuit of the maintenance of both, resources are allocated which indicate society's commitment to those practices with which social work is involved. Social workers, in turn, pursue maintenance by a wide range of supportive strategies designed to maximise self-respect and develop the abilities of individuals to survive and thrive under their own steam. While it is possible, at the conceptual level, to separate the maintenance strategy towards society and towards the individual, in practice, he thinks, they are not so easily disentangled. Rather, the two coexist in the actions of social workers in relation to the range of their work.

Davies's work has the merit of simplicity and clarity. Much of his writing goes on to show how an empirical examination of the practice of social work is consistent with maintenance theory. However, the simplicity also means that a deeper analysis of the processes involved are not subject to conceptual analysis. How, for example, do we recognise what maintenance is in practice? What exactly does a maintained client look like? How do we know what to focus on, or how to think about aspects of the client's situation, in order for maintenance to take place?

Furthermore, there are no related concepts at the level of the client which enable us to think about maintenance in more detail. Most of Davies's work focuses only on social work's place in society, a kind of 'consensus sociology of social work'. How, for example, are we to think about the interaction of environmental factors with the feelings and behaviours of the individuals and families themselves?

Indeed, how are standards set and what legitimacy do they have by which we can tell how maintenance is to be achieved? When should social workers be involved? And what should they be aiming for? Finally, his view of society is rather reified – that is, he tends to treat society as a thing or even a metaphorical 'person' which makes decisions and interacts with individuals rather than a relationship. Society is a relationship of people, rather than a thing.

Social functioning

Bartlett (1970), in writing about social functioning, draws upon a wider tradition which, as a result, provides greater possibilities than maintenance. It does so while – in general – falling within the broad conceptions characterised by maintenance. Social functioning and social adjustment have often been used interchangeably. Linn et al. (1969, p. 299) comment: 'effective functioning would suggest equilibrium within the person, and in his [sic] interaction with the [social] environment'. Katz and Lyerly (1963, p. 506) comment similarly about social adjustment: 'literally, social adjustment has to do with bringing into proper relation, behaviour to circumstances or oneself to one's environment: to free from differences or discrepancies'.

Bartlett's central focus (for social work) is the enhancement of social functioning. Like other authors, she sees this as relating to people's interaction with their environment. There were, she thought, two central subconcepts, the first being tasks. Tasks are the activities which people may have to fulfil, such as child rearing, transition from hospital to home, and so on. Their capacity to perform these tasks may relate to the person's abilities. However, an individual may fail in these tasks, not so much because of facets of themselves, but because of aspects of the environment which can make task performance extremely difficult. This may arise, for example, through some kind of disadvantage which can lead, in the individual, to stress or disturbance. If the social circumstances of an individual are too stressful, then task performance can become difficult. The mother whose partner has just left her, who is facing managing on social security benefits for the first time, and who has little support from others, may well be faced with stressors the severity of which would impact seriously on her capacity to care for her children.

Coping is another key concept. When the demands of the environment are excessive in relation to a person's coping capacities, they may become overwhelmed, or even helpless. Poverty, racial discrimination, lack of access to jobs and so on can lead, Bartlett thinks, to stress, alienation and anxiety. Thus, two key questions emerge in any assessment of social functioning: what are the environmental demands on the person? What are his or her coping capacities? There is what she calls an 'exchange balance', between people's coping and environmental demands.

Social workers, Bartlett considered, are concerned with the balance between people's coping efforts and environmental demands. She believed that 'as more adequate knowledge of social functioning is built up by the profession, practitioners will be better able to foresee the possible and probable consequence of the various patterns of exchange between people and environment' (Bartlett, 1970, p. 111). However, like Davies in relation to maintenance, an interesting idea is not explored in depth, theoretically at least. Goldstein (1973, p. 5) related improved social functioning to social learning. Social work provides a means through which clients can examine alternatives and work out solutions. It provides a context which maximises the possibilities of improved social learning.

139

This learning could occur thorough confronting difficulties and carrying out life tasks (the successful performance of tasks leading to social learning). Pincus and Minahan (1973) focus on the concept of 'life tasks' in building on Bartlett's work. They outline the key elements of the social functioning concerns of social work, adopting the same 'person in environment' focus characteristic of Bartlett's work. Social workers were engaged in (amongst other things):

- enhancing people's problem-solving capacities
- linking people with systems that provide them with resources, services and opportunities
- promoting the effective and humane operation of these systems.

Both Pincus and Minahan (1973) and Goldstein (1973) adopt models which focus more on the social systems which provide the context for the individual than is evident in Bartlett's work. That is because the issue of social functioning was considered theoretically within the framework of systems theory. Their concern was that the focus would be too much on the individual, in particular how the individual would *adjust themselves* to the system, rather than changing the system to fit with the needs of the client. By thinking interactionally, it encourages social workers to think less about the individual than about the interface between the individual and the social systems in society.

We are still left, however, with fairly general descriptions of the kinds of features which might be relevant to social functioning. There is no examination of either 'internal' psychological processes or 'external' social processes in any detail beyond the general terms such as tasks, coping and systems. Ecological thinkers provide a model for systemic interventions, which identifies different levels at which intervention can take place (Whittaker and Garbarino, 1983). These do suggest levels which would entail a focus less on individuals. Thus, while at one extreme there are micro systems, which are the immediate social network of individuals (their family, place of work, school and so on), at the other are the ideological and cultural expectations of society. These are macro systems which reflect shared beliefs, creating behavioural patterns. However, they are framed at a level of generality which does not allow us to think in more detail about a theory of social functioning.

Hollis (1972), whose systems thinking is more about 'person in situation' rather than an ecological approach, nevertheless introduces some key concepts which would allow us to examine social functioning in more detail. These are the concepts of reference group, and particularly role. While she does not go into great detail, there are others who do. The link with role is apparent in some long-established definitions of social adjustment and functioning. Garland et al. (1972, p. 259) suggest that social maladjustment 'has been defined as ineffective performance in the roles and tasks for which an individual has been socialised'. Likewise, Weissman and Paykel (1974) have suggested that 'in general terms, social adjustment concerns the individual's ability to function in social roles'.

To understand roles we first need to understand *positions*. Societies are neither characterised by members who are entirely alike, nor by people whose differences are completely random. What is characteristic of societies are groups or classes of people who behave similarly in certain areas of social life. We talk of classes of people called fathers, mothers, teachers, philosophers and so on. These are names where their similarities are collectively recognised in the society (Biddle and Thomas, 1966, p. 65). An individual may occupy a number of positions – he or she might be treasurer of a local sports club, parent, doctor and member of a school governors' committee. Thus, each position is an element, or part of, a network of positions.

Merton (1957, p. 369) suggests that each position includes a number of roles. This he calls a 'role set'. This is the complement of role relationships which an individual has as a result of occupying a particular position. For example, a school teacher has a role set relating them as teacher to pupils, colleagues, the school head, parent–teachers' and friends' organisations, trade union and professional organisations. For each of these role relationships there is a set of behaviours which is expected of the individual in a particular position. In a family, which is so often the focus for social work intervention, a mother would have a role set likely to relate her to her partner, son, daughter and so on, and a set of expectations in her relations with each of them.

These broad statements are helpful in considering social functioning, for we can consider the adequacy of social functioning in relation to role performance. How well, we might ask, is the mother performing in her various tasks as a parent? Is there anything that can be done to help her if she is struggling? What should that be? These are the kinds of questions which have considerable relevance for social work practice.

In principle then, we might think we can identify both the kinds of tasks which are involved in particular roles (because there are common expectations), and also the level at which performance might be considered to be adequate. The mother's role as parent might, for example, include setting appropriate boundaries to the child, providing adequate physical care and hygiene, engaging in meaningful joint activities (such as play), monitoring and encouraging progress at school, and so on. The social worker could focus on these particular areas in the conduct of their practice, enabling the mother to achieve adequate standards of child care. This takes us beyond the kinds of ideas involved in

Davies's work on maintenance, and expands and deepens our understanding of the idea of social functioning, as expressed by Bartlett.

However, things are not quite that simple. Part of the problem lies in the capacity for *role variability*. In different circumstances different kinds of roles and responsibilities may be attributed to an individual. Take, for example, the difference between the mother who adopts traditional role expectations and the mother who does not and, as part of that, takes paid employment outside the home. The mother with traditional role expectations may regard the home-keeping work to be her own, with no involvement by her partner (indeed, she may take considerable pride in this aspect of her work). Such a woman might regard involvement of her partner in home keeping to be a sleight on her competence, which could be the cause of distress and even conflict. Where she is employed outside the home, however, and where she does not take on traditional role expectations, she may well expect her partner to take on a major part of the home-keeping tasks. If he (or she) *did not*, then this could actually be the *source of conflict*.

Particular circumstances, therefore, can involve role variability, making it unwise to assume that a person in a particular position (such as that of mother) will automatically be involved in the same roles and have the same expectations in the performance of those roles. A second factor to consider is that of culture. There can be wide variations in cultural expectations and, indeed, between subcultures within a society. Take, for example, corporal punishment. We know that a greater tolerance of – indeed belief in the efficacy of – corporal punishment is more widespread amongst working-class than middle-class parents (McLoyd, 1998; Maccoby and Martin, 1983). In relation to certain perceived misdemeanours on the part of a child, corporal punishment might be the reaction of choice amongst some parents, whereas it would be frowned upon by others. On the other hand, those who believed in corporal punishment might consider that those who did not use this response to some child misbehaviour would not be acting in the long-term interest of the child.

This suggests that, in practical terms, the assessment of social functioning needs to be sensitive both to the specific circumstances of clients and to the culture or subculture in which they are operating. We know, for example, that some parents feel it is acceptable to leave young(ish) children (certainly below the age of 13) at home without adult supervision, even though this is not strictly legal (Sheppard, 2004a). One problem social workers face when, at times, this is drawn to their attention, is that the parents will not accept that what they have done is inappropriate or unacceptable. In this, they may have their views reinforced by similar views amongst people they know – in effect their reference group (reference groups are those groups in relation to which people set their standards, expectations and aspirations). Where their view coincides with others, it can be difficult to convince them that their behaviour is inappropriate or that their social functioning – in this case in relation to child care – is not adequate.

We may also find an older person struggling to cope at home, nevertheless wishing to remain at home. They may not find it easy to care for themselves, their hygiene may not be everything that might be expected by the social worker in their own life, they may have less contact with other people than is desirable, and their house may be a mess. However, unless they have mental health problems, or are in some sense a health risk, then they may judge for themselves what they consider to be adequate social functioning.

Where does this leave social functioning as a concept for social work? At one level, this means that, in the assessment of social functioning, it is necessary take into account the culture and expectations of the social groups of which the client considers him or herself to be a part. It is no good imposing external expectations on a person who will not recognise those expectations as valid. Indeed, in seeking to help, the social worker is best placed if he or she is working with a client to achieve their own aspirations, based on their own expectations. In these respects, therefore, norms and culture (or subculture) play a significant part.

However, there are limits to this. Does this emphasis on norms, culture and reference group mean that social workers must accept those standards and expectations of individuals and their reference groups? It does not, and cannot. Let us take, as an obvious example, the social worker's duty alongside that of the agency to respond to children's needs and, in particular, to treat the welfare of the child as paramount. What if a parent is behaving in a way which threatens the welfare of the child? We know, for example, that West African traditions mean that genital mutilation is not just accepted in relation to young girls, but encouraged. While the cultural emphasis on this makes the situation a little more complicated than might otherwise be the case, there can be little doubt that the welfare of the child is, indeed, damaged by genital mutilation. It would be inconsistent with the duty of social workers to treat the welfare of the child as paramount, for them not to respond in the face of genital mutilation.

We can take another example. There can be no doubt that paedophiles often have extensive networks, exchanging photographs and other communications. For an individual paedophile participating in such communication networks, the others within that network form their reference group, setting their standards and expectations. Does that mean that the social worker should not act if such an individual committed a sexual offence against a child? Would their defence – that others in their reference group regard sexual involvement with children to be acceptable – be adequate? Of course, it would not. It is imperative, indeed, that the social worker *does* act.

There are, therefore, limits to the extent to which it is legitimate to regard social functioning to be measured according to the norms of a particular culture or subculture. What is interesting about this, however, is the consistency of these limits with other fundamental aspects of social work which we have already defined. First, we have here two clear examples of 'objective needs', in which health, safety and autonomy are threatened. Social workers, therefore, are able to disregard – indeed *should* disregard – norms of a culture or subculture in circumstances where the objective needs of an individual are threatened.

Second, we have here a clear division between the work of a social worker: that which invests them with their authority role, and that which does not. Where the authority role is not involved, the social worker may legitimately incorporate cultural and subcultural norms into the assessment of social functioning. However, where the authority role is involved, the social worker takes as his or her point of departure levels of expectations which are not about a particular cultural or subculture. They employ, *in terms of the assumptions of social work*, objective measures of need. Thus, it is the existence of 'objective need' (in the assumptive world of social work) which both gives social workers the power to adopt their authority role and to disregard the norms and expectations of the client's reference groups.

It should be remembered here that all along, in relation to postmodernism, need, the possibility of objectivity and so on, I have been analysing the assumptions which underlie social work. Thus, it is important to remember that we are not talking here, or elsewhere, directly of what might be called epistemological adequacy. That is we do not *have to* assert that social workers are right in their adoption of an objective approach to need (although many might argue that they would be right to do so). I am simply presenting the way *it is necessarily the case that social work has, as an underlying assumption, a commitment to a limited objectivism*. This becomes very clear when we look at issues like the protection of children from sexual offences, and do so in the light of competing norms and expectations.

This works itself out in relation to social functioning, as with other areas, rather neatly. Where social workers have notions of objective need, they can disregard, indeed overrule, norms which are characteristic of particular reference groups. Where this is not the case, it becomes possible to employ those norms as a means for identifying adequate social functioning and desirable intervention outcomes.

Coping

Norms and roles, therefore, are important dimensions to social functioning. However, is it sufficient to consider role performance in terms of either objective notions of needs, or of norms characteristic of a culture or situation? Some of this relates to the particular capacities of an individual within their social environment. Bartlett alighted on the notion of coping, and this is a further important dimension of social functioning which we can examine further.

Coping theory has not been a major part of social work theory. This is little short of astonishing, in view of its obvious central relevance to social work and the extent to which that particular term is liable to emerge in practice. In the frequently chronically problematic circumstances in which clients are embroiled, the question 'how well are they coping?' is liable to emerge with some regularity. Social work, in this respect, would involve facilitating and enhancing the client's coping capabilities. The absence of 'coping' in the literature of social work theory, once noted, only serves to emphasise further the extent to which empowerment has been a focus for social work to the exclusion of other ideas with some potential.

The coping process is characterised by two underlying themes. The first is the (primary appraisal of) *threat*, a sense arising because of the stressor(s) which the person is encountering and with which they seek to cope. The second is *control*. In the face of the threatening stressor the individual seeks to gain control over the situation or themselves. This involves the (secondary) appraisal of the resources – personal and environmental – which are available for coping. There are various definitions of coping, but they all involve a focus on the individual and their environment. Sarafino (1998), for example, describes it as the process by which people try to manage the perceived disparity between the demands and resources they appraise in a stressful situation, while Lazarus and Folkman (1984) consider it to be the cognitive and behavioural efforts to manage specific external and/or internal demands that are appraised as taxing or exceeding the resources of the person.

All these writers, and others, are distinguishing between the demands a situation is placing upon an individual and their ability to respond. Where a mother has young children who – as young children do – demand a lot from their parent in a variety of ways, this can place pressure on her. If to this were added poor relationships with an unsupportive partner and financial difficulties, then the overall demands experienced by the mother would place a lot of pressure on her own coping capabilities or resources.

Coping occurs in relation to stress, or a stressor. Stressors are generally regarded to be facets of a situation which are threatening or harmful (or perceived as such) to the individual. In the example we have just given, the stressor could be the demands of the child(ren), the worry about financial problems or the difficult relationship with the partner. In social work, the term 'need' (or problem) is often used for that of stressor, but the term 'stressor' helps us to understand the potential psychological/emotional as well as practical demands placed upon an individual in a difficult situation.

Stressors gain their significance from the way they are perceived by the client. The same kinds of actions may be regarded by one person as stressful, but by another as unproblematic. For example, one mother could experience the behaviour of her children as demanding, while another could experience those very same behaviours as routine. This is referred to as *meaning*: the meaning that particular actions or events have for an individual.

Stressors often create a feeling of threat in a person. The difficulty in coping relates to the degree of threat felt. In this we are taken to the personal characteristics in an individual as well as norms and societal context, which we have discussed earlier. Factors, for example, in an individual's personal history can affect the way they see particular actions or events (the meaning those events have for them). Many of those women who are subject to social work intervention have themselves been abused in their childhood. Women subject to sexual abuse when they were children have described their own inhibitions when having to deal with the physical care of their own children, such as bathing, which they trace directly to their own childhood experiences (Sheppard, 2001).

Situations can be seen as stressful without referring to past experience. This can relate, for example, to current aspirations. A mundane example (though not necessarily for the individual) could be unexpected pregnancy. For one woman this could be a matter of uninhibited joy, especially if she has been 'trying for a baby' for some time and had begun to lose hope. For another woman, starting out on a professional career, pregnancy could come as a shock. She may feel a high level of ambivalence, experiencing the conflict between the news of pregnancy and the ambitions of a career. It may invoke a profound degree of dread, fear of the childbirth itself or of the unwanted responsibilities of child care.

When a situation is stressful or problematic, therefore, it involves some degree of felt threat. For the career-minded woman, the threat felt is that related to her career. Underlying coping responses is a different concept: that of control. The desire to gain some degree of control underlies an individual's attempts to cope. This attempt to gain greater control has been broadly divided into two: emotion-focused coping and problem-focused coping. *Problem-focused* coping is directed at altering the problem causing the distress (Lazarus, 1993; Carver et al., 1989). Where a mother has a child whose demands are, for her, excessive, she may put him in front of a television because when she does that the demands reduce. She may call upon her mother or friends to look after him from time to time, thus reducing her own face-to-face contact. By dealing with the problem in these ways, she will have a sense of greater control over the situation.

Emotion-focused coping is aimed at reducing or managing the distress caused by some stressor. If we take our example of the mother again, she may try to deal with her feelings about the situation rather than change the situation itself. Where she finds herself becoming angry, she may, for example, take herself out of the situation by going to her bedroom or going into her yard or garden for a smoke. By doing this she may find that she becomes less anxious or angry, and thus avoids making the situation worse. She gains some degree of control over her emotions.

These are quite recognisable forms of response for a social worker. When talking to a client, they may well look at methods for problem solving which focus on the problem itself. This can include drawing upon social supports available (such as friends or relatives) to help with child care tasks or, indeed, helping the woman manage the relationship with the child better (developing, for instance, parenting skills). It can also involve focusing on the emotional responses to a situation (how, for example, can we ensure that the mother does not lose her temper and hit her child?). This can lead to advice to take 'time out' from child care while nevertheless retaining responsibility. In this way, we might find having a cigarette in the back garden or leaving the child to watch television helps the woman retain some degree of emotional equilibrium. Mundane these may be, but they are forms of action that can be important for coping.

Within these two broad domains of problem-focused and emotion-focused coping, there is a wide range of possible actions which will relate to the specifics of the situation. There are two major groupings of problem-focused actions. One group is directed at the person's environment. This can involve the person's social support network, as we have described with the mother who gets help from her own relatives or friends. It can involve obtaining resources – for example, some kind of income support when there are money shortages. It may involve changing people's attitudes. Where a mother wishes to go out to work but is confronted with close relatives who believe that a mother's place is 'always with the child', she may try to change their attitudes so they accept her need to go out to work.

There is a range of environmental actions possible. All of these will be designed to enable the person to gain greater control. The social worker might facilitate the client's attempts to gain control by advising about their rights to claim income support (and the processes involved). They may help them with relatives who will not support their taking a job (even though it may cause no damage to a child, and actually enhance the woman's child care capabilities by providing a different outlet in her life), perhaps by rehearsing with her what she will say to those relatives.

Inward-directed coping is the second broad form of problem-focused coping. This focuses on the person him or herself, and involves strategies directed at motivational and cognitive change. They are often associated with counselling. Here the social worker may be trying to help a mother gain greater confidence in herself or her ability to carry out important tasks. She may, for example, see herself as a mother who frequently fails to live up to the expectations she has of herself, or who believes she is incapable of achieving adequate standards of child care. The social worker may engage in a process of highlighting where she has been successful in her child care actions, or where any limits may be entirely understandable in view of the pressures she may be under. They may be involved, together, in a 'little by little' process of improving her self-belief and her child care behaviour (which may well go hand in hand), until she (and the social worker) feels she is coping adequately with her child care responsibilities. Part of this involves developing self-belief, but part of it involves reframing – helping the woman see her existing actions in a more positive light.

Coping has significance because it has a number of facets which relate it closely to social work. The first is that it concentrates on the person–environment interface – that is, the demands placed upon the person and the action and resources available to meet those demands – a classic focus for social work (Hollis, 1972). Second, it emphasises the person's capabilities and their own actions to manage their problems. There may, of course, be actions which social workers so to speak, *do* for the client. But in general, it is widely acknowledged, social workers are seeking to enable the client, and without doing so, there can be no amelioration, maintenance or improvement in their situation.

A third key dimension of coping, arising from its person–environment interface, is its capacity to link with other key elements of social work. In relation to the environment, its scope enables it to incorporate the notions of stress and support. We have seen already how coping is itself focused on stressors. Support, though, is also important, forming part of the environmental resources on which the client may potentially call in responding to the stressor. However, the other side of the person–environment interface is internal. Coping allows us to link with one of the more important psychological concepts, that of locus of control. This refers to the extent to which the individual feels him or herself able to direct their own lives or, at the other extreme, whether they are at the mercy of external influences. Clearly much of social work, whether encouraging maintenance or social functioning, is about helping, as far as possible, an individual develop the confidence to be able to direct their own lives, and this aspect helps point to some of the 'internal-psychological' aspects of practice, which go alongside the external social-environmental aspects.

Conclusion

There is an obvious relationship between social exclusion and inclusion, and notions like maintenance, social functioning and coping. Inclusiveness is liable to be encouraged, in the ways outlined, by maintaining both (marginalised) individual and society, through better social functioning and improved coping. Furthermore, concepts such as maintenance, social functioning and coping have in common, but in contradistinction to empowerment, a more modest expression of the aims of social work. Helping maintain a client or helping them function better or cope more adequately are worthy aims, but do not carry the grandiosity attached to the notion of empowerment. That, however, may be a strength. Power, it might reasonably be suggested, is something wielded by characters such as the President of the US and to suggest, however modestly, a social work process or outcome which is any way comparable to this is surely misleading.

There is a clear relationship between coping and social functioning, which is not surprising in view of the place of coping in Bartlett's ideas. This relationship is illuminating, also, however, in relation to empowerment. We have mentioned frequently the position of a mother with child care issues. The woman's social functioning is improved to the extent that she is able to cope better, either through external action on the environment or internal action on the person's 'psyche'. Interestingly, however, some of these actions might, by some, be considered to be empowering. The woman who gains self-belief or is better supported by her relatives and friends might, some would argue, be 'empowered' as a result. To some extent this is a matter of nomenclature – names – although we have identified the extent to which the term 'empowerment' is the prisoner of the social and political assumptions of those who use the term.

However, even where we view it as a simple matter of nomenclature, we still may raise the question of proportionality. It may well be that to use the term empowerment in circumstances where a client has simply been helped to cope better is out of all proportion to the achievements of the practitioner. It gives social work a grandness which it neither merits nor, indeed, needs. The dangers, furthermore, of claiming too much lie in the raised expectations of others – those in society who might believe social workers can achieve more than they actually can. This is the last thing social work needs when expectations are already high, in areas such as child protection. If social workers claim to be miracle workers, they are in danger of being treated as if they *should* be miracle workers.

In other ways maintenance, social functioning and coping contrast with empowerment. Empowerment is an elusive concept with profoundly different meanings – meanings which vary according to the assumptions of the person using the term. For those interested in the more democratic 'empirical self' notion of empowerment, it is largely about democratising the practice process. However, for feminists, it is, to a considerable degree, about gender and conscientisation, by which is meant consciousness raising. Those adopting a Marxist position, in turn, are concerned with major structural social change. However, it goes further than mere different meanings. The different uses are fundamentally contradictory. To a Marxist, the adoption of a 'mere' empirical self, democratising notion of empowerment is anything *but* empowerment. In failing even to confront the structural unfairness of and alienation in society, social workers are serving to mystify and, hence, disempower clients.

Maintenance, social functioning and coping, on the other hand, are different concepts, but related and not contradictory. While they are consistent with each other, they together enable us to gain a deeper understanding of what they are about by relating them to each other. We can understand maintenance better in terms of social functioning and, in turn, social functioning better through considering coping. Together they enable us to incorporate a range of key elements in social work, including expectations, normative standards and the relationship of environment and person, and to do so in a way which helps us understand the social work task.

One criticism is that social work does not deal with all people who cannot cope properly or whose functioning in society is not all it could be. Social work does not deal with all those who are homeless or who are tramps or, indeed, all those who refer themselves or are referred for help. Surely, therefore, the notions denote a wider remit than social work actually possesses, and do not identify social work concerns with sufficient precision. Another that may be levelled at it is that it tends to adopt a consensus model of society. If society is unequal, unfair and alienating, do these concepts not simply serve to create an image of social work which, by focusing on individuals in their environment rather than the wider society, serves to perpetuate the existing, unfair social order? If so, it pathologises the individual and may even be regarded as oppressive.

Social work may indeed not be concerned with all those whose social functioning is in some respect impaired. However, this cannot be the starting point. It is first necessary to identify the realms of social work's concerns. In relation to this we have already shown that this realm involves social exclusion and inclusion. However, it does not involve all those socially excluded. That is because, as we have shown, social work is 'socially constructed' – that is the nature of its work, the meaning of it and its constraints are set as a result of social processes by which certain areas of social life are considered legitimate aspects of social work. Social work is concerned with social exclusion, but only certain aspects. It is in relation to these aspects that issues of maintenance, social functioning and coping arise. Hence, these concepts are not sufficient on their own to define social work. They represent key elements of social work, once its areas of responsibility, and how these are defined, within social exclusion, have been denoted.

Second, there may be a consensus theme to maintenance and social functioning, but some notions of empowerment have similar implications. There is nothing about the empirical self/democratising notion of empowerment which leads the practitioner to challenge the existing social order any more than that of maintenance, social functioning and coping. More significant, these notions of social work objectives are consistent with the underlying assumptions of social work – its 'assumptive world'. It is clear from our earlier analysis of social work, and from the extent to which a concern with social exclusion encapsulates its interests, that the problems which occupy social work are regarded as residual. There is no challenge to the overall social order, only an aim to be more inclusive with the diverse population of society. Social work can be part of the enterprise seeking to create social inclusion by focusing on individuals and groups in their immediate social environment. When seeking to help the mentally ill, those with learning or physical disabilities, children, parents and older people, social workers may reasonably be said to be aiming to help them cope better, or to function better in society. To function better in society, and to be brought to a point where that is possible, is to experience a greater degree of social inclusion.

Chapter ten

Interpretivism, reflection and social work as art

Interpretivism and the art of social work

Social work as an art form has been widely canvassed in social work. Its approach, emphasising the person of the worker, creativity and the importance of the relationship, has had a seductive charm. Its emphasis on the human aspect of the worker, and the values which underlie this, are very much what is meant when practitioners refer to the capacity 'to help' or to social work as a 'helping activity'. Yet underlying this is a more basic approach to the understanding of both humans and knowledge, one which is associated with what social scientists and philosophers call 'interpretivism'.

The interpretivist position may be broadly described in terms of the importance of meaning in the understanding of humans and society. This is about how people make sense of the world: how do they make sense of the behaviours of other people, or an interaction which might take place between one person and another? Does the discovery by a career-minded woman that she is pregnant mean she is distraught, because of the conflict between career and motherhood? Or does it come as a relief, a joy, because her career orientation had only grown from an inability, in the past, to conceive? The event is basically the same, but the meaning of the pregnancy to her is completely different.

Interpretivism also stresses that there is no one single view of the world, and that individuals and groups can interpret the world in widely different fashions. For one group of conservatively minded people, a strike may be seen as a disruptive action, undermining economic productivity, having a deleterious effect on both workers and owners of a firm. It may even be seen to affect negatively the economy as a whole. For another group of more left-leaning people, the strike could be seen as essentially good and justified, a proper assertion of workers' rights in the face of managerial power and insensitivity.

Individuals (and groups), therefore, actively 'construct' their view of actions and events and, as a result, develop perspectives on their 'world'. They can have a general attitude to parenthood or pregnancy (rather than a specific one about *this* child or *this* pregnancy). They can see trade unions in one way rather than another, society as characterised by inequality and unfairness or by reward and opportunity. These represent their perspectives, the meanings are generated in relation to humans and society. This is all predicated on the essentially subjective nature of human experience (that is, I, as a thinking experiencing subject, may see the same things in rather different ways from you). This gives considerable importance to the subject in understanding human beings (Hughes, 1990; Burr, 2003).

This approach has underlain two key facets of social work. The first is the idea of social work as 'art' – a creative, involved, intersubjective experience in practice. The second, closely related, is the transfer of learning in social work education: the idea that people are able to transfer ideas and meanings from one situation and setting to another. Both call upon similar fundamental ideas and perspectives, and create a particular 'image' of social work as a form of intervention.

Social work as art

Drawing on the American Heritage Dictionary, Palmer (2002) defines art as 'a special skill in adept performance conceived as requiring the exercise of intuitive faculties that cannot be learned solely by study ... a non-scientific branch of learning'. Study may play a part but there is something else to art – the personal capabilities of the individual practising the art, which links to their intuition. The social worker as artist is one who draws, in a major way, on their 'intuitive faculties'. The special characteristics of social work as art are apparent when compared with the notion of science: 'the observation, identification, description, experimental investigation and theoretical explanation of natural phenomena' (Morris, 1981).

Various writers have claimed that social work as science has been the dominant paradigm in recent years (Goldstein, 1992, 1999; Martinez-Brawley and Mendez-Bonito, 1998; Walter, 2003). While this claim has been contested by many of those whose allegiance is to a scientific social work – many of these claim science has not been sufficiently highly regarded (Kirk and Reid, 2002; Atherton and Bolland, 2002; Thyer and Gomory, 2001) – there are those who conceptualise social work in this artistic way. Siporin (1988, p. 178) drew attention to the practitioners' creative use of style, the helping relationship and metaphorical 'communication' as key dimensions to an inevitably artistic dimension of social work. This, he suggested, 'expressed the artistic, aesthetic dimensions of social work practice'. However, unlike scientific conceptions, social work lacked the language and analytical methodology which allowed for evaluation of artistic practice in terms appropriate to art. In other words, when practitioners sought to identify social work as art, it was difficult to express it in ways that others could understand or sympathise with. The danger would always be that social work was seen as 'woolly', lacking substance and without clear aims and ways of assessing what it had achieved.

Nevertheless, social work as art expressed a key dimension of practice. This is evident in its core form: the encounter between social worker and client. This is at the very heart of social work. All other aspects – meetings, report writing, attending court and the rest – are dependent on this. Salzer (1995) comments on this encounter in terms of a performance, rather like music or theatre. The social worker is interpreting experience (of the client) but is also herself performing, the performance including her narration and composition. She is telling a story (of the client), just as she is hearing the client's own story.

It is a creative enterprise, rather like theatre. The creation of a story occurs in the encounter between social worker and client, whether they are individuals or a community. The narration by the client, together with other information, leads to a construction of the situation, a process of making sense, which enables action to be undertaken. If we take the earlier example of the career woman who finds herself pregnant, the social worker would listen to the woman's account of her situation, exploring its context, both in terms of her current situation and aspirations and those life experiences which have led to these. It would be quite consistent for the social worker to explore these facets with the woman, contributing to the creation of an account of the woman's situation, her hopes and fears and some kind of idea of what should be done. It is both a professional act (or set of acts) and the creation of a story: the woman's story in relation to her pregnancy.

The very act of engaging the client and enabling them to present their story is itself artistic. Ragg (1977) considered a central part of this to be description. It is a very human activity. If the client is trying to express their emotions, making sense of them in terms of events happening to them, it is the social worker's job to help them to achieve this expression, to describe their feelings accurately and to their satisfaction. Indeed, the client realises his or her emotions through description. At the start they may be only dimly aware of the emotions they feel. Through the involvement of the social worker, the probing and prodding which accompanies that intervention, the client is able to describe these emotions. Likewise, they may, through the encounter with the social worker, be able to clarify their situation (not just the accompanying emotions) to themselves, describing it accurately and in detail.

The social worker is acting creatively by facilitating the client, by helping them to understand their situation better and formulating ways of dealing themselves with that situation. The woman who is ambivalent about leaving her partner, with whom she may have a stormy relationship, may find it difficult to think clearly. She may have to think not just of herself, but of her children. She may well have feelings about the relationship itself – its longevity, for example, endowing it with emotional significance for her, regardless of how she may view her partner. She may be concerned about the effect of separation on relatives and, indeed, their likely reactions to a possible separation. All these issues, and more, may leave the woman emotionally dazed, finding it difficult to make decisions. The social worker's role – through their humanistic relationship, their capacity to help the woman to describe, and hence to create, a story – is to help her come through her emotional haze, to a point where she can choose for herself what she can do.

This is a subtle affair, involving processes which are innate and non-scientific; indeed, these are, at times, not even conscious. Much of social work practice involves actions of which the practitioner is not fully aware and yet employs in the course of intervention. For example, an experienced social worker may be able to 'read' body language and react appropriately, according to Siporin (1988) without making explicit, to themselves, to others, what they have done. The realisation can be immediate, without conscious reflection on the meaning of the client's body movements. One may be able to explain later, through reflection, but the understanding, in the first instance, is immediate.

Social work and common sense

From an 'artistic' point of view, then, creativity and intuition lie at the centre of social work. What does this involve? England (1986) suggested that social work was a matter of common sense. This is not, on the surface, an idea of social work liable to increase its status as an occupation. Professions with a high status, such as law or medicine, gain their status to a considerable degree as a result of *their* lack of ordinariness. People, on the whole, do not consider they could carry out complex surgery, whereas this is the day-to-day work of some doctors. To suggest that social work is a matter of common sense invites the response: why should we require social workers to go through any form of training? Why can we not simply employ experienced, mature people for this work?

England's answer is that practitioners need to possess uncommonly good common sense. Social workers are able to make sense of situations confronting clients and to work with them in this in much the same way that everyone understands the experiences of others. It is the capacity of humans to relate to and understand each other, in relation to a widely diverse range of circumstances, which is employed by social workers in their practice. Social workers are involved, first and foremost, in communicating with clients, and this capacity can never be the sole property of any particular profession.

This, however, is the sort of thing required merely to carry out conversations. It is the very stuff of social life, of all relationships. What marks out social work (or should mark it out) is the degree of reliability with which social workers are able to communicate both their own ideas and perspectives and take on board those of the client(s). Social workers need to have mastered an *unusually developed* capacity for communication. For clients, it is this unusually developed capacity which matters. It is in the extent to which they are able to achieve that degree of exactitude in communication and understanding that they are able to offer something more than that provided by others.

This helps us to understand the importance of communication, interpersonal or psychodynamic skills for social work. The social worker is able to develop their intuitive capabilities by practising them, having had them identified. Thus 'reaching for feeling', being 'clear on role and purpose', 'active listening', 'challenge with support', 'reframing' and so on (Shulman, 1999) provide means through which social workers can develop their communication abilities. However, these are, for those of an artistic disposition, not skills which can be simply 'applied' but are only manifested when they have been incorporated into the practitioner's ordinary ways of working. They do not 'think of a skill' and then perform it. The communication goes on between worker and client, but the worker's appreciation of what is happening is itself immediate. It happens, so to speak, automatically.

According to England, because of the nature of this particular competence, it can never be the exclusive domain of social work. There will always be some people with particular talents in this area who have never received any training. They will be marked out by a high degree of sensitivity to others and a capacity to respond sensitively and honestly to them in ways they are able to understand and appreciate. These are unusually developed yet untrained capabilities. While some people may be seen to possess such abilities, able to employ them with most people, Thoits (1986) has pointed out that similarities between (speaking broadly) 'counsellor' and 'counselled' considerably aids the sense, in those being supported, of being understood. People respond to those whom they perceive to be 'like them'. Put simply (indeed simplistically), a single mother may well seek out another single mother to express her feelings, because of a sense that the listener will be able to understand her predicament. It is the combination of personal abilities and personal affinity which characterises those who are perceived to be most able to help.

Formal knowledge in social work is significant, it is suggested, not because of its capacity for some mechanistic application in practice, but for its capacity to create meaning. This is a matter we shall look at in more detail later. However, formal taught knowledge is very much secondary to the personal artistic qualities of the practitioner. It is important only to the extent that it facilitates communication and understanding. It is the extent to which it sensitises social workers to possibilities and increases the potential ways in which they can view situations, that it is helpful.

In England's memorable phrase, it is not the capacity to master abstract knowledge which is important, but the way in which such knowledge is 'plundered and fragmented' (England, 1986, p. 35) for use in practice. Understanding issues of loss and change can help the practitioner deal with such issues when they arise – they could be about the loss of a job, the death of a partner, a divorce or a host of other situations. Likewise, developmental psychology can sensitise social workers to a multitude of issues related to working with particular age groups. However, such knowledge does not have any particular priority over experience. It may be just as important that the practitioner has worked with people going through the process of divorce, or have been divorced themselves, when working with someone who is being divorced (or, indeed, is suffering any form of loss).

Creativity and holism

The notion of social work as art places a huge emphasis on the practitioners' creativity (Powell, 2002; Ringel, 2003). This is implicit in the rooting of social workers in their essential human-ness. The relationship is the means through which art may be manifested, but at the same time humans are themselves creative. They create 'pictures' of others, of their social life, of themselves and their actions, just as all humans do, in order to operate in the social world. Unless they have ways of knowing themselves, others and relationships, then they are unable to function properly in social life.

Intuition plays a core role in this creative enterprise. Intuition can both refer to innate processes involved in social interaction and also as a 'time of illumination'. In the latter sense it is about having no idea how a conclusion was reached, yet having a strong sense of knowing (Carew, 1987, p. 50). In the former sense the creative process is necessarily one of making order and sense of situations. As the different elements of a situation are constructed into a whole by the practitioner (all the time paying attention to the interrelationship of different elements), so an order is created. It is *this* kind of situation rather than *that* kind. He or she is this kind of person rather than that kind. Her relationship with others takes this form rather than any other. It is what we do as humans all the time in our relationships with others, and it is what social workers themselves must do in their conduct of practice.

It is a process of 'making meaning'. At any one time the social worker is faced with a vast array of facets of a social situation, all of which could command his or her attention. Paying attention to everything would be impossible, and in any case is not what humans do. Hence, practitioners pay attention to some aspects of the situation and bring them together in such a way that enables their picture to be drawn (metaphorically). Just trying to make sense of the client's circumstances is enough, but social workers are involved in an interaction and they are part of that interaction. They are not only painting the picture; they are actually *in* it. They need, therefore, to pay attention to themselves, what they are doing, how they are feeling, the contribution they are making. Indeed, beyond the client and practitioner him or herself are others involved in both of their social systems, relevant to that situation and which are the domain of the social worker.

The social worker is engaged in a process of synthesis, bringing together the elements of the situation to create a viable picture of it. In doing so, they create a whole picture of the situation. The quality of practice depends on the quality of the synthesis, the vividness of the picture which the social worker is able to create. As has been noted earlier, the practitioner may be guided by his or her formal learning, although they will be at least as likely to be informed by their own personal and practice experience. These will coalesce into a general perspective, or set of perspectives, which they will hold – their way of generally making sense of people and the social world. These will be evident in their values, their 'philosophy of life', their personal ideology, and the things they count as important in the conduct of their life. All these provide the 'meaning background' to the meanings which they will construct in relation to *this* particular client and *this* particular piece of practice.

It is not enough, however, for the social worker to be creative in their own right – they must involve the creative powers of their client(s) (Martinez-Brawley and Mendez-Bonito, 1998). This is, as it happens, unavoidable, because just as the social worker is drawing upon the common human capacity for creativity, so the client is doing the same. She, too, will be making sense of her situation, of the social worker, and her relationship with him or her (the social worker). It is also integral, as an aspect of the implicit values which are extended to the client in the artistic enterprise. The social worker may be seeking to help, and the client to be helped, but they are both humans. They are bound together by their common humanity and are thus, in a profound sense, equals.

Ragg's (1977) earlier emphasis on description, a process which is created in interaction with the client, necessarily entails client involvement in the creative enterprise. This is the case whether the client is an individual, organisation or community. The client must be allowed to exercise their own imaginative freedom, in order that they can transcend the limitations imposed by their existing perspectives, which are often – in the terms of the artist – the features of their life which are holding them back. The social worker both helps to set this imagination free and yet uses it in order to make sense themselves. The worker and client are, therefore 'co-creators' of the account of the client's situation and of any ways in which they may move forward.

The creativity is holistic. This means that there is a 'wholeness' about the social worker's approach. This is presented in opposition to what is deemed as a 'scientific' approach, one which compartmentalises, creating discrete and differentiated areas of the client's life for separate analysis and evaluation (Heinemann, 1981; Karusu, 1999). 'Holism' means understanding throughout the interrelationship of all aspects of the client's situation, and treating it in that interrelationship. It is about seeing the client and their situation as a whole, rather than in terms of their component parts.

If we are to be fully creative, we need to be holistic. The intuitive dimension makes sense of the penchant, it is suggested (England, 1986), of social workers to talk of 'how it felt'. It is the immediacy and wholeness of the experience which leads to an emphasis on feeling. Weick's (2000) view was that the capacity to engage all aspects of our humanity was the domain of women, contrasting characteristically male with characteristically female forms of communication. She distinguished the second voice from the first voice. The second voice – the male one –is that of objectivity, separateness and abstraction. These are the kinds of features attributed to scientific endeavour.

The first voice embraces feelings and intuition, absent from the second voice. Women use language rich in emotional meaning, intimacy and shared feelings. However, this 'authentic voice' is not one which is just involved in 'external' relationships, but is one that is involved in a silent 'internal dialogue'. This internal dialogue is one about the content of one's own experiences expressed to oneself. Such internal authenticity is considered important in itself. It is, however, also necessary if one is to have an authentic dialogue with the client. Honesty to oneself about oneself is a necessary prerequisite to true authenticity with the client.

The social work relationship, then, is one of a shared experience, of feeling as well as thinking, and of these aspects brought together on all sides in the process of artistic creativity. In the end, the artist can only be as good as the range of paints they have at their disposal, so the wider the range of paints, the greater the capacity to paint a vivid picture.

We cannot, however, limit ourselves to the 'here and now'. Palmer (2002) presents the idea that life is a process of continuous motion and change. Just as we need to be holistic in our focus on the client as he or she is at present, so we need to see that person as someone who is themselves in continuous process and change, a person through their life, rather than just the individual who is presented at this moment. Holism is longitudinal in its inclusion. To understand the client we must understand their past, how they make sense of it, and its connection with the present, in continuous process.

Meaning and understanding

Underlying the artistic edifice of social work is the capacity for empathy. This is an assumed dimension in the various aspects, such as creativity, relationship and communication, which we have already discussed. England (1986) refers to it as 'understanding others', and it is, he thinks, at the very core of social work. It is, he thinks, fairly obvious as soon as one thinks about it. Everyone knows that, when under stress, those who are able to help most are those whom we regard as particularly understanding. People actually seek out those they consider to have the capacity for such understanding.

England suggests that sometimes the manifestation of understanding is, on its own, enough. Some people are helped simply by presenting the problem to the helper and, through that articulation and understanding, they come to a solution. In other cases, it may not, of itself, be sufficient. It will, according to England, however, be necessary. It will not, where a person is genuinely distressed, be possible to move forward, whatever method is employed, without the client feeling understood. That understanding, more often than not, leads also to a sense of being valued, and hence provides some motivation for finding a solution with the practitioner.

It is, at one level, the capacity for listening which is important. It is, though, much more than that. It is 'listen and know what I mean'. It is not enough to hear the client's story; it is necessary to show that you have understood it, and understood it from where the client is standing. It is, metaphorically, 'standing inside their shoes', seeing what it looks like to them. As we noted earlier, some people seem to have very great natural abilities in this area. England suggests that we all know such people. However, we often actively seek out people like ourselves, either those who are in key respects 'like-minded' or in important respects similar to us (Thoits, 1986).

Those who are seeking help are often very careful about whom they choose, because of this need to be understood. It is, however, possible, when the right person is approached, for a sense of the isolation brought on by a problem to be lifted. The empathic person is able, in some way, to share in our distress because they understand it. Where, on the other hand, the person is seen not to understand, this can lead to a sense of increasing, not reducing, burden.

England considers that the helper goes on a metaphorical 'journey' with the client – so that they can see the 'sights and sounds' of the latter's experience. In making this journey, the practitioner will know better what it feels like to be in the midst of these events and 'places', not just for any traveller but for *this particular* traveller. Through making this journey, they will know the specific meanings, associations and memories which are conjured up for the client. The capacity of people to work for change is considerably enhanced by the shared experience of the client's distress, without, however, the practitioner themselves becoming disabled or distressed.

Palmer (2002) comments on the co-creation of empathy, a feature consistent with the creativity attributed to the artist. While the practitioner must have the requisite capacity for empathy, it is necessary for the client to participate, to provide the communication which enables that empathy to be accurate. They need to be able to recognise themselves where the practitioner manifests understanding, otherwise they are unable to pick up on the worker's empathy and hence unable to feel understood.

Interpretivist knowledge and reflective learning

Social work as art presents formal, written knowledge, if not as a side issue in the business of social work, nevertheless as an aspect quite subsidiary to the creative, interpretive exercise that is deemed to be practice. The formal knowledge of social work – that which is written and often an aspect of the various levels of education and training – has a status no higher than experience. Like experience it is seen as a 'sensitising' aspect of the interpretive capabilities of the social worker. It helps, in other words, social workers to interpret, and empathise with, the situation more accurately and to operate more imaginatively and creatively in seeking a solution. It is the imagination, interpretive abilities and creativity which are at the centre of practice. Knowledge application is, by contrast, relatively provisional.

The recent history of social work writing has had an interpretivist stream which places knowledge much more to the fore. While adhering to the same broad interpretive assumptions, the 'transfer of learning' – a concept which has been developed in relation to education, but which applies equally well to the constant process of informal as well as formal learning which can occur as a result of practice experience – focuses much more on formal knowledge. Thus, interpretation, as is the case with those who present social work as art, is crucial, but it is the way this both enables learning to be used and also facilitates the development of learning, from formal knowledge, that is emphasised in notions of transfer of learning, or transferable knowledge.

Practice ideologies

Hardiker and her colleagues (Hardiker, 1981; Curnock and Hardiker, 1979) understood knowledge as interpretation, and she suggested that this interpretive process underlay practice. She suggested that social workers developed and used 'practice theories', constructs which enabled the social worker to make sense of the client's situation and to act on them. Her view was that these did not come from nowhere or 'just' from experience, but that they reflected the process of assimilating frameworks of knowledge which occurred in formal learning situations. In other words, social workers had picked up, not always consciously, ways of looking at aspects of their work from their learning of formal social science knowledge. This learning was incorporated in the processes of practice and informed their conduct of that practice.

This is quite reminiscent of the description of practice characteristic of social work as art. The act of interpreting the client's situation occurs in Hardiker's account, as does the creation of ways of looking at it. However, rather than emphasising this process and placing the knowledge, if not as incidental, at least not as central, she sees formal knowledge at the heart of the social worker's creation. The actual constructions which occur are derived, and perhaps developed (in interaction with experience), from the kinds of theoretical frameworks existent in the social sciences. Hence the social sciences were crucial, not peripheral, and could be found in the implicit 'knowledges' of practice.

Hardiker identified three 'practice theories', in particular. The first was a 'judicial ideology'. This is where social workers saw themselves as part of the judicial system involved in the administration of justice. This involved notions of desert (in terms of penalties given to the offender) and consequences, as a response to their offending behaviour. It also involved notions of responsibility

– holding them responsible for their acts. Hence, a social worker operating a judicial ideology may well find themselves in a formal, authority-based role (indeed ascribing that role to themselves by their interpretation of the client's situation).

An alternative is a community development ideology. Here, the focus is on the community rather than the individual. The aim is to work within and change systems in the community. A great deal of weight is given to resources, or the lack of them, rather than to individuals. Practice is cooperative and enabling, involving groups. A social worker who adopted this ideology would not consider work with the individual as the appropriate means to deal with the problem with which they were concerned. Where, for example, an individual had poor housing conditions, but this was a problem they shared with many people in the area, it would be of little use simply to try to help them as an individual. Rather, the focus would be on the community, finding ways to ensure change so that all problematic accommodation was brought up to standard.

The third practice theory was a welfare ideology. This involved a personal social service, given to individuals and families. The focus was narrower than the community development ideology – individuals and families – and the emphasis was on personal need. Need, while not eschewing responsibility, meant the welfare approach was less judgmental than the judicial ideology, involving a supportive response to these personal problems.

These are rather general ideologies, and do not always represent the range of, and limits to, activities available to social workers (in the contemporary UK at least). Other authors have more recently taken on the issue of ideologies of practice. Robbins et al. (1999) suggest that social work is unavoidably infused with ideology in both theory and practice, while others argue that there are consequences to this in different areas of practice. Altman (2003), for example, argues that social work practice with children and families is rooted in traditional ideologies of womanhood, and that these ideologies need to be challenged by a more feminist agenda. Lynn (1999) suggests two fundamental ideologies of practice, those of social justice and personal caring (rather similar in these respects to two of Hardiker's conceptualisations of social work ideology), but also indicates the need for analysis of the impact of structural power. In relation to substance abuse, the ideologies of care, according to Burke and Clapp (1997), are disease/abstinence, psychosocial, ecological and harm reduction approaches.

These more recent studies serve to illustrate further Hardiker's point: that social workers are engaged in knowledge-informed interpretations, and that these have consequences for the ways they act. However, whether this point is up to close scrutiny is questionable. Does, for example, the social worker really need such detailed knowledge, as is acquired from a social science higher education, in order to make these judgements? Altman's (2003) study, for example, would suggest that social workers are actually employing ideologies widely present in the general population who have not undertaken social work education and training. Indeed, they would not appear to be particularly subtle or sophisticated ideologies and the processes are not inconsistent with social work as art. It may be that degree-level (and beyond) knowledge sophistication is not necessary to the creation of practice ideologies as envisaged by Hardiker and others. She notes anyway that these theories 'remain in the social worker's head and daily activities, rather than finding their way into the literature' (Curnock and Hardiker, 1979, p. 10).

The problem with this knowledge, then, is that it is not 'formal' – written down and available to read and learn from. It is not, therefore, possible to learn from it in the way that might be possible with other social science knowledge. Instead, social workers develop these ideologies as they go along in practice. The result is a tendency quite different from that advocated by Hardiker, one which emphasises the developing experience of the social worker rather than formal knowledge. Indeed, that route leads to, at an extreme, idiosyncratic personalised knowledge.

Aware of this problem, Curnock and Hardiker (1979) suggested that social work practice theories should be subject to research and turned thereby into formal written knowledge capable of being written down and learned (and hence employed in practice). This is, indeed, to some degree what has happened, as research, quoted above, has shown different orientations and ideologies manifested by social workers in the conduct of their practice. The extent, thereby, to which this is turned into crucial knowledge for social work, however, is questionable. If it were the case that the ideologies described by Curnock and Hardiker, and others who follow this 'ideologies' view, were generated in the first instance by processes similar to those described in the artistic process, then their generation would not appear to require such formal, written knowledge.

Knowledge transfer and learning

Transfer of learning was another notion which drew upon the interpretivist tradition. This was very much about the educational process, but described ways in which knowledge could be acquired and used generally in practice. The knowledge transfer processes identified could equally well continue to be carried out in practice by the qualified worker, as encountered during their qualifying training. It emphasised the ways in which learning was actively constructed by social workers and social work students.

Its orientation was to practice, in that the idea was that practitioners should be able to transfer learning from one area of practice to another (CCETSW, 1985). From the point of view of practice learning, and bringing practice together with its formal knowledge base, this was best conducted, in qualifying training at least, in a controlled situation that closely resembled the practice environment. This would involve working in an educational setting with real cases or those which closely resembled practice, encouraging processes which would enable the students imaginatively to bring their knowledge to bear on these practice examples (Harris, 1983).

These ideas created an image of the social worker as active and creative, able (through their interpretive antennae) to analyse situations, construct ways of understanding them, recognise other situations in which this understanding would be relevant, and create a further understanding of this new situation. Where, for example, the issue of child temperament was identified as a contributory factor in the parenting problems of a family, this would generate a perception of familial needs in which the child him or herself actually contributed to the instability of the situation (rather than, say, the issue being one solely of parenting). The formal knowledge about child temperament would be incorporated into the initial practice analysis and inform understanding of new situations through the capacity for transferring this more integrated (theory–practice) knowledge into new and different situations.

This relied on the encouragement of active rather than passive educational methods. Students would not simply be lectured to but would be engaged in problem solving. The process, while not being entirely heuristic (self-learning) would nevertheless involve a considerable amount of self-generated impetus towards the acquisition of understanding. While, however, one might argue for a controlled environment as the best initial basis for learning, the logic of this position was that practice itself would be the best place – ultimately – for such learning, based on the proviso that the influence of formal knowledge, once established in the controlled environment, would continue on into practice. It rested on an assumption, also, that such transfer of learning could take place; that the learned, knowledge-informed understanding developed in one situation could be transferred to another, and would be relevant to other situations.

This process, Harris (1983) felt, would benefit from the development of 'supra concepts', highly practice-relevant, but nevertheless formal, written knowledge, around which the learning process could be organised. These might conform, or be similar to, the kinds of practice ideologies suggested by Hardiker. Alternatively they could involve theories (or metatheories) such as ecological or systems frameworks for thinking. The capacity to view different practice frameworks in terms of interacting systems (such as the family, friendship network and community) or in terms of levels of social intervention (from micro to macro) could enable the practitioner both to integrate formal written knowledge with practice and to learn from that integration, applying that learning to new practice situations.

As with the processes involved in social work as art, these 'organising concepts' formulated within actual practice, give meaning and coherence to the range of information encountered by social workers. This is similar to the processes of generating understanding, as outlined by England, but occurred with the necessary injection of formal knowledge. The practitioner thereby actively 'constructs' his or her practice, but does so in a manner which both allows for this 'injection' of formal knowledge, yet enables its transfer from one practice situation to another. Expertise, here, is not just about the acquisition and exposition of formal knowledge, but in the capacity to create meaning through the incorporation of the knowledge into practice.

Enquiry, action and beyond

This general orientation towards integrated 'expertise creation' evident from knowledge transfer would be further developed in relation to active learning by the student, which would then carry forward into capacities required for the kind of 'lifelong learning' (Ruch, 2002) so favoured in contemporary social policy. In this model, the individual, in the process of qualification, learns means by which they are able actively to identify relevant formal knowledge and then incorporate it into their learning processes. In this, it is very much an extension of the active learning which formed a part of the 'transfer of knowledge' approach.

As with knowledge transfer, this involved a very practice-focused creative process. It entailed the presentation of a practice problem which was then used as the basis for group discussion and reflection (Burgess, 1992; Burgess and Jackson, 1990; Taylor, 1993; Burgess and Taylor, 1995; Burgess, 1999). Rather than learning being an individual matter (which it could be as well), the focus for learning was the group. In addition, it was not just a matter of bringing together formal knowledge and practice situation (rather cumbersomely described as theory and practice) but enabled experience to be valued. Hence, the tripartite elements of formal knowledge, experience and practice problem would be brought together in the learning process.

This approach was based on the premise that people learn best when they are engaged actively in their learning, rather than as passive recipients of knowledge. Rather than absorbing knowledge from the presentation of lecturers, they needed actively to pursue it. This active pursuit was not just in bringing knowledge and practice together, but extended to the very processes by which they looked for that knowledge. It involved making use of libraries to identify possible relevant knowledge and then bringing it together with practice to form transferable knowledge.

The process of identifying problems, relevant issues and responses, in effect, involved 'group constructions' of practice scenarios, just as the group would be able to construct appropriate interventions. This was very much a picture of the active, mobilised, cooperative (as well as creative) learner, able then to adopt this learning style in their subsequent, qualified, practice.

Gardiner (1988, 1989) wrote about processes relevant to both knowledge transfer and the action and enquiry approach. He was concerned with learning styles; that is, not just with what was 'on offer' as ways of learning for practice more effectively, but what the individual brought, in terms of their own ways of accruing knowledge. He identified a two-way process. The first was the application of theory to practice, which involved going from the general (formal knowledge applicable to a range of circumstances) to the particular (the practice situation confronting the social worker). The second was the ability to generate theory from practice, which involved a reverse process of identifying facets of, and themes in, practice situations, and generating knowledge from this.

Like knowledge transfer and enquiry and action learning ideas, this emphasised that, in developing educational techniques, we need to understand the way humans make sense of the world, while recognising the active nature of human enquiry. This extends to, indeed is especially involved in, practice situations. Social workers and social work students are not 'passive absorbers' of knowledge, but are actively engaged in knowledge creation.

Of course, this is a description of a learning process. There is, however, little guidance on the relative weight which should be given to, say, formal knowledge as compared with experience in seeking to make sense of practice scenarios. Furthermore, there is also no indication of the way in which one form of knowledge may be chosen in preference to another or the criteria upon which this would be based. Why should we choose this particular form of knowledge rather than another? Why should we construct the situation in this way rather than that way? The fact that 'it fits' is not really sufficient grounds. It needs to 'fit and work better', and that requires principles upon which we might choose one form of knowledge over another, principles which are not consistent, and *cannot be consistent* with the interpretivist assumptions underlying these approaches.

Reflection and reflective learning

All this is, of course, consistent with reflection and reflective learning which has become so influential in social work and social work education in recent years (Gould and Taylor, 1996; Ellerman, 1998; Ruch, 2002;). Indeed, the ideas may now be regarded as 'subsets' of the ideas on reflection. The ideas stem from the work of Schön (1983, 1987), who challenged the traditional idea of professional practice being the outcome of a deductive process through which formal knowledge was brought to bear on practice. He was self-consciously interpretivist in his orientation, but provided an overall frame through which to consider issues such as practice ideologies, knowledge transfer and enquiry and action learning.

He suggested that significant dimensions of 'theory' are only revealed though skilled practice and are implicit in action. This bears considerable similarity in its tenor to the work of Hardiker and those who followed on from her. Indeed, this knowledge is beyond conscious articulation. Likewise, situations are problematised – identified as this rather than that kind of problem – by professionals through their engagement in practice and alongside (in the case of social work) the client. In other words, problems are not predefined but are actively constructed in practice.

Much of the professional work of the practitioner is intuitive, in the sense suggested by England and others who promote the idea of social work as art. Social workers inevitably operate intuitively, constructing accounts and making sense of practice situations, and it is through these constructions that we get to know what practice is. There are no 'predefined' situations in social work. They are accomplished by practitioners who create their own definitions of them.

A consequence of this is that social work must be, in some ways, an art, but also that notions of knowledge transfer, practice ideologies and the active enquiring practitioner are necessary elements of the manner in which professionals, including social work professionals, operate. Practice becomes a complex process of negotiation and definition of what it is that the practitioner is actually dealing with.

Conclusion

Although reflection and reflective learning has come to the fore in social work from the 1990s, the tradition from which it emanates predates that time considerably. We may go back some way to the consideration of social work as art, which put forward many of the same kinds of tenets, and further still to the interpretivist paradigm which underlies the whole range of approaches in this chapter. The interpretivism outlined here underlies also much of that which is in postmodern approaches, and the criticisms which we have already noted there can be applied to the assumptions which permeate these interpretivist approaches to practice. In particular, the consequences for values and knowledge – that we are left with a relativism which means that we have no way of proclaiming one approach or explanation as superior to another – are particularly damning. If there is no way to choose generally, how can we choose one particular construction in practice as being better than another? How do we know the damaging from the supportive? In any case why should it matter that an approach is damaging? After all, we have no way of preferring a value which emphasises support and progress over one which emphasises damage.

The actions of the artist, furthermore, are shrouded in mystery. They are 'intuitive', laced with 'meaning' and achieved through the 'relationship'. Some of this, particularly the spontaneous aspects necessarily an aspect of intuition, are no doubt valid. Thoughts and ideas have to have some origin and, at the point of origin, they must be necessarily spontaneous. However, there is an avoidance of precision in much of the writing, in favour of the use of metaphor. There is little attempt to describe exactly what happens when social work is a creative, artistic endeavour. Indeed, by implication, that would be inappropriate because the process is intuitive. What, however, are the precise thinking processes by which these initial, spontaneous thoughts, move into more precise meanings? How do we move from 'hunch' to a full-scale account or understanding of the situation?

On these issues, nothing is said, other than the rather evasive repetition that social work is creative and intuitive. Yet it is the discovery of exactly these elements which is crucial to the credibility of social work, if these processes are indeed so important for it. Indeed, it is only through this that its validation is likely to be achieved and some way of facilitating learning undertaken, rather than a reliance on the unthinking virtuosity of the performer, a virtuosity which is difficult to express in language and is liable to be invisible to those other than the performer.

The approach of the artist, furthermore, rather like empowerment, is likely to engender a warm feeling in the practitioner – a sense that they are helping and getting in touch with the real humanity of the person with whom they are working. However, this turns social work into a merely personalised service, when in fact social workers operate so much under the auspices, directly or indirectly, of the state. It cannot therefore be a merely personalised service between social worker and client, which is perhaps more resonant of counselling.

Furthermore, it hardly pays proper attention to the authority role of the social worker. The 'artistic' orientation to social work paints a picture of assumed underlying harmony, of both worker and client working together towards common objectives, whatever short-term conflict may occur when, say, a social worker needs to challenge (with support) the perceptions of the client. However, we know very well how conflict can emerge precisely because of the authority role of the social worker, involving disputes over the validity of the underlying objectives of practice. One only has to peruse quite briefly the research on child protection for this to become obvious.

Likewise, the importance of worker–client equality can only, at best, be partially relevant. This has most in common with the democratic or self-realisation notions we discussed earlier in relation to empowerment. However, even the *potential* for taking an authority role, we know, has a huge impact on clients. Many clients subject to child and family social work intervention, even when it is designed to support the integrity of the family, predicate their own actions on the possibility that the social worker may, at any time, move from that support role to a child protection role, should circumstances require this. It is the sword of Damocles hung over all parents' heads when subject to child and family social work intervention, and they know this all too well (Sheppard, 2001). It can, indeed, have major psychological effects on them, to the extent of some mothers suffering from clinical depression.

This interpretivist, artistic notion of social work is, therefore, both inadequate at the level of knowledge validity and provides a rather too cosy description of practice. However, it is worth remembering also some of the strengths in an approach which is ultimately found wanting as a whole. There can be no doubt that social workers are involved, as a necessary part of their work, in the creation of meaning. This may not, of itself, be enough but it is necessary for them to make sense of the situations with which they are confronted. Any understanding of social work must incorporate this into its own framework.

The other major strength lies in the identification of intuition. There can be no doubt that the genesis of understanding has to be, in the first instance, spontaneous. There must be a moment when the process begins. We often call that moment a hunch, something which gives an insight into what may be going on. Insufficient as it is in itself, it is (like meaning) a necessary element of the social work process. It is, therefore, on an understanding of the necessity of intuition and meaning that one must, in art at least, understand social work.

Chapter eleven

Social work, science and technical instrumentalism

Technical instrumentalism

This term refers to areas of social life in which decisions are made in response to technical rules. The individual has some task to fulfil and the actions they should undertake are in accordance with some rule or other. At its most simple (as an example of rule following) we could consider the building of a cabinet from a kit bought from a shop. The person who has bought this cabinet in kit form would have the various parts from which it can be made, and a set of instructions about how it should be made. Provided the individual follows the instructions and does so in the order designated, then it is possible to turn the various parts into a cabinet. If the instructions are not followed, then it is highly likely that the cabinet, as envisaged by the producers, will not be made.

In this case and others like it, there is nothing to be gained from an imaginative diversion from the instructions (in terms of building the cabinet as envisaged by the manufacturers). It is not necessary to display empathy or construct meaning. The cabinet constructor is not an artist, in the sense displayed by a painter. They are simply following instructions which are instrumental to their ends of making the cabinet envisaged by the manufacturers. Indeed, such things are generally designed to be understandable to most people and to be within the range of quite ordinary skills. They are designed, in other words, to be made by those with no skills outside the quite ordinary, through following fairly straightforward rules.

The capacity for imagination (out of the ordinary) is not important, but the ability to follow rules is crucial. If we are talking of situations involving social life or social care we would be looking to rules which are general and which could be applied to particular situations. In social work, our general rule or procedure would, in principle, be applicable to practice. The assumption is that, although each situation may possess some degree of uniqueness, they are not so unique as to prevent the application of general rules common to these situations.

Take, for example, the response time to a referral to an Adult Services Team. The response time required by a local authority may be set at 72 hours. If it is a required procedure it is a rule which would apply to all referrals. They may have a range of distinguishing characteristics and all be unique in some way, but this uniqueness does not affect the general applicability of the rule. In more general terms, the depressed person may have particular unique characteristics or circumstances but they have, in common with others who are depressed, their depression.

Where rules are applied in this way (and we are starting simply here) the outcome is a practitioner who, in the requirement that they apply rules, may be seen as a technician. In an 'ideal' form', technical acts are those guided by some pre-arrangement which occurs in some institutional context. The pre-arrangement (in our general example) are the rules guiding cabinet construction and (in our second) the expectations of response times. The rules regarding depression are a little more complex, relating to formal knowledge application, but the principle of pre-arrangement applies.

There are three elements to this. The pre-arrangement involves *following guidelines, rules and regulations*, so that practice is carried out in a particular and regular way. We have covered this. They also *require skills*, rather than the ability to make and justify decisions required by ethical deeds. When we construct a cabinet, we are not actively making ethical judgements; it is an instrumental act. While it may be ethical to respond within a certain time period to a referral, the morality is already set. The practitioner is not weighing up the ethics of responding within that time period for themselves. Thirdly, these acts are based on some *operational knowledge*. In the case of cabinet construction, the knowledge is at its most simple – just following instructions. In the case of response time, it is knowledge of agency procedures. In the case of depression, it may well be some more academic, esoteric or professional knowledge.

As a starting position, it would seem that there are technical elements in the practice of social work. Social work, particularly when conducted within the state, is covered by a range of procedures and guidelines, all of which may be considered in some sense to be technical. Social workers are expected, in general, to be applying knowledge which provides some degree of guidance for their acts. This can be, for example, knowledge of the law or of child development. They are expected, furthermore, to be able to *do* the work required – they must in some sense be competent or meet required occupational standards.

Managerial technicality

The more mundane version of technical instrumentalism lies in the managed context of social work. There are various dimensions to this which, in the form of 'new managerialism', asserts that 'better management will provide and effective solvent to a wide range of social and economic ills' (Pollit, 1990, p. 1). Greater managerial control is bought at the expense of the degree of professional autonomy, a feature noted by many social workers in their practice in recent years. The greater effectiveness of increased managerialism versus greater professional autonomy is, as Pollit (1990, p. 1) notes, 'a seldom tested assumption'.

In the case of social work this 'new managerialism' emerged in a political context, in which the new right's agenda for public services as a whole focused in part on the need for what they considered to be more effective management . 'Efficient management', according to Hesletine (1980), a former British cabinet minister, 'is a key to the [national] revival'. He argued that this ethos needed to permeate all aspects of public life. Social work in state organisations, it should be remembered, has always been a managed activity. However, the extent of managerial control is potentially variable and was, by common consent, extended in social work in this general context of a political commitment to a new managerialism (in the UK at least) (Harris, 1998, 2003).

The growth in managerial control *vis-à-vis* professional autonomy is associated with deprofessionalisation. A second element in this is the degree of public confidence in the capacity of social work to exercise a high degree of professional autonomy responsibly and safely. This is a complex issue but, as it relates to managerial control, it provides a context for the development of processes designed to increase the power of managers and, in so doing, increase their capacity for the direction of the actions of social workers.

It is in those areas of greatest social work responsibility that the claims to professional autonomy have been most damaged. Child protection work enables practitioners to claim that they have the heavy responsibility of dealing with life and death situations. Whatever the reality of their effectiveness in preventing child fatalities (Pritchard, 1992, 2004), social work's claims to professional autonomy have been undermined by a series of very public child death tragedies of children under some form or other of social work supervision. With the 20:20 vision of hindsight it has been easy to criticise the actions of social workers, and for commentators to express surprise that even the dictums of common sense, let alone standards of professional behaviour, had been transgressed in such cases. While these cases are the huge exception rather than the rule (as a proportion for all child protection work these cases are a very tiny minority), the concern generated has provided a context for the development of greater managerial control to 'ensure' the safety of the child.

Indeed, in other areas of practice social workers may seem to need only quite routine or ordinary skills and capacities to carry out their work. Much of their practice may appear to be the stuff of everyday life. Just how much abstract knowledge is required to arrange residential care for an older person no longer able to cope adequately in the community? This is something which might easily be arranged by a relative with no social work experience and certainly no training. A family where a teenager seems to have behavioural problems may seem to differ little in principle from the kinds of 'teenage problems' suffered by many families. Perhaps being an experienced parent is more useful to the social worker than any form of complex professional knowledge, if they wish to be really helpful in such situations.

In these cases, the imperative may seem to be to ensure that practitioners 'do their job properly'. By implication, this requires some oversight and becomes the responsibility of managers. Social workers would have set roles and tasks which they could fulfil in relation to particular practice situations and which are 'ensured' through managerial oversight. Having defined their work as more or less routine, it becomes possible to prescribe the actions – in advance – which should take place in order to carry out these roles. Elements of this managerial control include, of course, direct instruction, in which a manager directs a practitioner to do or not to do something. (In the latter instance this could, for example, include closing a case where the risk had been reduced to manageable proportions, which the social worker, left to themselves, would not close because there might be some unmet needs.) A less obvious control is normative. This is where the legitimacy of managerial control and the expectations of behaviour arising from this permeate all those in the organisation, including non-managers. The result is that direct instructions are not required in order for non-managers (or practitioners) to carry out the kinds of actions which are expected of them. They simply *know* what to do. The commitment, on the part of non-managers, to the managers' expectations and aspirations, involve what Clegg (1979) has called hegemonic control – control exercised by managers without others being directly aware of it, or of the potential for conflict.

It is the third area for managerial control, relating to technical instrumentalism, that concerns us. Control by rule or procedure is one means for control, which involves the social worker as technician. As with the constructor of cabinets, it is the capacity to follow rules or guidance, not for imagination and creativity, which lies at the core of this form of social work as a technical activity. Where procedures are set, for example, in relation to responding to particular kinds of referrals, there are certain expectations about the behaviour of the social worker. We have already given the example of response time. The social worker is competent or not to the extent that he or she has responded within the expected time period. 'Incompetence' would be defined, in that instance, as responding outside the expected time period, or not responding at all.

There is little that is complex about this. It is about applying a general rule (response time) to a particular situation (the referral with which the social worker is dealing). The capacity to use these general rules depends on the extent to which the task involved can be said to be routine. Where a task is not routine there are no fixed responses to a situation. The individual has to think up their own response (having analysed the situation), decide what should happen and carry it out. Solutions to problems are novel and unstructured. This is exactly the kinds of process envisaged, in our analysis so far, in social work as art (although this is not the only way of conceiving responses to non-routine situations). The creative, imaginative social worker is using their individual capacities and skills, responding to the uniqueness of particular situations and recognising their complexity, a complexity which cannot be distilled into sets of routine instructions.

Routine activities (those which have been 'routinised') are characterised by the extent to which the degree of choice has been simplified by the development of fixed responses to a situation. In the case of response time, there is nothing, in principle, which is problematic. The choice is to respond within the allotted time (and be competent) or not respond within that time (and be incompetent). The capacity to generalise this rule to all situations is in direct relation to its simplicity. Of course, that is the case in principle. In practice, other factors, beyond the capacity of the individual to follow these instructions, come into play. Most obvious is the pressure of work, which may be such that it is not possible to respond within the expected time period to a referral.

The image created here is one not just of reduced professional autonomy but of reduced complexity. This approach implies that the nature of the task is sufficiently simple to create these general rules or procedures which may govern the conduct of practice. This is one reason why some of the more managerial developments in social work in the UK in the past few decades have been so uncomfortable for many social workers. It can be seen as a 'dumbing down' process, one which, indeed, does not so much *simplify* the task of the social worker as make it *simplistic*. Indeed (the argument would go), it may be that the developments of procedures are seen as a focus on the irrelevant or, at least, less relevant. If the practitioner believes that the creative, responsive analytical skills, together with the person of the worker, are what is important in social work practice, then rules governing response times might be seen as trivial irrelevancies.

The degree of discretion inherent in these rules, guidance and procedures, however, has some importance. It is in the level of discretion that some headway can be made in the gap between the prescriptive nature of the rules and the complex nature of the individual situations with which they are designed to deal. Dunsire (1978) distinguishes between those who may respond to procedures or guidance with wide discretion or narrow discretion. Managers are able to exercise most control where the work involves low levels of uncertainty – that is, where situations are largely straightforward and similar, and it is possible to predict the likely variations in that situation. We know fairly easily whether a social worker has responded within a particular time period. Dunsire calls these 'rule followers', and monitoring of their activities is relatively simple. Routine clerical work may fall into this category (and social workers are forever complaining these days about form filling).

Other groups may work in an environment where wide discretion is required. Dunsire calls these 'judgement makers'. This applies to situations which are not routine, where it is not possible to predict the possible alternative circumstances that may arise, and there is, therefore, considerable scope for uncertainty. It may be difficult to ensure lawyers working for a local authority follow prescribed solutions (or difficult in some areas) because it is their expert understanding of the law, together with the wide variety of individual circumstances of each case, which is most important. Managers cannot tell them what to recommend because the combination of these factors make it impossible to develop rules which precisely outline all possible alternatives, and all possible responses to those alternatives.

Dunsire's classification, though helpful, is perhaps too dichotomous. It is perhaps better to envisage practitioners potentially operating along a continuum, at one end of which are rule followers and at the other end of which are judgement makers. This can help us look at further dimensions of rule following as an aspect of technical instrumentalism in social work. Governments, as we have noted, have been concerned to develop appropriate responses to cases of potential risk to children, and a whole host of procedures have developed. Some of these have been further along the continuum towards judgement making.

One example of this, again from the referral process, but this time including initial assessments, involves criteria by which cases are allocated priority. It is widely understood that a social services department is bombarded with far more 'in need' cases than they have the resources to deal with. Furthermore, it is necessary, particularly in child protection (for reasons we have already mentioned), to distinguish those cases most at risk. The result is that departments have developed classifications through which priority can be given to the various referrals which are received. This contains elements of 'rules set in advance' and judgement made on individual cases.

Sheppard (2004a, p. 79) outlines how this has been achieved in practice through departmental procedures. The child care teams researched here have five different levels of priority, with definitions attached to each, as follows:

- *Priority one: safeguarding.* 'An immediate response is required.' Children who are suffering, or have suffered, significant harm or are likely to suffer significant harm. Timescale: within 24 hours.
- *Priority two: safeguarding.* 'An early response is required.' Identified factors exist indicating unacceptable risks to the child without intervention. Timescale: within three working days.
- *Priority three: safeguarding.* 'An assured response is required.' Children for whom there is significant concern about their care, health and development. Timescale: within three working days.
- *Priority four: promotional.* 'An assured response of support is likely to be required.' Children who are likely to be moved up to priority one, two or three unless services are required. Timescale: within seven working days.
- *Priority five: promotional.* Cases where advice, signposting (advice or direction to appropriate alternative services) or access to a service is required. Timescale: within seven working days.

These are multidimensional, containing a variety of interconnected rules. These priorities operate (rather obviously) as a hierarchy, in which those with highest priority would be seen first. The timescales are intended to be maxima before the family is seen. 'Safeguarding' refers to safeguarding children at risk of significant harm, while 'promotional' refers to the promotion of the welfare of children and families in need, but without children at risk of significant harm. Alongside this are different descriptions of what each priority means.

While these are clear rules – for example, that priorities should be adhered to (priority one before the rest), time periods should be adhered to, that priorities had particular kinds of characteristics (for example, for priority one, an 'immediate response is required') – these rules are not, with the exception of time periods, especially precise. How do we define, in particular cases, where 'significant harm' has been experienced by a child? Some circumstances may be straightforward where, for example, a child has suffered a violent attack from a parent which has left them with broken bones, but (even here) social workers will be interested in exploring in detail the whole context of the case. How do we know where there is 'unacceptable risk without intervention'? This requires not just an awareness of acts which have already been carried out, but the capacity to speculate into future possibilities or probabilities. What is 'an assured response of support'? What, indeed, is support? And how do we know when it is assured?

What we have are department rules and guidelines which nevertheless require, by implication, the exercise of judgement. The person allocating priority (the manager) must judge where 'significant harm' has occurred, what constitutes 'unacceptable risk' and where an 'assured response' has occurred. In order to do this, he or she relies not just on the information provided at referral but on the assessment and investigative capacities of the social worker(s) who has explored matters with the referrer, and further. Thus the rules do allow, in advance, for responses to be dictated and for the circumstances of those responses to be defined by the decision-making process, leading to those responses requiring the exercise of judgement.

Another example of technical instrumentalism in the managed process is the proliferation of forms which have to be completed in order to carry out the work of the case, or even the department. These have increased significantly since the advent of care management and, indeed, were central to its processes. One example taken from the *Practitioners' Guide* (DoH, 1991a) exemplifies certain characteristics:

- as far as possible these are prescriptive, clearly designed to exercise some control over the work of practitioners;
- they are written in a manner which gives a very routine 'feel' to the conduct of practice;
- they clearly delineate when a task is 'done', and if it is not;
- they are often in the form of a checklist, with tick boxes attached.

The form itself is an 'Assessing Need Checklist', and is therefore absolutely central to the practice process (DoH, 1991a, p. 91).

1. Has the scope of the assessment been negotiated with the potential user?
2. Has the appropriate setting been chosen?
3. Have expectations been clarified about the resources both practitioners and users bring to the assessment?
4. Have the potential users and carers been enabled to participate with due sensitivity to their ethnic, cultural or communication needs?
5. Have users and carers had appropriate access to advocacy support?
6. Have the differing perceptions of need been reconciled or, if not, any differences recorded?
7. Have decisions on eligibility for assistance been explained to the user?

8. Have the eligible needs been prioritised?
9. Have objectives and criteria for measuring them been set for each of the prioritised needs?
10. Has a record of the assessment been shared with the user?

Each of these is accompanied by a box to be ticked, provided each of those tasks had been undertaken. Rather neatly, there were ten tasks prescribed.

Presumably, where the boxes are ticked the work undertaken is deemed to be adequate (or that is the implication). However, each of these contain potentially complex tasks. While there may be some recognition for the potential complexity of the tasks, the emphasis, in focusing on these checklists, is on the routine aspects of work, and gives the impression of relatively straightforward actions being required. This is backed up by the increased employment of non-social workers in areas which had previously been social work terrain, and the development of National Vocational Qualifications – 'on-the-job' learning based on the premise that lower levels of thinking and complexity are required in work in social care than that required for social work.

Alongside this, forms have been developed for core and comprehensive assessments. These focus not just on the completion of tasks, but are designed to channel the ways in which practitioners think. Need is divided into broad categories which provide the focus for assessment (DoH, 1991a, p. 12). Thus we have personal/social care, health care, accommodation, finance, education/employment/leisure and transport/access. It is in relation to these areas that social workers are expected to formulate their account of client needs. However, the 'channelling' can go further. Each of these areas can be further subdivided in order to ensure practitioners focus precisely on those kinds of areas which are prescribed, by the agency, to be of interest. Thus (Sheppard, 1995a), under the broad area of 'relationships', we have family/partner, others, the carer and social interaction with others. These, of course, overlap but they serve to illustrate the extent to which the manner in which assessment is carried out becomes prescribed. Indeed, a range of 'levels of need' can be attached to each of these areas, further prescribing the outcome of the assessment.

We again return to the core element of technical instrumentalism in these checklists – that they are, to a considerable degree, rule-governed actions. In this vision, social work becomes (to a considerable degree) a technical act in which certain tasks are carried out, within predefined parameters and according to certain predefined characteristics. The competent practitioner is the one who 'follows the rules', by assessing those areas prescribed, rating them appropriately, following the prescribed processes and by *recording* that they have done so.

This is a very different picture of social work from that encapsulated in 'art'. It is less creative than rule following. It limits autonomy, whereas art encourages individualisation. It focuses less on the relationship than on the performance of actions and appropriate processes. It appears to limit the capacity for the display of virtuosity, rather emphasising the importance of uniformity and conformity.

However, many might suggest that it achieves its aims by ignoring those factors that are most important in social work. If social workers cannot form a relationship, many would argue, they have nothing at all. Indeed, some clients have problems of a degree that special skills may be required to form and maintain the relationship, developing on essentially human qualities. The managerial-technical-instrumental approach to social work says nothing about this. Likewise, the creation of meaning, it might be argued, is at the heart of social work. This requires the development of empathy and understanding, and of an account or narrative which makes sense of a situation. There is nothing in the arid approach of ticked boxes which takes account of the importance of meaning creation, yet the capacity for meaning creation is a necessity if these forms are to be completed in any meaningful way. They are, at one and the same time, both a presentation of the situation without meaning emerging from it (as would be the case if a narrative were written down), and yet require the development of meaning before they can be properly completed.

They have a tendency, finally, to emphasise the routine and general, yet often require the exercise of considerable judgement in order that they can be completed properly. By not focusing on the knowledge and skills required to make a proper completion, they encourage the possibility that lower levels of skills than those actually required might be acceptable. In other words, just because an untrained social care worker is able to tick a number of boxes, it does not mean that the assessment has been carried out as well as it might have been by the more sophisticated understanding of a social worker. However, it gives the appearance that this has been achieved, increasing the scope for 'lower-level' practitioners conducting the work.

We should not dismiss, however, the use of technical approaches, even those using tick boxes as aids to practice, where these can be a highly sophisticated support to the work of the skilled practitioner. It would be foolish, for example, to deny the value of the Beck Depression Inventory (Beck et al., 1988) in work with people who may be suffering from depression; the inventory can be used both as a diagnostic tool and as an aid to identifying the most efficacious interventions. This, though, takes us on to areas other than technical instrumentalism as part of managerial control.

Technical instrumentalism, science and professional knowledge

Technical instrumentalism also represents an approach to professional knowledge use. In general, to the extent that the term is employed, it is used as a term of derision by those whose commitment is closer to notions of professional work as 'art' or as 'reflective practice' (Schön, 1983; Miller, 1979; Grobman, 1999). At the same time, those who so fervently criticise it assert that it has been the dominant model of professional knowledge use in recent times.

It is, however, an approach which has implicitly dominated the theory–practice debate in recent years. This debate has, to a considerable degree, construed a relationship between the two as based on separate domains, one of theory and one of practice. Theory refers to formal knowledge, researched and written down and which, therefore, is widely available for consultation. Practice, on the other hand, is what practitioners do, in the case of social work, intervening in the social world. Furthermore, the relationship has one particular direction: from theory to practice. The practitioner learns the theory and then is able to apply it, as appropriate, to practice. If the practitioner is looking at issues concerning a child aged (say) five or six, they may wish to draw upon developmental psychology to guide them in their responses.

Finally, there is an additional assumption that theory – written down, researched, formal knowledge – is superior to knowledge from other areas, particularly experience. This is based on the idea that researched formal knowledge is more carefully and rigorously constructed than can be the case with personal experiences, and that it is subject to more systematic and widely based critical scrutiny, the result being that we can have more confidence in such knowledge. In addition, because of the less idiosyncratic nature of the knowledge development process, it is more possible to apply such knowledge generally. In other words, if we find out certain things about parenting – for example, that a woman who has lost her mother before the age of 11 is more likely as an adult to be vulnerable to depression (Brown and Harris, 1978) – we can apply this generally, keeping an eye out for the problems of women who have lost their mothers before the age of 11.

Rein and White (1981, p. 21) suggest this approach comes from 'an objectivist-scientific' approach of a sort associated with positivism, that 'science makes knowledge [whilst] practice uses it'. Certainly, positivism has developed, to a considerable degree, into a term of derision in recent years, and it is very important to realise that positivism is not the only 'theory of knowledge' which is objectivist (many critics seem to fail to realise this). This is something to which we shall return.

However, positivism does attach particular meanings to theory and practice. First of all, positivism asserts that we live in an objective world, and that includes society and the social world. We do not 'construct' our perceptions of reality, as individuals and groups. It is not the case that individuals and groups can validly see the same things in different ways, each view having equal merit. Rather, reality is 'out there', we observe it and are able, using appropriately rigorous methods, to discover it.

This approach sees *theory as a general rule, or law, which is tested against observable evidence.* We may present the hypothesis: 'where relatives of people suffering schizophrenia have good support networks, the person suffering schizophrenia is less likely to relapse' (cf. Anderson et al., 1984; Taylor et al., 1984). We look, using appropriate methods, for evidence on this and come to a conclusion about the accuracy of this proposition. *Practice, on the other hand, involves the use of theoretical knowledge, deductively, primarily to control events.* Suppose we found evidence to support the aforementioned proposition. We might, as a mental health social worker, be working with a person suffering from schizophrenia and their family. Using the theoretical knowledge about support groups, we might focus specifically on the adequacy of the support networks available to the relatives. If they were poor, the social worker might take actions to improve the network.

The deductive process is as follows:

- (Theory): where relatives of people suffering schizophrenia have good support networks, the person suffering schizophrenia is less likely to relapse.
- (Practice situation): in this case the relatives have poor support networks.
- In this case (theory indicates) the person suffering from schizophrenia is more likely to relapse than if his relatives have good support networks.
- Our aim is to minimise the likelihood of relapse in the patient.
- It follows (from theory, the particular practice situation and our objectives) that we should seek to improve the quality of the relatives' support network.

This approach thus entails an instrumental engineering conception of the relationship between theory and practice. It involves (social) engineering in that there is the conscious manipulation of certain key facets of the client's (and relatives') social life in order to achieve some objective. It is instrumental in the sense that we are not concerned with querying whether or not the objective being pursued is a good one or a bad one (even though most would, I am sure, agree that the objective in our example is a good one). Our concern is with achieving the most effective way of achieving our overall objective (to prevent relapse of the patient).

Evidence-based practice and positivism

In practical terms we can look at this in various ways. The notion of 'evidence-based practice' has gained considerable influence in recent years and, to a considerable degree, is linked to this technical-instrumental notion of the theory–practice relationship. Sackett et al. (1996, p. 2), in a widely quoted passage, have defined evidence-based practice in a way which implicitly involves this rule following the instrumental notion of the theory–practice relationship. It is, they say 'the conscious, explicit and judicious use of current best evidence about the care of individual patients'. They were referring to a medical context, but the term 'patients' may easily be replaced by 'clients'.

Those most firmly in the positivist camp have strongly pursued an approach to the use of knowledge in social work which follows the deductive model outlined above (Macdonald and Winkley, 1999; Macdonald and Sheldon, 1998; Thyer, 1993). The idea is that as A is applied to circumstance B, C will result. This appeals to universal laws which lie at the heart of positivism. These are generally seen to be generated in 'hard sciences' such as physics, but to the extent that social sciences *are* sciences (in the positivist sense) such universal laws may be developed. The relationship between social support of relatives and relapse in patients suffering from schizophrenia might be presented as just such a universal law.

However, since it is not possible to be as certain about the social world as it is about the physical world, it is the probabilistic version of these 'laws' which are presented (this probabilistic version is one which is adopted by realists also). The problem is that there are so many factors potentially impacting on a situation that there can be cases where factors other than those we have examined affect the situation. For example, it may not be enough to examine the quality of support provided to relatives of people suffering from schizophrenia. It may be that limiting contact between the relative and the person suffering schizophrenia (particularly where the relative tends to be critical) could have the effect of reducing relapse. There may be no need, in those circumstances, to improve the quality of social support to relatives.

Thus, rather than a 'cast iron' law – that where the quality of social support for relatives is poor, relapse in the person suffering from schizophrenia will occur – we are left with the *probability* that this is the case – that a person with schizophrenia is *more likely*, in these circumstances, to relapse. Of course this posits a more complex relationship between theory and practice (while nevertheless being rule-based) in which judgement must play a part (of which more later).

Those of a positivist view, however, largely also subscribe to a 'hierarchy of knowledge' approach. This is one in which knowledge gained in certain kinds of ways is deemed superior to other forms of knowledge. In particular, the randomised control trial (RCT) is viewed as the 'gold standard' for knowledge. The RCT is an experiment in which two groups are compared, one of which receives a form of treatment and another which does not. We might, for example, look at the impact of cognitive behavioural therapy (CBT) on people suffering depression: we may hypothesise that depressed people receiving CBT would improve more (that is, have a reduction in their depression) than those not receiving CBT. In this case, one group of depressed people would receive CBT (the experimental group) and the other would not (the control group). Considerable importance is ascribed to the need to allocate people to each of the two groups randomly. Significant importance is also ascribed to preventing either group being affected by other factors which might impact on the change which would occur. Finally, measurements are taken at (at least) two points, a baseline and follow-up point, and the two groups are compared to see where the improvement (if there was any) was greater.

This is considered the 'gold standard' because the findings are regarded to be most reliable. Not everyone subscribes to this view, and this claim has been contested by many (see Sheppard, 2004b, pp. 129–34 for a summary). Not least of these are the observations that:

- it is impossible, in social life, to insulate research subjects from factors other than those which are being examined (CBT in this case), and hence we cannot be as sure of the relationships (in this case between CBT and improvement in depressed state) as the advocates of randomised control trials would suggest; and

- anyway, in trying to 'insulate' the experiment from social life, the researchers are also limiting the applicability of findings to social life, since the former cannot reflect the complexity of the latter.

Having said that, many who would criticise its position of being the 'gold standard' would nevertheless accept that RCTs do make a contribution.

Below this 'gold standard' are other approaches to research. For positivists, these generally follow a similar hierarchy. Thyer (1993), for example, identifies four approaches at the top of the knowledge tree:

- Outcome investigations involve *single subject groups* – that is without a comparison control group – focusing on change over time.
- *Experimentation*, for Thyer, involves a comparison group, hence involving one group which gets the treatment, and the other which does not.
- *Comparative effectiveness studies* involve the comparison of two groups, *both* of whom get some treatment. One, however, is a new treatment, and the central issue is: 'is the new treatment superior to the conventional treatment?'
- Finally, there is *componential analysis*. This involves the gradual addition of first one, then two, or three components, to see whether in fact multiple components (that is, interventions involving various elements, such as (a) counselling (b) support group and (c) material help, are more effective than one alone.

While Thyer describes these as 'steps', it should be emphasised that he regarded all of these forms of knowledge as 'experimentation'. By implication, non-experimental methods did not produce the same quality of knowledge.

Macdonald and Winkley, 1999, p. 8) assert that 'the confidence that we can have that a particular set of outcomes is attributable to our actions depends in large part on the research design used and its careful execution'. Thus, while qualitative studies have their place, 'the development of effective services requires other kinds of evidence'. They consider RCTs to have 'the edge' (p. 10) over other designs, using the conventional argument of the importance of random allocation. Below this come, in order, quasi-experimental designs (which do not involve random allocation between experimental and control groups), non-experimental designs (which involve either no comparative group, or no matching of one group with another) and, finally, 'other research methods', such as client opinion studies, surveys and cohort studies.

For the reader unacquainted with these methods in detail, the important point is that, for these authors, if we are to be serious about the use of knowledge in practice, then (a) it should focus on effectiveness and (b) certain methods, most especially the randomised control trial, are simply more reliable than others. Hence, it is this kind of knowledge which we should seek to apply to practice.

Non-positivist technical instrumentalism

The technical-instrumental approach to the theory–practice relationship is not confined to positivists. There are those, even amongst positivists, who consider that different kinds of methods may be employed in relation to different kinds of problems (whilst nevertheless regarding effectiveness studies to be the most important, and experimentation the gold standard for effectiveness studies) (Macdonald and Sheldon, 1998). However, others have emphasised not just the importance of employing different methods for different problems within social work, but for the use of multiple methods in examining individual problems (Davies, 1994 ; Sinclair, 1992; Cheetham, 1992). This group is more circumspect, less committed to the supremacy of RCTs. There is, this group would suggest, considerable need for research, but it may be simply investigative rather than experimental in design.

From a knowledge point of view, furthermore, not all those who adopt a technical-instrumental approach would subscribe to a positivist conception. Realism, as a philosophy of knowledge, has become highly influential in recent years. However, those who wish to dispute the idea that knowledge can be scientific, or who wish to assert that the technical instrumental notion of knowledge use is not valid, rarely (if ever) confront the challenge presented by realism (a summary of realism as it relates to social work can be found in Sheppard, 1995a, pp. 145–9). Schön (1983) is particularly complicit in this, implicitly contrasting positivism with social interactionism, as if they were the only two options, and failing to look at realism as an alternative and more dominant (and sophisticated) notion of science. There are those who trenchantly argue that major aspects of practice must involve some notions of an objective reality, but who do so on realist rather than positivist assumptions (for example, Hagge, 1996; Moore, 2000). In other words, it is not necessary to confine ourselves to a positivist approach to adopt a technical-instrumental approach to knowledge application.

In brief, realists hold that there is an objective world 'out there', but our capacity fully to understand it is limited. It is necessary, therefore, for us to accrue evidence and develop frameworks which enable us to understand and explain the world better. These, properly developed, are called theories.

Because we cannot understand the world fully (due to the limits of human understanding), we may develop more than one way of understanding any particular aspect of the world, including the social world. Thus, in the social sciences, we may develop competing theories. We might, for example, attribute juvenile delinquency to the experience of poverty and disadvantage, to the influence of peer groups or to inadequate socialisation as a person was growing up. From the point of view of the realist, we should choose the theory which contains the most comprehensive explanation and for which the best evidence has been accrued.

However, because of the limited nature of human understanding, it may be that one explanation is more adequate for one set of circumstances and another is better for other situations. In that case, the theory or explanation chosen should be the one which best fits those circumstances. This is about a complex world, allied to imperfect human understanding. However, overall, realists emphasise that all knowledge is provisional, liable to be overtaken by new knowledge which more adequately enables us to understand the social world (and, indeed, the world in general).

The greater uncertainty inherent in the realist position, compared with positivists, is consistent with a more all-embracing approach to methodology. This position, in contrast to that of positivism, might be called an *applied social science* position. Cheetham (1992, p. 53) remarks that 'evaluation of social work effectiveness [is] one of the best ways [of] developing the knowledge base of social work and bridging the gap between theory and practice'. However, her concern is not limited to what is conventionally called 'outcome', but also to evaluation of 'process'. While 'outcome' focuses on what happens as a result of intervention, process looks at what happens during intervention (Cheetham et al., 1992). This is not, therefore, just about whether or not a form of intervention (say) improved parenting or reduced depression, but how it was experienced by the client. Or it could be about the extent to which the manner in which the service was delivered fitted with policy or practice expectations. Or it could be about the extent to which delivery of the service was fair and just.

Inevitably this leads to different types of research. On purely pragmatic grounds, some issues may be more suitable for one kind of research than another. Where, for example, we wish to discover from clients what they consider to be important in the provision of services, it may be a loose semi-structured interview which is required. If we wish to examine the interaction of clients and workers in a child or family centre setting, this may be be undertaken by a process of observation. In neither case is experimentation in any way the most appropriate means for investigation, and so cannot be seen as the 'gold standard'.

Beyond this, multi-method research may be pursued. This involves the use of more than one method in order to understand better the social world. We might bring together surveys with in-depth interviews, client perspectives with some form of experimentation. The idea behind this is that the world is a complex place and it is in the *combination* of different methods which have different things to offer the researcher that we are most likely to obtain the clearest picture. Thus, if we look to quantitative data, this is suited to the measurement of magnitude (how much, what degree of change and so on), association (between different facets of the social world, for example depression and quality of parenting), change (where a precise notion of change is required) and so on. Qualitative methods, on the other hand, offer the opportunity to understand meaning, the capacity to examine relatively few cases, but in depth, and to be very responsive to humans' understanding of the world in the process of carrying out research (see Sheppard, 2004b, chapter 11, for a more detailed analysis of this perspective).

All this may be seen as a pragmatic response, arising from identifying the most appropriate method being applied to the particular issue which is being studied. Some might (broadly) be quantitative, others qualitative. There can be no doubt that many of those engaged in this broader approach to relevant knowledge are, indeed, being pragmatic. They are simply responding to the problem at hand with the approach which seems most efficacious. However, there are those (amongst whom I count myself) whose use of research consciously reflects a realist position. While, therefore, there is a commitment to the use of knowledge in practice, this group of 'applied social scientists' may be considered to be a combination of pragmatists and realists.

A *third* approach to evidence-based practice is still more all-embracing, one which might be termed the '*extended evidence*' position. Those we have examined so far focus on research, written, formal knowledge as the 'evidence' in evidence-based practice. However, there are those who go beyond this and include more experiential knowledge, such as that learned while carrying out practice, as legitimate 'evidence'. Indeed, there is some suggestion that this may have some official backing, since this kind of wider notion of evidence is apparent, for example, in the Department of Health's work on assessing needs in children and families (DoH, 2000).

This position is explicitly outlined, in relation to health, by Rycroft-Malone et al. (2004). However, this is also evident in social work (DoH, 2000; Cleaver et al., 1999) and in any case, the notion of 'evidence-based practice' transcends both health and social work and social care boundaries. Rycroft-Malone et al. (2004) suggest that the prominence given to research, and quantitative research in particular, has meant the 'relative neglect' (p. 83) of other forms of evidence. They suggest that evidence should be considered to be knowledge 'derived from a variety of sources', including contextual, individual practitioner and patient/client.

In particular, they argue for the importance of knowledge derived from practice, part of the 'professional craft knowledge' of practitioners. It has particular potential when articulated by practitioners and hence made manifest, rather than remaining only as idiosyncratic knowledge of individual workers. In this way, it can be verified through the wider communities of practice. In order to maximise the use of what is known, it is suggested, it is necessary to draw upon and integrate multiple sources of knowledge.

Broadly, Rycroft-Malone and her colleagues identify four sources of evidence. The first is 'knowledge from research evidence'. They do not distinguish between types of research nor, for example, do they have notions of more or less valid knowledge, such as those who assert RCTs to be the 'gold standard'. They point out both that research evidence is evolving and developing (hence may change over time) and that research knowledge only covers some of the issues, circumstances and situations confronted by the practitioner. Knowledge from research alone is not adequate for the needs for the best possible evidence base.

Knowledge from 'clinical (or practice) experience' is another area. This knowledge is expressed and embedded in practice, and is often tacit and intuitive. Steetler (2001) argues that, to be credible, such knowledge needs to be verified from various sources. For example, they could be gathered through accounts which have been obtained from various practitioners. The two other areas are knowledge from patients, clients and users and knowledge from local context. The former involves the identification and expression of clients' experience of problems and needs and of their experience of intervention. The latter refers to areas such as audit and performance data, knowledge about local resources, knowledge of the culture of relevant organisations and local policy.

Comments

Knowledge is, in principle, relevant to social exclusion and inclusion to the extent that it helps social workers promote inclusion. Nevertheless, there have been some trenchant criticisms about the relevance of knowledge in practice, particularly regarding technical instrumentalism. In the past (though this seems to be less the case more recently), there has been widespread scepticism about the use of applied knowledge. A number of studies on practitioners' use of knowledge have found a lack of 'theory' use. Practitioners do not seem to have applied knowledge in the way suggested by technical instrumentalism (for example, Carew, 1979; Stevenson and Parsloe, 1978; Corby, 1982; Marsh and Triselliotis, 1996). In the absence of evidence of direct knowledge application, some have adopted a 'subconscious assimilation' theory, whereby theory informs practice without practitioners being directly aware of it (Paley, 1987). Personal and practice experience are implicitly and explicitly given a higher value than formal applied knowledge.

Others have suggested that this limitation in knowledge use is inherent in the nature of social work. Davies (1994) was concerned that some of the disciplines (particularly sociology) taught to social workers would have little relevance, even a damaging effect on social workers undertaking education and training. More generally, he felt that the constraints of the practical circumstances in which social workers found themselves undermined the usefulness of formal knowledge. For example, a range of information from attachment theory, including that on child temperament, might potentially be relevant to practice when seeking substitute care for children. However, the brute reality is such that it is often difficult to find sufficient foster carers at all, let alone worry about the extent to which there is a well-defined 'fit' between the needs of a child and the precise qualities which foster carers have on offer.

However, on the other hand, recent reviews of findings have shown the potential relevance of formal knowledge for practice. In particular, they have been able to show the effectiveness of particular forms of intervention, such as cognitive behavioural therapy and task-centred practice, on some of the problems confronted by social workers (Macdonald et al., 1992; Sheldon, 1994; Kirk and Reid, 2002). Likewise, decades of research have helped inform law and policy in relation to child care. It is only logical that this should be extended to more detailed educational processes, such as (in the UK) the Child Care Award and Approved Social Worker award (in mental health), as an addition to basic qualifications. The issue, some would argue, is not the relevance of knowledge, but its dissemination (by those who conduct the research and relevant agencies) and uptake (by social workers).

However, even the evidence-based practice movement has quite varied positions within it. Firstly, it is important to emphasise that a technical-instrumental, even science-oriented, approach does not have to be positivist. Some, to be sure, adopt a positivist position, but many do not. Three positions have been outlined here: those who are *positivists*; the *applied social science group* (who are either pragmatic in their approach to knowledge and its application, or who have a coherent realist approach); and the *extended evidence position* (which includes non-researched information as evidence). It is clear, therefore, that the notion of being 'evidence-based' papers over quite significant gaps between different groups who are commonly committed to the general notion of using evidence in practice.

The last of these groups – the extended evidence group – clearly seek to transcend the limits which would otherwise be placed on them by a focus on only research-based knowledge, indeed a hierarchy dictated by a positivist position. However, in doing so they open themselves up to a considerable weakness. First, it is not clear that they are adopting a 'rule-based' approach to knowledge, with its focus on a single direction, in which knowledge is applied from theory to practice, not practice to theory, or practice to practice. More problematically, however, their adoption of 'practitioner knowledge' as an evidence base is in danger of fêting personal idiosyncrasy in the guise of formal knowledge, when it cannot be so. They offer no real solution to the problem of rigour. Either this professional knowledge is subject to rigorous research (for example, we could ask a social worker about their practice strategies in relation to handling child abuse referrals), in which case it is written up and becomes formal knowledge about the processes of intervention. Or, without this rigorous knowledge creation approach, it remains primarily in the realm of personal anecdote, not subject to critical appraisal or other appropriate means for developing rigour. While it would not be wise to dismiss areas of information such as knowledge of local resources and audits of aspects of the organisation (which Davies (1994) considers to be important aspects of practice knowledge), a rather more coherent notion of evidence-based practice is required from the 'extended evidence' group.

This, of course, relates to the use of formal knowledge as a form of technical instrumentalism. Managerial technicality, while also adopting a rule-following process, is far more restrictive. While the evidence-based approach involves practitioners being the 'repository' (at least to some extent) of knowledge, and therefore experts, who call upon the rules which are derived from professional knowledge, managerial technicality does no such thing. Rather the rules developed seek to determine how social workers should act in particular situations. While evidence-based practice enhances the professional position and autonomy of practitioners, managerial technicality entails greater managerial control. Indeed, it may be said to involve deskilling and reduced status also for the practitioner.

A key issue, as we have outlined, is the degree of appropriateness with which such a strategy is pursued. Is social work really the kind of activity suited to restrictive determining technical-managerial rules? Well, to the extent that it needs to be evidence-based (on an individual level), or even art, it cannot. The key here is where social work lies in what Jamous and Peloille (1970) have called the 'technicality-indetermination' ratio.

Social work, like pretty well all professions these days, operates within organisations, which need managing. As such, they need managerial hierarchies, and social work has even been termed a 'bureau profession', one which operates within, and whose actions are entwined with the operation and aims of, bureaucracies. As we have seen, technical-managerial rules operate effectively where there is some degree of predictability in the conduct of practice. However, not all elements of practice may be determined in advance. Indeterminacy arises from the notion that an occupation works within an area of uncertainty which, because of the special skills of the professionals involved, can only be fully understood by those with those skills and knowledge – people in the same profession.

To the extent that the range of possible practice situations cannot be determined in advance, technical managerialism is restricted. Where there is indeterminacy in social work, this means that its practitioners must treat each situation on its own merit and, between worker and client, create an understanding of and response to the particular concerns exercising the client. The indeterminate aspect of work broadly refers to specialist skills possessed by practitioners of a profession, not reducible to managerial rules.

The areas of social life which are the concern of social work are often characterised by high levels of uncertainty. We only have to look at the difficulty which child care practitioners encounter when seeking to predict outcomes of their work on an individual family-by-family basis to recognise the degree of uncertainty involved. There is always an element of calculation in choosing one intervention over another and there is no surprise if matters do not quite work out as anticipated. It is here that we have to consider both the need for more abstract forms of professional technical knowledge and the judgements of practitioners, interwoven between that technical knowledge and which they have learned from practice experience. This can involve analytic, creative elements of practice.

Derber (1982) has also referred to the concept of 'technical proletarianisation'. This occurs when the degree of autonomy experienced by professionals is reduced because of the control exerted by management. It is a feature of some social workers' experience of recent efforts at technical managerialism in practice. While this is, to some degree, an inevitable part of social work, it is necessarily limited by the degree of indeterminacy which undoubtedly exists in practice and the extent to which rigorous but more abstract forms of knowledge are required to conduct practice (evidence-based practice).

There are, therefore, dimensions of technical instrumentalism in social work, with a tension between the determinate and indeterminate aspects of practice, the managerial and the evidence-based, and the rule-following and the creative. While we can suggest that evidence-based practice can have a place in social work to the extent that it makes a difference, and to which rule following is appropriate, there are limits.

Conclusion

Clearly there is a real problem with technical instrumentalism, including evidence-based practice, in that there is no consideration of the processes through which knowledge may be used in practice. That there are forms of knowledge which can be relevant to practice and inform practice situations, we should have little dispute. However, the idea of a straightforward 'rule-governed' application of theory to practice is really rather simplistic and gives no attention at all to the psychological processes through which the analysis of situations can be brought together with the choice of forms of knowledge which may inform these situations, There is, furthermore, no consideration of the ways the two can be integrated in individual instances to inform the processes of intervention generally, and specific practice strategies in particular.

There is clearly an element of 'making meaning', though not in the sense outlined by interpretivists. Their commitment to a relativist perception of the world, with an absence of an 'external reality', is itself not coherent and does not fit with the practice assumptions which we have outlined of social work. However, based on various factors – the salient features of a particular practice situation, the capabilities of the individual practitioner, their professional responsibilities and the various forms of knowledge available to them – it is necessary for social workers to construct 'on-the-job' ways of viewing the particular practice situations they are confronting. We need, therefore, to begin to understand these further.

Chapter twelve

Judgement and decision making: practical reasoning, process knowledge and critical thinking

Our last two chapters leave us with a conundrum. Notions of social work, both as art and science, have something to offer. The importance, in particular of meaning, is evident from the 'art' concept of social work. We can hardly, however, neglect evidence gained from research and, in using such research, there must inevitably be some element of deductive logic used – that is (in short) we have to be applying that knowledge to relevant practice situations. It would be foolish, then, entirely to dismiss elements of science in social work.

The tantalising nature of both notions (apart from the limitations inherent in each) arises because of the gaps they leave, the questions that are not asked, let alone not answered. Some of this arises because of the dominant notion of what constitutes knowledge. Whatever the knowledge commitment of those who are considering the matter (whether, for example, they are interpretivists – or by extension postmodernists – or positivists), 'knowledge' is largely considered to be that which has been thought through, and/or researched and written down. It is then available for practitioners to consider and apply in whichever way they consider appropriate. To be sure the 'extended evidence' position outlined in the last chapter does seek to include 'practitioner knowledge' but that aspect becomes a little incoherent upon critical appraisal.

In order to make this clear, it is helpful to identify and name this approach, which may be called *product knowledge*. This is knowledge formally collated and written down, and available for consideration by practitioners. This may be usefully contrasted with an alternative form of knowledge – *process knowledge*. This form of knowledge refers to our understanding of the mental processes by which practitioners reason, judge and make decisions about practice. We know very little about this – in relation to social work – at present, although Sheppard and his colleagues (Sheppard et al., 2000, 2001; Sheppard and Ryan, 2003) have begun the process of excavating its various dimensions.

It is possible, however, to focus on process knowledge as a theoretical concept (as a process of 'emergent understanding'), one which can go some considerable way to informing our theoretical notion of the idea of social work. Our focus here is: how can social workers go about thinking and reasoning about situations they confront in practice? In what ways is this a reflection of common processes of human understanding? How does this inform us on how practice may be made rigorous?

Common human capacities

In order to proceed we need to start off where 'social work as art' finishes. In its emphasis on intuition and on creativity, those thinkers who present this view fail to analyse the very facets which require detailed explication. What exactly is involved in this creative process? What are the psychological processes in constructing meaning? Furthermore, is understanding enough? Do social workers not need to go much further than mere 'understanding' in order to carry out their tasks properly? What exactly is involved in taking these further steps? And how can we know they are conducted rigorously? Furthermore, what is the relationship between these processes and the circumstances both 'out there' in the social situation and 'in there' in the construction of that situation?

Those who proclaim social work to be 'art' are right to draw attention to the notion of common sense as an important dimension of practice, but they are both vague in explicating this idea and rather limited in a focus on understanding. Humans do use 'common sense', but they do so far more than just to gain understanding. They do so in order to respond, to know what to do, to know *how* to know what to do, in order to make decisions, judge and gain control. They do this, it should be said, in the conduct of their everyday lives.

However, these common-sense ways of knowing are also those characterising – admittedly in a more rigorous way – social research and, arguably, science generally. In focusing on 'ways of knowing' and 'ways of acting', we relate social work both to this 'common sense' and also to the rigour of social research. Rigorous social work, in other words, may be characterised as practical social research and social workers as 'scientists of human life' precisely because, on the one hand, they call upon common ways of knowing and acting, but on the other do so while seeking the rigour characterising social research and science.

'Common sense', in one meaning, refers to commonly held assumptions about the world. The most fundamental and widely held of these is that there is, indeed, a world 'out there', which exists and is independent of us as individual, perceiving beings. In technical terms this is an ontological statement – one about what exists. While really rather obvious, it is of considerable importance, for many interpretivists deny the possibility of a potentially knowable (even provisionally) external reality. Social work, we have shown, is implicitly (and at times explicitly) committed to an objectivist view (at least in part) of the social world, one which is consistent with this common-sense assumption. In adopting this view social workers are, in the technical sense of their knowledge commitment, realists.

However, we may also look at things in terms of ways of knowing. It is, of course, a truism to suggest that social research, and indeed any attempt to understand and act, cannot go beyond the limits to human understanding. As this is the case for academic disciplines, so it is the case for social work. Medawar (1979) has commented that the common device of experimentation is widespread, while Huxley (1902, p. 42) argued that science is no more than trained and organised common sense. Likewise, the qualitative methods of social science, some have suggested, are simply refinements or developments of those used in everyday life (Hammersley and Atkinson, 1983; Sheppard, 1995b).

It is, however, in the rigour with which academic disciplines are pursued that they differ most markedly from common-sense ways of knowing and acting. Wallace and Bruce (1983) suggested that social scientists are more routinely and professionally concerned with explanation than lay people; that common-sense formulations are more superficial and more easily satisfied; and that common-sense formulations are more concerned with the personal than the general.

However, if it is important that social science is pursued with greater rigour than lay understanding and since it *can* be pursued with greater rigour, then this must surely be the case for social work. Social workers, in dealing with people's lives (with crucial decisions about psychological well-being and health, with matters of personal liberty, and even, on occasions, life and death), have at least as much claim upon the need for rigour as social scientists. It is vital that their ways of knowing are as rigorous and accurate as possible; that their ways of acting are clear and lead to precise formulations; and that their monitoring and review are characterised by clarity.

They must, therefore, go far beyond mere intuition, although intuition can provide the starting point for social work acts. In so far as social workers operate in and on the social world, they do so in a world of meaning and interaction. We need, therefore, to focus further on this issue. However, ways of understanding and ways of acting involve understanding the processes of thinking through which social workers act in and on their social world around their tasks. This takes us beyond mere constructions of meaning making to the more 'scientific' processes of acting in and on the social world.

Humans as rule-using analysts

At the heart of meaning, of social life, is the notion of *verstehen* (Weber, 1949). *Verstehen* is about the understanding of people's understanding, of making sense of the ways they make sense. It is necessary, both for social science and to operate in the social world, to understand the ways others – individuals and groups – make sense of their social world. It is the process of gaining interpretative understanding. The meaning of an event (which itself can be the same) can be quite different for two different people. Family members may view their emigration from Britain to Australia quite differently. For a father it may represent hope, a new start, work opportunities that he no longer has in Britain – the chance to reclaim his self-esteem. For his daughter, however, it may involve profound feelings of loss, leaving her friends, school and environment she has known all her life. The same event, the same family even, but quite different meanings are attached.

Just as meaning is an aspect of everyday life, so *verstehen* – as it is in social science – is a critical aspect of social work. If an Australian social worker were to become involved with this family because the daughter had become depressed or violent or was 'acting out', an understanding of the meaning of the emigration to the daughter is liable to be highly significant. Indeed, gaining a sense of the father's feelings of optimism may be important in becoming aware of his lack of understanding of, and responsiveness to, his daughter's distress.

What is true in understanding individuals is equally true of understanding groups (including families) or societies. Three key human capacities are involved in this. The first, *intuition*, we have discussed to some degree already. Understanding others, as we have noted, must involve some innate human capacity or intuition. It is our capacity to perceive that enables us to know that the other person is perceiving. It is our capacity for feeling which enables us to know the feelings others have. It is our ability to think that enables us to know that they, too, are thinking.

Furthermore there has to be some starting point, some moment of direct apprehension of others. It is sometimes called 'hunch'. Hunch involves a direct understanding – or more precisely a belief of understanding – of the other person's feeling or situation. They may, for example, present a smiling front, but we just have a hunch – we do not know why – that they are actually rather desperate, perhaps depressed. Having had that hunch we may then observe the tightness with which they grip the arm of the chair, the brief delay in answering about emotion-filled topics, a tendency to look away when certain sensitive issues arise. Such observations take us beyond hunch, for we now have evidence relating to our sense that they are rather desperate. However, there is a necessary starting point, an initial moment of apprehension, and that is intuitive.

In seeking to understand others we do so on the assumption that they are a subject, one whose actions involve *motives and intentions*. We cannot fully understand the acts of others unless we know also, or think we know, exactly why they did them. The act of a parent beating a child describes an event. However, we do not properly understand this even without knowing the intentions or motivation of the parent. The beating may be perceived by the parent as an appropriate form of discipline, a means of setting and maintaining boundaries. It may be an act of sheer frustration, the behaviour of a parent at the end of his or her tether, weighed down by money worries, subject (perhaps) to violence from their own partner, and simply unable to cope with the child under this pressure. It may, indeed, be the act of a malevolent, violent individual, one for whom such violence is simply something they do, and have no compunction in doing, and who has no care for the child.

In this case, the event is the same but the acts are profoundly different and have potentially differing consequences. For a social worker, the differing intentions have profound implications, also, for their actions. The presence of a psychopath has rather different likely consequences from that of a concerned, but frustrated and despairing mother.

We make sense, further, in relation to socially communicated expectations. This is about people living in a social world, in which the norms and expectations of that social world affect the way we understand the actions of individuals and groups. Formally, these elements refer to social *rules*. Rules act as guides as to what to do, how to behave. They are closely related to roles. If you are a teacher, what are the kinds of things you do? If you are a mother, how should you behave? In making sense of individual forms of behaviour or actions, we do so against rules which are often implicitly held but which enable us to give meaning to what we may be observing or what we may be doing.

How do we decide whether or not someone is a good teacher? We may look at the way he delivers his lectures, the degree of preparation he puts in, his attentiveness to the questions of his pupils. In doing so we are looking at implicit rules; rules which govern our judgements of good and bad. Thus listening carefully, not interrupting the student, checking out that he has understood what they were trying to say, directing his response carefully to the content of their query, and doing so in a way which draws on his knowledge and expertise, could comprise key characteristics of the good teacher who is attentive to the questions of his pupils. On a more abstract level these represent implicit rules of behaviour. The rules are that a good teacher prepares well, presents clearly, listens attentively to queries, and responds clearly and coherently in a manner which is understandable to the pupil.

The point here is that ways of knowing involve a *socially contextualised understanding*, with which the psychological processes outlined earlier interact. It is part of being human that we are social beings. Social context may work in a further way – giving the same (apparent) actions quite different meanings. An individual with his head down and on his knees in a church is likely to be praying. If he is doing this in the presence of his monarch he is probably being knighted; if he did so in front of a guillotine he may well be about to be beheaded. Different contexts, different meanings, but all related to implicit rules, which we can state: people kneeling in church with their hands together are praying; people doing the same in front of a monarch are being knighted; and so on.

However, humans are not hopeless dupes, condemned merely to see events in terms of some pre-set rules. Humans are *rule users*. They use their analytic capacities to make sense of and act within the social world. Rules are there as guides, but the person themselves must look at the scene, make sense of it and decide what is going on. They are *rule-using analysts*. This brings together the cognitive-rational elements of being human with the features of intuition, and the capacities for (and for recognising) intention and motivation.

The teacher may be quiet, apparently listening carefully to what the pupil is saying to him. In reality, this may be a sham. In reality he may have his mind on other things, and is uninterested in what the pupil is saying, and even in the pupil himself. This may not be immediately apparent, but his response may be not quite right, not entirely focused on the content of the pupil's enquiry. In this case, we may think back to our earlier observation, and notice that his eyes were glazed when the question was being asked. This enables us to draw conclusions different from those we initially held. He is *not* such a good teacher after all. But we could further measure this against past observations – he has in the past listened carefully. So what was different this time? Was he troubled by something? Did his preoccupation make him fall below his usually high standards. We are, in other words, *analysing* the situation.

We cannot, therefore, separate the features of understanding and acting in the social world from humans' own innate intellectual capacities for reasoning and analysing. We are not simply 'making meaning' by some arbitrary exercise, or by being intuitive. We are not simply 'being creative'. We are rather careful analysers, gaining understanding by complex processes which involve meaning and, importantly, involve testing our perceptions against the evidence we have before us. He is apparently not a good teacher, but is this really so? What does our knowledge of him, our past observations, tell us about him? How does this influence the way we should see him? Indeed, should we define the intuition in terms of good or bad teaching? Should we instead define it in terms of a perhaps troubled individual? Is that what is really going on?

Translated into a social work context, these are hugely important questions, questions which could even make the difference between life or death. Let us go back to the example of the mother beating her child. The woman who is finding it difficult to cope because of external pressures may nevertheless provide a safe home for the child if the social worker can help to reduce the pressures on her and the stress she feels. Indeed, an attentive caring mother may emerge. The parent, however, who beats the child through malice, who has a psychopathic tendency, with no care and no remorse, provides an altogether more dangerous proposition. To leave the child with this person could involve injury to the child and even risk to their life. The capacity for analysis, for understanding and using rules, for contextualising them, and imputing motives are absolutely crucial to social work. *Social work then, has an absolutely crucial (necessary) content of practical intelligence, or practically orientated intellectual capacities.*

Social interaction and reflexivity

Understanding and acting in the social world, then, can occur through, at one extreme, intuition alone and, at the other, through a conscious analytic process (which incorporates intuition, but at the outset). Where, however, it is important to seek an account which is as accurate as possible, then the use of conscious analytic processes assumes greater importance. In social work, where practitioners are involved in actions which can have huge consequences for people's lives, it is incumbent on them to seek, as far as possible, an accurate account of the situation but also to operate themselves with the greatest care and in a conscious manner.

In rigorous practice, therefore, there is a necessary relationship between meaning making and intellectual processes which helps ensure rigour. However, social workers are not simply involved in meaning making. More profoundly, they are involved in social interaction, and its complex nature further emphasises the importance of analytical processes of thinking and reasoning.

An action is social when a person assigns a meaning to his or her conduct and, through this meaning, is related to the actions of others (Weber, 1969). If I were to wave at someone passing by on the other side of the road, then my intention would be to provide them with a greeting. They may be too far away to hear me say hello, but I will nevertheless be able to convey my meaning by a commonly understood action. Waving, in that way, is a social action.

Social interaction occurs when actions are reciprocally oriented towards the actions of others – that is, when I act in response to the action of someone else, or in anticipation of some response they might make. When I wave, they may wave back or smile. Social work is constantly characterised by this kind of social interaction, but an interaction which, even at its simplest, is liable to involve some complexity. The client who is recently bereaved may be talking about their deceased partner, then look away, biting their lip, trying to hold back their tears. The sensitive social worker will both know the emotional content of that action and the attempt by the client to 'hide' their feelings, perhaps through some sense of its impropriety or embarrassment. The social worker, recognising the layers of meaning, may wish to reassure the client that it is okay to express feelings, and to give some sense that they understand that the client is finding it tough. They could do so by a simple action of reaching out and holding the client's hand. In doing so, they are engaging in social interaction.

All social work actions are social interactions. However, these social interactions can – and frequently do, in social work – involve a high degree of ambiguity. It may not, in other words, be immediately obvious to the social worker what the most accurate interpretation of a situation is likely to be. If we take the example of the teacher which we discussed earlier, it was not, perhaps, immediately obvious what was going on, or how we might more accurately understand his behaviour in responding to the pupil's query. Likewise, with the bereaved client, it may be that they pull away following the offer of a hand by the social worker. Maybe that is because they are not a 'touchy' kind of person. Maybe it is because they do not want to 'make a fuss' or that they want to 'be strong'. Their response to the social worker is ambiguous but so, also, it transpires, was their biting of their lip and looking away.

Indeed, the same may be said for the client, which can make matters still more complex. If each is unsure of what the other is saying, or of how to interpret what the other is doing, then this may be a factor which needs to be recognised and taken into account. The social worker, in seeking to understand accurately what is going on, may well need to take into account the client's own uncertainty. Suppose a white social worker were interviewing an Afro-Caribbean mother in relation to possible child protection concerns. She may respond to questioning defensively and perhaps aggressively. This response could itself be important information. Yet its meaning may not be clear. It could be an attempt to bluster her way out of a situation where she had non-accidentally injured her child. It could also, however, arise because she feared she may be subject to discrimination. An aggressive response, where injuries to the child were, in fact, entirely accidental, may be understandable in such a context. Getting this wrong (on the part of the social worker) could have huge consequences either way, so it is necessary for the social worker to work through this ambiguity. This clearly requires something more than mere intuition (though intuition may well have a part to play, and be a starting point).

There is, almost inevitably, considerable ambiguity in much of social work. It is the nature of the beast. Often, say, in child protection, it is in the interests of some of the parties to be 'economical with the truth'. Only the most naïve social worker would assume that clients were always telling the truth and the whole truth. However, it is not necessary to impute Machiavellian purposes to the actions of the client. The sheer complexity of the situations with which social workers are asked to deal can make it difficult to unravel exactly what is, or has been, going on. There may be a number of individuals involved, each with their own story to tell. They may themselves be giving accounts of situations which were, in some degree, ambiguous. The people giving the accounts may have not been careful in trying to understand what was going on – they may have 'jumped to conclusions'. It is incumbent on the social worker, often with huge responsibilities, to work through the complexity of these situations, and the accounts of them, in the search for the most accurate way of viewing it.

In social work, the term reflexivity has increasingly come to be used to refer to this process (Sheppard, 1995a, 1995b, 1998; White, 1997). It refers to the capacities by which we, as humans, naturally 'process' in everyday life. However, it is a process informed by an understanding of social location. The social location of social worker and client are determined by the roles they play (which, as we have seen previously, anchor their social interaction). Social workers' analyses occur from their social state *as* social workers, with all that entails about their purposes, roles and responsibilities. For example, where they involved with children 'at risk' their first responsibility is child protection, and that provides the social 'anchor' for the analysis they undertake in relation to work situations and social interactions.

The reflexivity, informed as it is by social location, involves self-reflection (considering their own motivations and actions and their effects), other reflection (understanding situations being observed and people with whom they interact), and the cognitive processes by which we understand situations. It is also 'forward looking' rather than mere reflection, involving considering possible future actions and events and their consequences. (What if I do not remove this child from their family where they are at risk? What will happen if I undertake one form of intervention rather than another? And so on.)

Reflexivity arises because of the ambiguity of the kinds of situations confronted by social workers, the need to gain an accurate understanding of the situations, and the likely consequences of different acts. Where a social worker undertakes a child protection investigation, it is likely they will look at the way the mother or father and child relate to each other. Is the child comfortable in the parent's presence? Does he or she avoid going near the parent, or having eye contact? Do they sit on the parent's lap when the interview takes place? The social worker is seeking to discover the relationship between parent and child, in a manner relevant for our child protection concerns.

However, the social worker also needs to be aware of the impact of his or her own presence. What is the impact of having a social worker in the house on the actions of both parent and child? Does the child have an idea of what is going on? Is he or she reacting to the situation, rather than behaving as normal (the same goes for the parent)? Likewise, what is the effect of the social worker him or herself? Is the manner of their questioning likely to generate hostility or trust? And so on.

Hammersley (1983), while focusing on social research, identifies three aspects of reflexivity relevant to social work. First, the researcher's (and social worker's) own actions are open to analysis in the same terms as other participants. All are, in their own way, trying to make sense, and trying to make sense of others making sense. Secondly the researcher and the social worker need to be aware of the decisions they are making and the motives which underlie them. Social workers, like others, carry 'personal baggage' around with them. How far, for example, is this social worker's assessment of an investigation of possible sexual abuse influenced by their own experience of having been abused in the past? Likewise, their authority role in child protection can impact on a situation. Thirdly, they need to take account of their own actions on the interaction generally, and on those with whom they are interacting (particularly clients). An insensitive or aggressive approach can engender an aggressive response which might not have occurred but for the initial behaviour of the social worker.

Categories and schemas

The common-sense way of understanding and acting within the social world involves an acceptance that there *is* an external world and that it exists independently of us. That much we noted earlier. We have noted also that key elements of assumptions which exist in social work involve an implicit commitment to a realist position. Social work, we have shown, has an objectivist core while nevertheless recognising limits to humans' capacity to understand fully their world, including the social world. There may be an objective world, external to us, but our ability fully to 'know' it is limited by our own limitations as human beings.

Indeed, we are unable fully to apprehend what is going on around us in all but the most simple and straightforward of situations. If we attend a party, with many people in the room, we may engage one other person in conversation. Many others may be in the room, all within earshot, and they may all be talking to each other. However, we will only be aware of our own conversation. The rest is likely to appear a cacophony of sound. This is because we are attending only to our own conversation. We are unable to do that and to hear all the other conversations at the same time. We have to be selective about those aspects of the immediate social world which we are able to take in.

We are, therefore, neither able to attend to all aspects of the social world in our immediate social interactions, nor appreciate some total, objective external reality. Instead, humans select information, which they seek to put together in a way which enables them to understand and act in the social world. In order, for example, to relate to another person, it is likely that you will have some 'image' of that person, one in which you have identified certain key characteristics which have been put together in a way that 'makes sense' of them. That person may be kind, welcoming, talkative, responsive to others, positively seeking out others' company. Your general view of them, therefore, would be of an extrovert. That may not, however, be the view some other person may have of them, from which they might be viewed as a little intrusive, garrulous, rather taken up by themselves or their own interests.

These represent different ways of viewing the same person, based on the information which an individual has 'received' in the course of knowing them. In social work, this assessment of personality is a key aspect of practice, closely related not just to the understanding of the client, but also to the responses and interventions of the social worker. We know, for example, in child care practice, that a social worker's 'way of seeing' the personality of the mother, particularly to the extent that it links with the degree of risk to the child, is central to the decision about what to do and the process of intervention (Sheppard, 2001). Indeed, as we have shown earlier, it is crucial that social workers develop the most accurate 'way of seeing' the parent, because the welfare of the child – even its very life – could depend on this. Like all good realists, therefore, social work does not assume that all ways of seeing are equally valid. One way may be more accurate than the other, and it is this which should be adopted. Indeed, in order to stand the best possible chance of identifying the most accurate 'way of seeing' the social worker needs to proceed in the most rigorous manner possible – which involves using the analytic capabilities we have noted earlier.

Again, in doing this, social workers are calling upon common human capacities, refined, however, by a rigour which has been more characteristic of the academic study of the social world. The 'way of seeing' which enables people to understand social situations involve interpretive schemas. A schema is 'a naïve theory' about an aspect of the social world (Berkowitz, 1986, p. 82). Schemas are critical aspects of everyday understanding of the social world, and serve the same kind of function as theories do in social research. We can make sense of apparently problematic behaviour in a fourteen-year-old by reference to 'teenage problems' – a stage that teenagers go through which somehow makes them 'difficult'. The same might go for tantrums in two-year-olds – 'the terrible twos'. Each of these are commonly held schemas – lay theories – about why furious arguments may occur between teenagers and their parents or why young children may scream and shout in public. Thus, if a specific instance of teenager–parent conflict were to occur, the 'teenage problems' schema is an 'off-the-shelf' explanation available to make sense of the situation (whether or not that is the real reason why problems are occurring).

Categories are the 'building blocks' of social schemas. They are the different elements which come together to create a coherent framework for understanding, available to be used in relevant social situations. We know how to identify a police officer by their uniform. We also expect them to act with authority in situations where the law may have been broken. However, they may also be there to help members of the public. We may walk past two police officers talking to a young man next to a car. The young man may be wearing a track suit, trainers (sneakers) and a woolly or baseball cap. We may assume that he has exceeded the speed limit, stolen the car or gone on a 'joy ride'. This could be, in part, because of the police's law enforcement role and also our assumptions about the kind of 'look' which we think characterises a 'joy rider'. However, an alternative (we might discover) is that the car was not working properly, or that the young man had lost his way and had approached the police officers for help. We are categorising the man (and those who are speaking to him) in terms of particular characteristics or categories.

There is a huge range of potential categories available to be applied to social situations. People are old, young or middle-aged; attractive or less attractive; kind or selfish; ill-mannered or polite; and so on. Categories and schemas are central to social work, as they are in everyday life. If we take the previous example of the police officer, we are saying to ourselves as passers by, 'what is going on here?', 'how can I make sense of this situation'?

The same processes, in principle, are involved in social work practice. If we are conducting a piece of family therapy, we are likely to be interested in the interactions between different family members. What kind of seating positions do they take up when left to decide for themselves? Do they have eye contact when they talk to each other? Does the father act with anger when the child tries to maintain the reasonableness of their behaviour? Does the child's sister respond by touching her brother? Does the child seem to avoid saying much? In asking these questions we are trying to work out the relationship between different family members. When doing this, the social worker will be employing categories. The child may be 'withdrawn', the father 'aggressive', the sister 'responsive' or 'caring' and so on. Each of these categories exist independently as ideas, but are available to be applied to situations.

The social worker may use categories and schemas widespread in the lay population to provide them with ways of knowing and ways of acting in practice. They may also use formal knowledge – the rationale for the use of the latter lying in its capacity to 'go further', to provide new categories and schemas, or alternative ways of knowing and acting, to those widespread in the lay population. The ultimate justification for the use of formal knowledge in social work, then, lies in the way it may be utilised in the specific context of practice. That it *can* be used in practice is the first requirement, and only once that is fulfilled can we consider the issue of whether it adds to what could already be known by the use of 'lay knowledge'.

Of course, the latter is also of considerable importance, since there would be little point in emphasising the acquisition of formal knowledge in the process of social work education and qualification if it added nothing to lay knowledge. There are, of course, strong grounds for considering that formal knowledge does have a significant contribution. An understanding, for example, of the issue of race in psychiatry can alert the social worker to the risks of discrimination in specific instances. We may take particular care in considering a young male Afro-Caribbean for compulsory admission, knowing their over-representation in this process and in being admitted. We may be wary of too easily considering teenager–parent conflict was just a matter of 'teenage problems' if we have an awareness of attachment theory and the possibility that the rejecting actions of the parents may have been a contributory factor. In this case, an understanding of formal knowledge avoids the adoption of a seductive, but perhaps inaccurately applied, lay schema.

The consequences, furthermore, in terms of 'ways of acting' (as opposed to just 'ways of understanding') are significant. The two different explanations have profoundly different implications for intervention. While a 'teenage problem' explanation might indicate a focus primarily on the young person, one which drew upon attachment theory could easily lead to a focus not just on the young person but on the parent(s) as well. Indeed, it may require an exploration of the behaviour of one or both parents and their feelings towards the child, as we follow the implications of their having made a contribution to a situation where the teenager is 'acting out'.

It is in the accuracy with which they are able to categorise a situation (and the different aspects) that good social workers (in part) may be marked out. It is apparent that a key aspect of this involves the employment of categories and schemas. While such workers necessarily use common human capacities, it is not enough for these to be used to common standards. This, though, is not simply about the adoption of formal knowledge – of 'product knowledge' as we have termed it earlier. The gravity of their responsibilities requires that the greatest accuracy occurs and this, in turn, requires rigorous *processes*. We can understand this better by a more formal representation of these analytic processes.

Social work as practical reasoning: the process of analysis and response

Social work is about practical reasoning. It is worth stating again that at the heart of social work is the need for a high level of practical intelligence. That is, social workers need to manifest considerable intelligence in their processes of analysis, a capacity to examine the various dimensions of (at times) hugely complex situations, put these together in a way which most accurately represents the situation, formulate a response and continue to analyse the situation, while in the process evaluating what is happening. Hypotheses are central to this.

It is in the nature of reflexivity and humans as rule-using analysts that they are constantly making hypotheses – and these are at the heart of our formal understanding of the processes involved in social work. We have noted that social workers – indeed people in general – necessarily start with intuition. They need to make an initial appraisal of a situation, and that appraisal is necessarily both immediate and intuitive. In our previous example, involving the police and young person, we are presented with a scene which have various facets – the participants, a car, our awareness of relevant roles and responsibilities – and we make an initial definition of the situation, a perception of what is going on. In doing so, as we have seen, we draw upon categories and schemas which are, so to speak, 'free-floating', available, independent of particular social situations, but which may be used to define relevant situations.

Our initial observations or definitions, drawing upon relevant categories or schemas, are (in fact) hypotheses about that situation. Our first apprehension of the scene involving the young man and the police was that an arrest may be taking place. That is a hypothesis: this young person has offended and the police are about to charge him with an offence. Thus the observations are merged with the situation-relevant categories and schemas to produce a hypothesis.

We do this on the basis of the cues provided by the situation we are observing. The clothes which are worn, the age and sex of the person to whom the police are talking, the fact that they have a car with them and the interaction (seen from a relative distance) between the police and the young man. However, upon closer observation, we find that the police officer and the young man are smiling, apparently having exchanged a joke. There is a relaxed 'air' to their interaction. One of the officers points and seems to be giving directions. This, it seems, is not about an offence, but is about the young man (who has lost his way) asking directions and the police responding. An initial hypothesis seemed to fit the situation but additional observation was not consistent with that hypothesis, leading to its revision. We have a new way of viewing the situation, one which is better than the first, in that it is consistent with more of the data (observations) which we now have.

The interesting point here is the combination of intellectual processes: that an initial hypothesis is made; that it is, however, not a 'once and for all' definition; but is capable of (and indeed is subject to) revision, and that a new hypothesis is made. Our perception or definition of the situation is, in other words, provisional and this points to a matter of huge importance to social work. *All knowledge, and this includes situations confronted in practice, can only ever be provisional.* We can never be absolutely certain that our definition of that situation is accurate. It is always possible, in principle, to find information which may fatally undermine our perception or definition and, if that is what happens, then it is incumbent upon us – if we are seeking to be as accurate as possible – to change the ways we define that situation, in line with the new evidence.

Hypotheses are at the heart of the analytical processes which necessarily occur in social situations. We are involved in a constant process of hypothesis generation and testing, and this is undertaken in order to obtain the best possible 'fit' between the interpretive schemas we are using and the situation we are observing (or, indeed, in which we are involved). The situations we are observing (or in which we are involved) can be relatively straightforward and the process of accurately 'categorising' it can be equally straightforward. Others can be much more complicated, filled with ambiguity and far less amenable to a clear and early definition.

This is frequently the case with social work. Social workers will often – and rightly – comment on the complexity of the situations with which they are involved. As greater complexity is confronted, so there is a need for greater use of analytic capacities, of making and revising hypotheses. Indeed, cases are also subject to change – change which needs to be detected, accounted for in terms of developments and changes to hypotheses. The capacity, therefore, for social workers consciously to adopt and use hypotheses in the conduct of their work is quite central to practice. This is a cognitively difficult ability.

This ability requires social workers to be good 'scientists of human life'. We can formally present the foundations for the necessary reasoning process as 'retroduction' (Hanson, 1958). This is implicit in the employment of both intuition and analysis that we have outlined. It is a rigorous methodology for discovery and explanation. The idea is that our understanding is developed both deductively (through the testing of hypotheses by examining relevant data – in this case observations of social situations) and inductively (in which ideas are developed from those situations). If we take our earlier examples, such as that of the police and young driver, we find that there is a 'dual process' going on. On the one hand we observe the situation, put the elements together and draw an initial conclusion (that an arrest is being made). This process is arguably inductive. On the other, that 'initial conclusion' is formulated into an implicit hypothesis (that an arrest is being made because the young man has committed a motoring offence). Having been formulated in that way, it can then be tested through further observation. In this case it is falsified, since the further observations suggest something quite different is going on – that the police are offering advice and help. We have moved from the inductive to the deductive.

However, in doing this we have not just stopped at the second, deductive, stage. We have falsified our hypothesis that the police were making an arrest. However, in reformulating the situation in our minds, we have created a second hypothesis – that the police are offering help and advice. This hypothesis, though, has been achieved inductively – by bringing together the additional information with the initial information to create a hypothesis which seems to cover the situation better. We have moved from the inductive to the deductive to the inductive to the deductive.

Categories and schemas are of considerable importance here because they enable the social worker to create interpretations, which may be formulated as hypotheses which are capable of accurately presenting the situation. Thus, categories and schemas concern the *generation of understanding*, while hypotheses, observations and analyses involving falsification or confirmation concern *the reasoning processes*. There is a constant interplay between categories and schemas on one hand and observations of reality on the other, an interplay which occurs through a process of reasoning, at the heart of which is hypothesis generation and testing.

The logic and consequences of falsifying

If science and social research may be presented as using commonly held processes of human understanding and acting in the world, but doing so more rigorously than occurs in everyday life, it is incumbent on social workers to be able to be equally rigorous. This is because of the enormous implications of the interventions they undertake for those they work with. It is commonly held that the reasoning process involves constantly seeking information which might falsify one's hypothesis or interpretation of the situation. That is, we should be constantly on the lookout for information which is not consistent with our existing interpretation. This is a position held by Popper (1963) and sociologists who employ analytic induction as their methodology of social research (Znaniecki, 1934; Lindesmith, 1968; Robinson, 1951). In the process we should seek to develop categories and schemas which better present the situation we are confronting.

As a process, in principle, this sounds fine, but in social life it is more easily said than done. Psychologists have long been aware of the phenomenon of 'confirmation bias'. This is the tendency in humans to look for facets of social life or situations which are likely to confirm their pre-existing ideas about that situation. At the same time, they tend to ignore elements of a situation which are liable to contradict their existing ideas of a situation or aspect of social life.

This is especially the case where a situation is complex. Where information is not simply ignored or resisted, it can be dismissed as 'implausible', 'untrustworthy' or not worthy of attention. Snyder (1984; Snyder and Swan, 1978; Snyder and Campbell, 1980) has shown how this 'tendency to bias' is manifested through characteristic lines of questions when our schemas are tested against our observations. For example, when individuals were told that someone was 'introverted', and asked to investigate matters further, they did not try to discover whether the person had ever acted extrovertly, through which disconfirming evidence might have been accumulated. Rather, they investigated further the introvert facets of the subject's personality. The kinds of question asked was: 'what factors make it hard for you to really open up to people?' They are, of course, likely to accumulate further evidence of the subject's introvert nature by asking such questions.

Social workers, however, do not just deal with complex situations: they work with considerable time constraints. Because of the tendency in humans towards confirmation bias, this means more time is required to digest and accept alternative points of view, as compared with those consistent with our interpretation (Kruglanski and Freund, 1983). This is frequently not a luxury open to social workers, as the pressures of work can provide a poor environment for combating the tendency towards confirmation.

The consequences of the complexity of situations, the pressures of work and the tendency to confirmation bias, have, it has been suggested, made a contribution to child abuse tragedies, where children have died while under the supervision of social workers (Sheldon, 1986). Social workers have, in some cases, been busy confirming their interpretations of situations (which seem to discount the real danger to the child) which, in retrospect, seem astonishing – as in the cases of Maria Colwell and Jasmine Beckford (DHSS, 1974; Blom Cooper, 1985). Of course, reports are written with the benefit of hindsight, but there is, for example, no escaping the awestruck incredulity of the majority report on Maria Colwell that the professionals involved should have failed to recognise the extreme dangers under which she was living.

Of course, hindsight is a wonderful thing. The cases were complex, and the social workers were harassed and under pressure. The fact remains, however, that these (and other children) died, when a greater attention to evidence pointing to the dangers could have prevented their deaths. That is the most extreme consequence of getting things wrong (and shows, furthermore, that there *are* objective outcomes in social work, which means that not everything is a social construction or a personal opinion). However, even where social workers are not dealing with life-and-death situations, they are often working in situations in which their decisions can have huge effects on their clients' lives, their psychological well-being and future prospects.

These may be less obvious. There is a danger that a case may develop an 'accepted wisdom'. It is quite possible that a mother, perpetually having difficulty managing her children, is defined as a 'non-coper'. Every act she performs, or fails to perform, may be seen in this framework, confirming the accuracy of the existing assessment. What, however, if she is really depressed, and her difficulty in coping arises directly from the effects of the depression? It may be that with appropriate action her depression can be dealt with, and as a consequence her parenting may improve. Yet the continuous re-confirmation of her as a 'non-coper' may prevent the appropriate action from taking place. Yet it is clear that social workers do, at times, fail to recognise the presence of depression in mothers, and hence do not respond at that level to the child and family needs (Sheppard, 1997).

To err, of course, is human. But in social work, mistakes costs lives, or can damage them. *While, therefore, on the one hand, it is vital we understand that social workers can only use common human abilities for 'knowing about' and 'acting in' the social world, it is incumbent on social work that it does not adopt 'merely' common standards in this respect.* Social workers must adopt common capacities for practical reasoning, but must do so *far more rigorously than is commonly required in everyday life*. If science and social research have been able to develop methods based on everyday understanding but far more rigorous, then social work must do the same. The knowledge which emerges from a full understanding and adoption of rigorous processes of practical reasoning should be called 'process knowledge' precisely because it is focused on the processes of human reasoning.

Conclusion

At the heart of social work is the need for practical intelligence, for social workers are necessarily involved in reasoning processes, and that reasoning is frequently applied to highly complex situations in which social workers have huge responsibilities. Social workers must seek to gain an understanding of a situation that is as accurate as possible. However, they need, as accurately as possible, to be able to identify the range of possible actions and consequences of each of those actions, were they to be undertaken in a case. They need to be able to look forward to what is likely to happen, how clients are likely to behave, what they may think and so on if one action is taken rather than another, or no action at all.

These are high-level cognitive abilities, requiring appropriately able individuals properly trained in the rigorous thinking processes required for practice. The capacity to interpret or gain meaning is simply not sufficient. Neither is the availability of some formal knowledge or evidence base (and certainly not the simplistic technicalising of managerialism). The capacity to think, and think clearly and well, are necessary conditions for the conduct of practice. In this, reasoning processes, involving hypotheses, analysis and precision, are absolutely central.

What are the *key elements of these reasoning processes?*

- First, there is the capacity for imagination. This involves an availability of a wide range of interpretive schemas through which individual situations may be understood. What is the range of possible ways by which a particular situation may be understood, and which is most consistent with that situation?
- Secondly, the capacity for forward thinking or 'speculative reasoning' is necessary. Social workers need to be able to speculate intelligently about the range of future possibilities, according to potential ways in which a case may develop, the actions of the social worker, responses of the client, interpretations of both, and so on. If they do not undertake this process (with the question 'what would happen if

I did this?'), then their actions are entirely arbitrary, undertaken with no idea that one action might lead to a better outcome than another.

- Thirdly, they need a capacity for generating hypotheses. This is something which happens in everyday life so, in principle, this should not cause too much concern. However, it is in the recognition that they need to develop hypotheses, and the clarity with which this is done and the clarity with which they are aware of this process, that social workers are able to have the best chance of gaining the most accurate (or plausible) picture of what is going, and what may occur as the situation develops and actions are taken.

- Fourth, it is necessary for social workers to be routinely precise in their formulations. The greater the precision, the greater will be the clarity of the formulations, and the extent to which these 'fit' with the observations made and the information collected. Likewise, it will be clearer where these do not fit or are not adequate (or less adequate than alternative formulations).

- Fifth, they need to pursue understanding which seeks to create the greatest possible 'adequacy of fit'. This implies that there may be more than one possible way of understanding a situation, as (indeed) is frequently the case. That which should be chosen should be the one which best fits with the situation being observed. In this, there will be an interplay between observation and evidence and the way the situation has been understood by the social worker.

- Sixth, a consequence of this is that the capacity to generate alternative possible formulations (or ways of understanding) a particular situation is important. Where one view is pursued, the likelihood of confirmation bias, as outlined earlier, is greatly increased, with all the accompanying risks attached to this.

- Seventh, a recognition of the importance of, and the preparedness to adopt, falsification as a principle for moving forward, both in the understanding of a case and in that case itself, is likewise important. The presumption of correctness which is associated with confirmation bias is one which presents a serious threat to practice which seeks the best outcome for clients and, as we have seen, can even threaten their lives.

- Finally, social workers need to recognise that all their formulations are, and can only ever be, provisional. This is generally the case for knowledge and it is most certainly the case for practice. Any way of understanding a situation, or future possibilities arising from that situation, may well be found to be inadequate. Evidence may come forward which profoundly challenges a particular way of understanding a situation. Other ways of viewing it may prove to be closer to the observations and evidence collected.

We may add one caveat to this. In principle, with the identification of falsifying information we should reject our hypothesis. However (and also in principle), this would mean rejecting our hypothesis as soon as we find one piece of information with which it is inconsistent. This is likely to be unwise, unless that piece of information is of such profound importance that it utterly undermines the current way of viewing that situation. Rather, such contradictory evidence needs to be 'logged' and social workers remain flexible enough to be able to reject their current way of viewing that situation should further falsifying evidence arise.

This reflects the kinds of processes which occur in science. One single study or observation contradicting a commonly held theory is unlikely to overturn that theory. It is more likely that the data will be noted as contradicting the dominant theory and, dependent on further findings, may or may not influence the rejection of that theory. A build-up of evidence contradicting a dominant theory may well, in the end, lead to that theory's rejection, but it may even take the replacement of one generation of scientists by another before that replacement fully takes place (Lakatos, 1978). Such is the difficulty of replacing one theory in the scientific community by another.

Thus, social workers are not adequately characterised as artists or scientists, but as professionals involved in a process of practical reasoning which, alongside commonly held human capacities, requires a high level of practical intelligence. This is applied to frequently highly complex situations, providing a process by which they are able to draw on various sources for understanding and acting, including life experience, professional wisdom (gained from frequent contact with clients) and formal knowledge. It is this process of practical reasoning which is at the heart of social work.

Chapter thirteen

Social work intervention and human nature

Throughout this book, while looking at a diverse range of issues, we have had recourse to consider the 'material' with which social work works – that is, human beings. Indeed, we have looked as humans as 'social beings' – that is, humans-in-society. For example, we have referred to humans as people who may seek self-realisation, who take on roles and exist in role sets, who act and socially interact with others; in other words, humans as self-directing (although not always) creatures, who are involved in relationships with others.

Many of the attributes ascribed to humans (or, put another way, assumed in social work) have been discussed in relation to the various themes which have been the focus of this book. Nevertheless, there are certain core characteristics which, in particular, are apparent when we examine the kinds of interventions which social workers undertake. Underlying social work methods, in other words, are assumptions about the kinds of creatures humans are, and those interventions only make sense if those assumptions are made.

If we are to understand social work fully we also need to understand what it is social workers do in order to work with a situation, ameliorating its problems, maintaining or improving it. The actual 'nuts and bolts' of methods are widely discussed elsewhere and do not require recapitulation here. However, the 'idea of social work' – an understanding of the kind of entity that it is – does require to explicate how these interventions perceive humans who, after all, are what social workers work with, providing the *raison d'être* for the discipline's very existence.

Purposeful acts

There is a general tendency in social work to assume a capacity, amongst its clients, for purposeful activity. This is especially the case for approaches such as task-centred practice or problem-solving approaches (Perlman, 1957; Reid, 1977), but it would be difficult to envisage much of social work without the idea that human have conscious purposes and that they are, in principle, capable of conscious directed activity. There is some limit to this, one might argue, for some people with learning difficulties but even here, social workers often go to considerable lengths to enable such people to be able to express their purposes.

The capacity for purposeful action is, therefore, assumed in much of social work. Task-centred practice (TCP), however, actively seeks to enhance the capacities of clients to act in a (directed) purposeful manner, and the method seeks to mobilise those capacities. Hence TCP emphasises problem definition (and precision in this definition), development of plans, delineation of tasks, and review and evaluation of outcome. All this involves the capacities for purposeful action.

It emphasises *conscious* actions also, in that it emphasises the primacy of the client's expressed wants or wishes (the term 'wants' is strongly endorsed in TCP). The idea is to help the client be more effective in the pursuit of their wants, by helping them to learn an efficient means for doing this. At the heart of this is the development of problem-solving abilities, so that problem solving is a central feature of purposeful actions by humans. One can view humans as constantly seeking to deal with and solve problems, in the most mundane areas of their lives as well as those which might have a major impact. How can I get the kids to school on time? How do I ensure this report is typed up in the appropriate way? How can I make sure my young daughter eats more vegetables? And so on. Humans are involved in constant problem solving without which, frankly, their lives would grind to a halt. TCP seeks to engage the capacity for problem solving in relation to the major areas of concern in social work practice.

Indeed, a further emphasis on the conscious and purposeful nature of the approach is its concern that intervention should be essentially short-term (generally six to eight weeks). This, in part, arose because of empirical evidence purporting to show that longer-term intervention has no particular added value (Reid and Epstein, 1972). However, an approach like this assumes people are likely to be quick learners and that their capacities for purposeful actions can be mobilised relatively quickly.

Purposeful acts are those with a particular aim in mind. One acts in a particular way because one seeks to achieve some outcome, and that is the purpose of the act. This involves two important features – the issues of intent and motive for action. Hart and Honore (1985) suggest that an action is intentional when it is purposeful and carried out by human agency. This means that the action is voluntary, the person is considered to be the perpetrator of the actions and that, hence, the action is not somehow 'caused' by some external factor. We have seen, of course, that some actions are assumed in social work to have been

220

somehow externally caused (frequently those involved in the authority role), but this basic assumption of voluntarism as part of being *fully* human is widely evident in social work. The person aims for some end result; they seek to bring it about; they seek to do so in a particular manner. That is voluntary action.

Motivation is a second element of purposeful, voluntary action. A motive, according to Weber (1949, p. 98) is a set of interrelated subjective meanings which provide an adequate ground for the particular action envisaged (to the person themselves or, indeed, an observer). Motive is something most frequently brought up in relation to crimes. What, it is asked, was the person's motive for the crime in question (why, for example, did the woman murder her husband?). It might be suggested that it was in 'self-defence' – that she was being attacked and she killed him. Alternatively, she could have done it because there was a nice insurance to be collected on his death, which she wished to have. Or it could have been to do with some love pact with another man – they may have wanted him out of the way because he refused a divorce – and so on. It is the 'because' which provides the clue to the motive – they did this because they wanted to achieve some end.

These may be criminal cases, but motivation is as much attributed in everyday life. Why, it might be asked, did you buy that Play Station? (because it helps me de-stress after a long day). Why did you get a red dress? (because I think red suits me) and so on. One is seeking, in these cases, to discover the reason(s) for a particular action. We can even present this in formulaic terms: 'my reason for doing X was Y' where 'Y' was some goal or other. Thus, 'my reason for crossing the road was to get an ice cream' would be plausible on a hot day, where an ice cream parlour was on the other side of the street. The goal, quite understandably, would be the purchase of an ice cream.

These same features characterise the more problematic circumstances and the decision making which confronts social work clients. Problems with parenting are the very stuff of intervention in child and family care. If a child is having tantrums, we may want to help the mother to take decisions which will reduce the strength and frequency of those tantrums. That would be the goal of the action. If we were to assume that these tantrums were somehow related to lack of involvement by the parent, the action proposed might be to engage more in play. Hence, if we were to ask the question (drawing on our formula): 'why are you playing with your child more?' the answer would be 'because the increased attention will reduce his tantrums'. However, if it was felt that it was the mother's attentiveness during and following tantrums which encouraged them, the mother might deliberately seek to ignore him. In answer to the question 'why are you ignoring your child?', we might say 'because that will help reduce his tantrums'.

In so far as social work seeks to enhance or draw upon purposeful acts, it is dealing in a central facet of what it is to be human. Goals, as a key part of this, are an important feature of everyday life. What, though, is it that influences goal selection? There appear to be two key factors, one of which is expectation. This is the perception, on the part of the person undertaking the act, that a particular action or set of actions will achieve the desired goals (Kirsch, 1985; Bandura, 1982). In general, people go for the achievable – although they may have fantasies about goals that are unattainable or in relation to which they have a low probability of achieving a desired outcome. If one were considering a promotion in a social work department of some sort, where one was currently a basic-grade social worker, one might seek to become a senior or team manager. One might believe that one was capable, even now, of a great deal more but setting a goal (say) of becoming Deputy Director would probably be seen as unrealistic.

Self-conception is a second key factor. People have fairly enduring images of themselves. We might see ourselves as essentially intelligent, or kind/caring, or a 'mover and shaker', a good sportsperson, or someone with considerable energy and drive. These are all likely to influence the choice of goals. We will seek goals or achievements which are consistent with our self-image. If we are caring, we might seek a career as a nurse. If we see ourselves as a 'mover and shaker', we might seek a career in politics or industry. Having got into one of these jobs, we might then be highly motivated to seek promotion (Markus and Nurins, 1986).

This same sense of achieving the realistic, interestingly, underlies task-centred practice (TCP). TCP emphasises the importance of aiming for outcomes which can be achieved. It is not about trying to change overnight all aspects of a person's life but about focusing on particular aspects, precisely identified. If one is successful in that task, then one might be able to move on. If not, one might undertake a different, less challenging task. The concept of 'incremental tasks' – where tasks undertaken become more difficult by increments – draws both upon the importance of achievability (and achievement) but also of, once *having* achieved, undertaking more challenging tasks. If a mother finds it difficult to engage in play with her child – where the outcome sought s a closer relationship between the two – she may start with supervised play over a limited time period. She may then go on, by increments, to play more independently with the child, over more extended time periods.

There are a number of further features in goal-directed actions. One is self-conception, which is extended through social workers being social beings (more of which later). This is important where someone is trying to *shape a particular identity* in the mind of their audience. This could occur during a particular interaction, or over a period of time, over a number of interactions. In this case an identity is an image of oneself that one tries to convey to others. We may wish others to see us (as we might see ourselves) as a decisive person, able to make decisions on important issues, and to stick to them. If so, we would wish to act in such a way that we felt would lead others to see us as decisive (Goffman, 1959). We might recount incidents where we felt we had been decisive (and to have been so to good effect). Or we might, in the course of interactions at work, make clearly and defined decisions relatively quickly. We are, in other words, in the business of 'impression management'.

Another feature of purposeful acts – underlying the idea of goal *selection* – is the *capacity to choose between alternative strategies*. If one is to select a particular goal, it implies there are potentially more than one, and hence that selection is required. Over the course of their lives, people develop a repertoire of strategies which they can draw upon in relation to a range of situations (and potential situations). This repertoire can involve strategies which tend to 'kick in' semi-automatically when required. We have, for example, people who are diplomats and who respond to possible conflict by seeking to calm the situation. We have others who may be concerned that they do not get 'pushed around' and respond to potential conflict by asserting their position.

Very often, however, there is conscious selection, and exactly the kinds of analysis which we have discussed extensively in previous chapters. When seeking to deal with a difficult situation, for example, the individual may call upon actions which may have worked for them in similar situations in the past. However, where these do not seem to work, they may seek to develop new strategies and to try them out in the situation. Where, for example, we go for an interview, we may try to behave as we have in the past, by giving clear, concise answers. If, however, this does not appear to be working, we may change to answers which are fuller and where we can sketch outcomes of the implications of what we are saying. In doing so, we are gauging what we think might be effective in the interview, or what the audience wants. Hence, we have a repertoire of actions from which we can draw but we can also develop new actions which, so to speak, go into storage for future use.

Arising from this is another capacity – that for *self-monitoring*. This involves a process where we judge how well our actions are being executed and how effectively they are enabling us to achieve our goals. This is exactly what was happening in our example of the interviewee, who would be looking at how effectively their behaviour was helping them achieve their goal (getting the job) and, if it was not working, changing the way they were acting. Carver and Sheier (1982) suggest this involves at least three dimensions: attending to oneself, including one's actions; comparing oneself to some standard which the individual considers appropriate; and attempting to reduce the gap between the way the individual is acting and the way they wish to act.

Reid, the main initiator (with Epstein) of TCP, recognises connections between this form of practice and the capacity for purposeful acts. Because this is all, in terms of TCP, a conscious enterprise, he emphasises wants rather than needs (the latter may be ascribed, and it is possible for someone to be unaware of needs). He emphasises humans' autonomous problem-solving capabilities, and relates this to a state of psychological deficit which helps galvanise their motivation. People with wants are in a state of dissatisfaction – dissatisfied people want something they are not getting. The connection between wants and problems arises because of the difficulty someone has in achieving satisfaction. If you want something you have not got, or cannot have, then you could be considered to 'have a problem' (Goldman, 1970).

Reid (1977) is aware that, by focusing on wants, the opportunity exists to mobilise the client's motivation. Wants have two elements, he thinks: 'direction' (what a person wants) and strength (how much he or she wants it). Of course, the more difficult it is to solve the problem, the higher is likely to be the level of motivation required. Also, there can be conflict between different wants. A desire on the part of a parent to have more money from paid employment may conflict with the desire to be involved more in the care of their young child.

Beliefs are also important. A person's actions are influenced by their beliefs about how a problem can best be solved. Likewise, the extent to which they want to solve a problem is influenced by beliefs about how important that problem is (either to them alone or in terms of the importance ascribed through societal or group values). If 'being a good parent' is a belief regarded to be important in the social group, an individual may be galvanised to become one if they feel they fall short.

We are brought back, through this, to the notion of intention, which we have shown is central to purposeful actions. Wants and beliefs create intentions, which in turn determine what a person does. In TCP, these intentions are formally expressed as plans, leading to tasks (actions) which are designed to fulfil a purpose (to ameliorate or solve a problem). Hence, in TCP, we have (in quite structured form) a means for achieving client purposes.

Conscious, unconscious and preconscious states

Social work is a psychodynamic activity. This is a wide term which, however, refers to work which focuses on the psychological, particularly affective (emotional), states of an individual in order to help them make better decisions for themselves. This, then, encompasses a wide range of activities, including the use of interpersonal skills, counselling and psychotherapy. The latter two, in particular, are associated with some kind of healing function, and there are some who are reluctant to use these terms in relation to social work.

Nevertheless, this whole area remains an important stream which underlies much of the ways social work operates (Biggs, 1998; Donavon, 2002; Sudbery, 2002; Fleming, 2004). When some kind of individual 'empowerment' is talked about – notwithstanding our earlier critique – this may well refer to the development of a greater understanding (and response to) an individual's personal circumstances. When working with families whose children have been placed in care, the issue of loss is often significant, not to mention a need for greater understanding of the parents' behaviour as parents. Of course, much of mental health work can involve 'working through' painful issues, some of which can stem from periods in a person's earlier life.

None of this undermines the notion of humans as purposeful beings. Indeed, it simply serves to enhance and deepen our approach. If we are to ask the question: 'why did X do Y?', we are looking for a statement of purpose. However, some would argue that at times people can be only dimly aware of their real purposes, affected as they are by unconscious drives or overwhelmed by the emotions of the moment. A young person may be performing poorly at school. Is this, as they suggest, because they have limits to their ability, or is it to 'punish' their parents (who are ambitious for the young person) for some hurt they have suffered? What lies behind the anorexic tendencies of a young woman, in a family whose dynamics have left her feeling very pressured? There are purposes here, but they may not be those expressed 'on the surface'.

Meaning, as we have discussed, is a major part of social work. *Verstehen*, as we have seen, is about understanding others, about understanding *their* understanding. In order to consider purposes we also have to understand meanings. In social work, the centrality of meaning, of understanding their understanding, is encapsulated in the term 'starting where the client is'. This means that, before any action can be taken or help given, the social worker needs to know how the clients sees him or herself. It is only once you know 'where they are', that you can begin to move to where they (or you) want them to be. Indeed, it is generally considered a prerequisite to discovering where they want to be, in an informed manner.

It is often assumed that the person knows best what they want. I know whether or not I want an ice cream on a hot day. I know whether I want to buy a car. An individual may even be considered to know best what they need (Smale et al., 1993): This is the client as the 'expert' on themselves. In taking this stance, the assumption is that clients are, to a considerable degree, conscious of their wishes and purposes. However, this is far from always being the case – or at least this is how it may be seen in social work. Some may be quite clear about what they want, and why, and what they need to do to go about getting it. Others may have varying degrees of clarity about each of these aspects. Some may only be dimly aware of their true purposes or even the reasons for their behaviour. That, at any rate, is the position in much of the literature in social work and is a clear implication, as we have seen, of the concept of 'need' in social work.

Where this is the case, clients are considered to have behaviour which is driven by purposes which lie in their unconscious or preconscious. Goldstein (1981, p. 438) makes this clear when he writes of social work as involved with:

> ... changing personal or shared misconceptions of reality that obstruct healthy adaptation and problem solving. The individual may unwittingly misunderstand himself, others, or conditions in the environment. It is possible that his reasoning is confused, resulting in personal meanings that tend to distort reality in unhelpful ways.

This is a fundamental statement about human beings – that in some circumstances they can perceive situations that distort reality and that this arises from flawed reasoning. There may, in short, be some sort of unconscious or preconscious motivation present. This, of course, leads us into the terrain of psychoanalysis. Many have been concerned to distance social work from psychoanalysis, concerned as they are that this may individualise problems or pathologise individuals. However, it continues to be a major and widespread influence in social work (Biggs, 1998; Donavan, 2002; Sudbery, 2002; Fleming, 2004).

This is not just a matter of the social work literature but reflects a widespread perspective in practice. Indeed, the very notion of 'need' at times involves notions that the client is not fully aware of their true motivations. In this, certain fundamental elements of psychoanalysis, particularly those related to the unconscious, continue to exercise considerable influence. The social worker may consider the client to be 'defensive', or to be 'projecting' some of their views or feelings onto others. They may be 'angry' (that is, possessing a generalised anger rather than one specifically focused on some object). In all these, and other, cases, the social worker will be calling upon concepts related to the unconscious (or at least preconscious) and hence psychoanalysis. This suggests that psychoanalytic thought has an influence on social work which transcends the limits of those who overtly and deliberately practice psychoanalytically.

Howe (1988) points out that people often behave – even distort reality – in ways which, given the circumstances, do not make sense. We see this when someone responds angrily to another who seems to have behaved quite reasonably, or when they react strongly (overreact) to an apparently inconsequential statement. They may even deny the importance of issues, or facets of a situation, where their importance is blatantly obvious to the observer. To those of a psychoanalytic disposition, it is clear that the individual is using defence mechanisms, mechanisms which are designed to ward off the anxiety generated by those issues.

Defence mechanisms are unconscious strategies through which an individual may protect themselves from pain or anxiety. For example, a person may lose their temper easily in a social situation, particularly when their view is challenged. They may themselves argue that it is understandable that they lose their temper because others are changing the subject or avoiding the issue. To the observer, however, this may occur whenever his or her view is challenged in any meaningful way. As that challenge becomes extended by discussion, so the person, no longer able to deal with those alternative views, particularly in the light of the influence they seem to have on others, loses their temper.

To the observer, it may seem obvious that the subject becomes angry when challenged, and even angrier when the prospect of 'losing the debate' occurs. It is an issue, it seems, of control. However, to the extent that the individual is not prepared to accept this – and really does not believe this to be the case – he or she could be said to be in denial. Indeed, to the extent that this is a recurring pattern, the individual may be generally in denial about the link between their temper and their wish to dominate (or, indeed, their anxiety about losing control).

The preconscious is another dimension, which is discussed by Hollis (1972). This, she thinks, is of particular interest to social work. Unconscious memories and feelings are those which are actively repressed. They are very 'deep' and consist of material that cannot be recovered 'at will'. The reason is that they are actively repressed by the very defence mechanisms which make it difficult for individuals to recognise their consequences. There are particular and long-term specialist psychoanalytic techniques which are appropriate for dealing with the unconscious. These techniques are not those characteristic of social work. Nevertheless, there is no doubt that psychoanalytic ideas permeate social work and influence considerably many of the judgements made.

The preconscious concerns material of which we are not aware or not fully aware but which are, relative to unconscious material, much easier to recall or become aware of. A parent might have feelings of hostility to her child, perhaps because of resentment felt that their birth had impacted hugely on her life, creating major restrictions and preventing the development of a career. This can be part of a complex set of feelings which includes genuine care and concern, affection and protectiveness. It is, in principle, possible to help the woman identify those feelings of hostility, by discussing examples of when they have occurred, drawing inferences from the circumstances of their occurrence and developing an awareness of the relevant 'life history' impacting on those feelings.

For Hollis (1972), the caseworker's concern with the preconscious draws them into counselling activities focusing on feelings. Casework may be used therapeutically and, while it does not employ the methods of psychoanalysis, it can promote an awareness of the less accessible parts of the preconscious. When an individual is not immediately aware of their purposes – or not fully aware – these reside, in Hollis's terms, in the realm of the preconscious.

If we take the example of a mother who finds herself, in her own view, to be easily losing her temper with her child, then the task of the social worker would be to work through the various feelings and perspectives of the woman, until she is able to identify the relationship between her frequent expressions of hostility and the circumstances of the child's birth, as well as its impact on her life. Her strong feelings of love towards him may make it, in the first instance, difficult for her to understand why she loses her temper with him so easily. Indeed, she may feel considerable guilt about this.

The development of understanding occurs through the 'surfacing' of her feelings of anger about the impact of his birth on her life. Ragg (1977) suggests that the task of the social worker is to facilitate the woman's own capacity to provide an accurate description of her situation and its context, both socially and in relationship to her life history. She would understand that her expressions of hostility often has little to do with his behaviour, but much more to do with these residual feelings of anger which she has not acknowledged. In developing this understanding, she is in a better position to decide how she wants to behave and what she intends to do about the situation.

In undertaking this process, the woman is working through feelings of ambivalence. She loves the child, yet feels anger towards him. Once she locates the origin of this hostility, she is able to recognise her fundamental feelings of love towards the child, while those feelings of anger are rather more about herself and her situation than they are about the child. She is able to begin to address the real issues, which are not about hostility towards the child but about the development of a career. Rather than pursue destructive feelings of anger towards the child, she can take action which would enable her to set in place the development of a career. Alternatively, she may be in a better decision to accept the limits to her career, and the need to defer its pursuit, until the child is older.

Humans as social beings

While attention to the more psychological aspects of what it is to be human is highly significant, it is equally important to recognise that humans are essentially social beings. Humans, as we have noted (and as is pretty obvious), live in a social world and are constantly engaged in social interactions. They are involved, in one form or another, in relations with other people, with varying levels of commitment and interest. This is so obviously an assumption in social work that attention is not always drawn to it. Yet it is crucial to our own understanding of the practice of social work and its assumptions.

While it is clear that pretty well all social work literature – and the same goes for practice – relies on the notion of humans as social beings, this aspect of social work is most strongly presented in relation to social support and its allied concepts. This is hugely influential in social work, encapsulating, as it does, writing on social network, systems theory and an ecological approach, as well as social support. While frameworks, such as that evident in ecological approaches, enable the practitioner to look at different 'levels' of society and social interaction, and hence encompass issues even related to social structure and ideology in its most extreme ambitions, social support can operate quite immediately in the client's environment. One might, for example, receive support from formal agencies, such as social or health services. However, it is equally the case that one might receive support from a partner, husband, wife, parent or children. These, obviously, are people to whom an individual is likely to be closest. However, as with all other elements of this general 'social support' approach, social interaction is at its heart – that is, those aspects involving reciprocal relations between people.

This, indeed, is (as we have seen) an essential aspect of social work. Social work is a nonsense without social interaction. Social work involves, at base, social encounters in which the relationship between client and worker, however defined, is pivotal. At the very least this is a role relationship (the role of social worker, the role of client and the role of carer being obvious aspects). However, it is also social in the senses that it must also be informational (information must pass between at least two people for communication to take place) and affective (there is inevitably *some* degree of emotional content to the encounter and, at times, this can be quite acute).

Social work interactions involve at least three assumptions about what it means to be fully human, and these assumptions permeate its perspectives. The first is the importance of attachment or affiliation. We know a great deal about attachment from attachment theory which, in social work, is generally applied to child development. However, attachment is also of considerable significance in adult–adult relationships (as well as adult–child and child–child relationships).

Attachment refers to an emotional bond that exists between two or more people. This is not, however, some passing interest between two or more people, but represents a strong and deeply felt relationship between them. There are generally considered to be two types of these social bonds. One, most generally associated with attachment, involves a very close (generally dyadic) relationship with very powerful emotional content (Weiss, 1974, 1978). The loss of a relationship of this sort is liable to be the cause of extreme emotional pain. Such a relationship can exist, for example, between a parent and child, or two life partners, such as a husband and wife. *Affiliation* is the term used for a second form of attachment, one which is less intense. However, there is some emotional content (and hence commitment from those in such a relationship), whose stronger defining characteristics are, nevertheless, shared interests, which provide for mutual loyalty, and a community of interests. This kind of relationship is more characteristic of friendships and other non-partner relationships (Bee and Mitchell, 1984).

While these relationships are expressed in terms of emotional bonds and personal commitment, their underlying feature is a form of biological determinism. We are, so to speak, 'hard-wired' to need to have attachment relationships, and this is most evident where they are absent. These may vary in form, but the need for them appears to be a (close to) universal characteristic. People who are isolated are more liable to have impaired psychological well-being and mental health problems, to feel lonely and to seek out relationships with others. Henderson (1977) suggests that this penchant for attachment is innate and arises through species evolution (hence its biological core). The capacity for forming bonds would facilitate species survival, and this would then be a matter of 'preferential selection'. Humans, in other words, who do have the capacity to form attachment relationships would be more likely to survive, pass their genes on to succeeding generations, as a result of which this aspect of humanity – the capacity to form attachments – would become an aspect of humanity as a whole.

There are, of course, exceptions to this. We do, for example, find people who choose a hermit's lifestyle, eschewing relationships with others (though whether they nevertheless feel lonely is another matter). Also, psychopaths are generally defined in terms of their inability to empathise with others and a lack of concern for others (except perhaps as an instrument in the pursuit of their own self-absorbed interests). These, though, are relatively unusual, and we may question whether most people would regard the psychological 'make-up' of the true psychopath to be sufficient to identify them as 'fully human' (especially if the capacity for empathy is a mark of humanity).

Social integration is another aspect of the social aspect of humanity which underlies social work. This is less related to the affective side of human relationships, as is the case with attachment, than the idea of group cohesion. Social cohesion represents and encourages a sense of belonging and of knowing one's place. In this conceptualisation of humans the sense of identification with others, of shared values, of involvement with others, and others' involvement with us, form a key and important aspect of the human condition. This again makes sense in terms of species selection, since the capacity for humans to work in groups is important for species survival. Societies characterised by greater social integration would provide a more fertile base for continued human existence and, over a period of time, those who manifested these characteristics would be 'selected in' – that is, they would be more likely to survive.

While the beneficial effects (at the individual, social and species levels) are clear, the effects of the absence of integration are also evident. Where poor integration exists, *anomie* is, according to Durkheim (1897, 1947; Wright Mills, 1960), likely to develop. Where there is an absence of shared norms and beliefs (and commitment to them), anomie will occur. This may be characterised by a sense of individual futility and meaninglessness. It can be characteristic of the social group or it can be manifested in the individual (and has some of the elements of clinical depression). When the latter is the case, it is referred to as anomia.

Anomia was, according to Srole (1956), a continuum 'self to other distance' or 'self to other alienation', or, according to Laswell (1952), a state of feeling cut off, unwanted, alone and unvalued. Others have identified a feeling of 'moral emptiness' which can include despair, demoralisation and hopelessness (Meir and Bell, 1959). It is, in other words, a form of psychological emptiness (depression if you will) arising from a sense of being 'cut off' from others by an absence of social integration.

A final element of humans as social beings is one normally used in relation to the psychology of people but which has profound implications in the light of their relations with others. This is the notion of 'locus of control' (Lefcourt, 1991). The locus of control refers to the sense an individual has of where control of the direction of their life, or of factors influencing important matters in their life, resides. What control do I have over the direction of my career? Or my love life? Or the way my kids turn out?

People can be identified according to whether their 'locus of control' is 'internal' or 'external' (or at some point on a continuum between the two). An internal locus of control is where a person's perceptions of events which are significant in their life is experienced as being under their control. It arises because of their actions and behaviour, and they can enable a situation to change, or remain the same, by their own actions. An external locus of control is where the corresponding events are experienced as outside their control, or in the control of others, or other factors. They are not related to one's own behaviour. I can feel I have control over the direction of my career, my love life, or the way my children turn out. Alternatively, I can feel I have little control over these things. If the former, I have an internal locus of control. If the latter, the locus is external.

This relates to perceptions, but it can also reflect the reality of people's situations. A black person who believes that they may experience difficulty pursuing a career, because of factors outside their immediate control (such as racism), is not being unrealistic. A person aged 51 and who has just been made redundant, who feels that factors other than their own abilities will ply an important part in the likelihood of future employment, is also not being unrealistic. Poverty and disadvantage generally can provide poor environments in which to pursue lofty ambitions. Hence, while a sense of internal or external locus of control can be essentially 'internal' arising from the person themselves, it can also reflect the reality of social relations, which have a profound impact on their life.

Conclusion

Social exclusion and inclusion focuses on humans in society and hence, as the location for social work, an understanding of humans is central. We have, through much of this book, alluded to elements of the construction of social work, which is incorporated within the idea of social work, which make reference to our human status. Where, for example, we focus on humans as conscious subjects, who construct meanings and so on, we are observing human nature. There are, though, core assumptions about human nature which are both widespread in social work and which are particularly encapsulated in some approaches to intervention. Hence, we view aspects of humans as social beings which both permeate social work as a whole but which are particularly represented in ideas like social support and social network.

The assumptions are so taken for granted that they are rarely expressed, yet are readily identifiable when written down. Social workers will hardly be surprised to find that there are assumptions about the capacity (in principle) for humans to seek goals (however imperfectly), to choose between alternative strategies, and that there are unconscious and preconscious factors which may impact on this capacity to choose, the choices they make and goals they pursue. Likewise, it is not really possible to imagine social work which does not assume humans are social beings.

That these assumptions are core elements of social work, therefore, is clear. However, it might be identified as a form of 'essentialism'. This is the idea that humans have fixed qualities – a human nature if you like – and that these are identifiable. Some thinkers criticise this idea, suggesting that human nature, like all aspects of social life (in their view) is socially constructed. There is no 'real' or 'true' core to human nature. Rather different people and different societies construct human nature, and these constructions reflect the ideologies and beliefs dominant in that society.

This is a contentious position, but I do not intend to appraise it in detail here. As a general comment, this does involve the adoption of relativist ideas which we have already subjected to pretty extensive criticism and which, we have seen, are entirely incompatible with the idea of social work.

However, that, in any case, does not matter greatly. The issue here is not with the validity in general of the idea that we can identify human nature (or key aspects of it). What is important is the extent to which the idea of a human nature, and of particular facets which might be identified, is *assumed* in social work. This is clearly the case. The very idea of social work would be incomprehensible without reference to the notion of humans as social beings. The capacity for self-directed behaviour is another key aspect, and what is interesting here is that social work is so often concerned to identify reasons why behaviour may not, in principle be self-directed. In fact, very often we are talking of levels of ability to direct one's behaviour. Some are quite simply more able than others. Among the factors, furthermore, which can influence the capacity to direct actions and behaviour, are those often attributed to psychodynamic factors, such as unconscious and preconscious motivations.

It follows therefore, that *social work is an essentialist activity*. It is essentialist in that certain assumptions are made about human nature, and those *assumptions are necessary for the very existence of social work*. They are, therefore, embedded within the idea of social work.

Chapter fourteen

Conclusion: the discipline of social work

Social exclusion and the discipline of social work

It is the position of this book that it is possible to identify in social work elements of continuity which enable us to go beyond mere responsiveness to social policy developments or changes, or the positions of particular academics. First and foremost in this is the recognition that social work has been continuously involved with social exclusion and exclusion, and that this is necessarily the case. Social exclusion is, of course, a term of relatively recent origin and use. However, it encapsulates much of what has been discussed in relation to social work from its modern genesis in the nineteenth century.

Thus, for example, we find earlier discussions, as noted in preceding chapters, on the position of social work between 'civil society' and those excluded from it; of its place between public and private spheres of social life; and of it working with marginalised groups. These are all entirely consistent with the notion of social exclusion and with social work's concern with those who are (or have been defined as) socially excluded. Of course, social work is not (and has never been) focused on all aspects of social exclusion, and in this the occupation is subject to (in its state form) the changes of social policy. Social work, in other words, while consistently focusing on social exclusion (or on those have been defined as having been socially excluded), may nonetheless have concentrated on different aspects from time to time and carried out its work, to some degree, in different ways. Thus, for example, while care management may have inaugurated changed ways of working (such as, for example, the purchaser–provider split), it remains focused, overall, on those who are socially excluded.

Social exclusion also contains implicit meanings which are consistent with social work. Most overtly, the implication of the very term 'social exclusion' (and certainly its use) is the idea that it is somehow a *bad* thing. The very use of the term seems to imply that something needs to be done about it (and that is certainly the way it operates in social policy). Where social work is involved with those who are socially excluded, its practitioners are engaged in an activity which is, at its most general, about social inclusion. It emphasises the practical, positive and socially inclusive elements of the social work enterprise. Indeed, the very language of social work is consistent with this (even where common concerns are not identified). Thus social workers may claim they are concerned with 'empowerment', or with 'social functioning', or 'maintenance', or 'coping' or, indeed, 'responding to need'. These terms can have quite different meanings (and may, indeed, as we have seen, be flawed), but all are consistent with some kind of social exclusion–inclusion agenda.

Social exclusion and inclusion, therefore, are at the very heart of the social work enterprise and, paradoxically, this has been the case in its modern form, long before these terms were coined. Just as nurses and doctors may be (respectively) concerned with health and medicine, as lawyers focus on the law, teachers on education, so the 'stuff' of social work is social exclusion. *If practice were to abandon social exclusion (in whatever verbal form it was manifested) as its defining characteristic, it would no longer be social work.* It would be something else.

This does not mean, it should be emphasised, that social workers are not concerned with people who are ill (and hence with health issues) or that they do not use the law in the conduct of practice. This is quite obviously the case. However, they are interested in health (or more precisely ill health) as an aspect of social exclusion. Hence, involvement with someone suffering mental illness, or because of long-term physical disability, arises because they reside within socially excluded groups. How do we know this? We know this because social work is not always involved with people suffering ill health. Social workers are, for example, involved with young offenders, older people who feel isolated or families who are economically disadvantaged and have difficulties in parenting. All these groups have in common that they are socially excluded, and this is the case with all social work.

It is, of course, also possible to suggest that, say, health professionals are involved quite frequently with people who are socially excluded. Older people with health problems are socially excluded; those suffering mental illness may be considered socially excluded; those with disabilities can be socially excluded. However, firstly, their focus on these groups is because they are suffering ill health. The *raison d'être* of the professionals lies in their work related to health and illness. Secondly, they tend to deal with patients covering the whole spectrum of the population. People can suffer ill health without being socially excluded, but they are still the legitimate focus for health professionals.

What this, of course, helps us to understand is how professionals' concerns can both overlap and yet entail a difference in roles. This is not always properly understood. The move towards – and it sometimes looks like a headlong dash – the idea of a generic 'mental health professional' runs the risk of losing the distinctive contribution of different occupational groups, precisely because such moves fail to understand the important differences. Community psychiatric nurses are mental health professionals. Social workers are welfare professionals who work, in some cases, with people suffering mental illness. The focus and orientation, and hence what they have to offer, of these professions are different, even when working with the same client group (Sheppard, 1991).

The appreciation of social work as essentially concerned with (aspects of) social exclusion and inclusion, while being an observation on practice, has potentially profound implications for social work as an academic discipline. It becomes possible to identify a distinctive discipline of social work. This is rather important. It is possible, for example, for applied subjects to be taught at university level which are just about preparing intending social workers for practice. The key issue here is: what do students need to know in order to practise competently (or successfully, or adequately, or whatever the current jargon might be). That would simply entail obtaining relevant 'knowledge' from one area or another, facilitating student learning, and enabling them to get to a point where they may practise.

There is no doubt that social work education is centrally involved in this process. However, it is more than this. Just like sociology and psychology (or, for that matter, chemistry and aeronautics) have their own disciplinary area, so does social work. This we have sought to outline in this book. This is rather important, because it means that social work cannot *merely* be the creature of government whim or transient fancy. Although social work – in its state form – is an arm of government policy, it is not *just* an arm of government policy. It has an existence – it is an entity, if you like – which may be defined, at least in part, independently of government policy. Thus, just as social policy influences the areas of social exclusion which are the concern of (state) social work (and independent social work funded by the state), so we find that policies mandating social workers to act in particular areas conform to certain fundamental dimensions of social work. This may not be conscious, and it can involve variation in the forms of practice, or even areas of work, in which social workers are engaged. Nevertheless, there are themes and continuities which underlie social work. It is through these themes and continuities that we are able to locate social work as a discipline.

We should not, furthermore, confuse the notion of a discipline with that of a 'profession'. A discipline is an academic form, describing an area of knowledge which is its concern. A profession may use some of this knowledge, but it is essentially an occupation form, one which practises in some way or other. Thus, we can outline the key elements of a discipline without worrying too much about the issue of whether or not there are professionals whose practice is based on that knowledge (even though that may be the case).

Practice paradigm and the discipline of social work

Social exclusion is, of course, an interest in various academic disciplines (as a topic for study), such as those of sociology and social policy. However, in the case of social work its disciplinary focus comes from its manifestation as a practice form. Social exclusion, then, provides a *necessary*, but *not sufficient means* for identifying social work's disciplinary status. Other dimensions, which are linked to social exclusion and through which social work is manifested, have been narrated in this book. However, of central importance to its disciplinary status is its practice form.

It is, paradoxically, its practice form which provides social work with an important element of its disciplinary distinctiveness. Nigel Parton (2000, p. 450; see also Parton, 1999) has commented that 'ironically, the characteristic which is perhaps central to its rational and *raison d'être* – its commitment to something called practice – has until recently been seen to undermine its claim to being a proper intellectual pursuit'. What has changed this are the twin concepts which have been developed, those of the *practice paradigm* and *practice validity*. Underlying these (which we shall discuss later) is a further notion – that social work is, and must necessarily be, a practice-led discipline (Sheppard, 1995a, 1998; Parton, 2000; Houston, 2001). We should be careful with this notion, because it is not about the discipline somehow being led by what happens in practice or, even more, that practitioners are somehow ahead of those who study the discipline, in their understanding the nature of social work. This does not undermine the position of practitioners, but is merely to affirm that such a position would imply the degeneration of the definition of social work to the nuts and bolts of its practice at any one time. It is, in fact, much more than that.

Social work as a discipline – if it is to exist as a distinctive discipline – must be 'practice-led'. For the discipline of social work to be practice-led means that its knowledge forms are consistent with the assumptions underlying social work. These, as has already been noted, have key elements of continuity. This is the reverse (for the purpose of illustration) of a 'theory-driven' approach. Here, instead of the knowledge forms being consistent with practice assumptions, the forms of practice reflect the particular theoretical commitment of whichever commentator happens to be writing about it. There is a major problem with the latter, for if social work were 'theory-driven', then it could take, in principle, whatever form with which that commentator wanted to provide it. Social work, in that case, could look like anything at all and nothing in particular.

We can explore this further. It is widely understood that there is huge theoretical (and paradigm) diversity in the social sciences and, given our extended analysis, the discipline of social work could be nothing other than a social science. Social work, if 'driven' by these disciplines, could take an equally huge range of forms. Yet, in practice, it does not. Indeed, we find that some forms of knowledge, which may have a big impact within academia, pass almost unnoticed in practice. The major example of this is Marxist social work (Corrigan and Leonard, 1978). This was a major theme in social work literature, creating an image of social workers as participating in a social and politically revolutionary process, the ultimate focus of which was at the level of social structure, and the aim nothing less than major social (indeed societal) change. Of course, no such thing happened (whatever individual sympathies people may have had with the analysis), precisely because the approach in no way fitted with the assumptions underlying social work.

Feminist thought, however, did have a large impact on social work. Obviously the reasons for this are complex (and relate, in part, to the impact of this thinking on the wider society), but it differed from Marxism in that some aspects of feminist thought, at least, were not inconsistent with the assumptions underlying social work. Hence, it was possible for a feminist social work to develop and, even more, a wide feminist influence on social work as a whole to emerge. Indeed, this thinking allowed for an exploration of just how far the practice assumptions allowed social work to develop (Sheppard, 1998) – a kind of boundary-testing process.

What, then, are these assumptions? This brings us to the notion of a *practice paradigm* for social work. This term, in a social work context, refers to the commonality of perspective which binds the group of practitioners together in such a way that they may be regarded as operating within the same broad 'world view' (cf. Kuhn, 1970). It does not imply complete unity of thought, and there can be different theoretical stances within the same overall paradigm, but there is an underlying unity in 'taken-for-granted' assumptions.

Three key elements of the practice paradigm may be identified. These are all consistent with our preceding discussions on various themes (including, for example, those of authority, need and empowerment). We are first concerned with the nature and definition of social work's concerns and the extent to which they may be considered 'real'. Social work is committed to a *'core of objectivism'* in its practice. As we have seen, this entails that the world 'out there' is real and exists independently of the individual perceiving it. This is apparent in our earlier discussions on authority, need and postmodernism. This does not mean that there is no room for uncertainty or dispute. However, it does mean that, at the heart of social work, in particular in relation to much of its central concerns (such as child abuse or mental health), social work assumes that such matters are real and have an objective core.

A second underlying assumption in the practice-led discipline of social work is one of *limited voluntarism*. This relates to the capacity for autonomy in decision making amongst humans – it is essentially a 'human nature' assumption. As we have seen throughout, social work assumes a world of meaning – that is, one in which individuals and groups, as subjects, make sense, or seek to make sense, of their social world, and where they act on the basis of this understanding.

Limited voluntarism implies that human actions are assumed to be voluntary except where some circumstances indicate there has been some 'external' cause. The most obvious example of this is where compulsory admission is deemed to be required in relation to someone who is mentally ill. This is a clear example (not the only one) because, as Peters (1960) has observed, we are likely to give a causal (that is, a non-voluntaristic) account where the person's actions appear considerably at odds with normative expectations – that is, they are acting oddly or incomprehensibly.

The third dimension relates to the social form of social work's commitment. This, in Burrel and Morgan's (1979) terms, fits most closely a 'regulation' position, one which is not concerned with broad (structural) social change but with the relationship between individuals and groups in their social environment, in a 'society as it is'. This is consistent with *an 'order' or 'consensus' view of society*.

This means, in effect that social work does not involve action which is concerned with major social change. Rather, its tendency – though this is not entirely the case – is to operate at an individualist level, that of individuals and families. Social work's focus tends to be on the *micro-social level*. This is apparent in both state social work and that carried out voluntarily or individually. It reflects an assumption, outlined earlier, that social workers are concerned overwhelmingly with need as a residual issue in society. It is evident in the structural constraints which are apparent in the organisation of social work and with the 'meaning' given to its work, as we discussed earlier. The reader will recall that we discussed the way in which child abuse was defined individualistically, a matter of individual acts, rather than something which may equally be defined societally – for example, where infant mortality worsens as a result of growing poverty and inequality.

This does not, however, exclude a legitimate involvement with social groups (such as community social work), and the extent of social work involvement with such groups largely depends on the degree of political will for such involvement. This form, it should be said, is far less widespread than more individualised forms of social work, which appear to be 'core'. Nevertheless, there is no reason, in principle, why social work cannot be involved with community groups, networking and seeking to enable them to gain greater control over and improve their immediate social environment. However, this does not extend to wholesale structural change and may, it could well be argued, be about helping existing society function more smoothly and consistently with its underlying beliefs. It continues to work, then, within a broad order or consensus approach while recognising that this requires a commitment to human dignity and minimum standards of social justice (which are widely held).

Practice validity and the forms of knowledge in the discipline

There is then a core of objectivism, a limited voluntarism and a series of micro-social-focused, broadly consensus-order assumptions which underlie the humans-in-society practice paradigm of social work. Why should this be important? It is important, in one respect, because it tells us something quite fundamental about the discipline of social work, enabling us to draw up its disciplinary 'area'. However, it is equally important in what it tells us about the forms of knowledge which are consistent with it as a discipline. Since a discipline may be considered in terms of the knowledge area which it occupies, this has great significance. However, in the case of social work, it is also about the knowledge orientation which it must adopt for it to exist as a discipline.

This brings us to the concept of *practice validity*: that is, the extent to which a knowledge form is consistent with the underlying assumptions of social work. The validity of any knowledge form for social work, in other words, is to be assessed in terms of the extent to which it is consistent with social work's practice paradigm, the 'taken for granted' assumptions of social work we have just outlined. This involves the core of objectivism, limited voluntarism and micro-social-focused, consensus orientation which characterise social work's practice paradigm.

In terms of knowledge forms, it is this requirement which distinguishes social work clearly from other disciplines. In 'pure' disciplines, knowledge forms are considered in terms of their 'epistemic validity' (White, 1997). Epistemic validity refers to the extent to which knowledge generated is rigorous in terms of its methodology and its assumptions about what we can know. What, we may ask, are the knowledge assumptions of the particular knowledge generated (for example is it relativist or objectivist)? How consistently are these knowledge assumptions adopted in a study? Are these consistently reflected in

241

the methods used? The requirement here is that the knowledge form adopted is 'true to itself'. The social sciences are characterised by a range of positions on knowledge and theories (we have extensively looked at some underlying themes in this book, in the form of relativism and objectivism). Each may be criticised from the standpoint of another, and the result is that the social sciences are riven with disputes about the legitimacy of one position on knowledge versus other positions.

Social work does not have that luxury, and the concept of practice validity helps us to understand how this works. If we take again the example of Marxism, it becomes immediately clear why it had such little impact on practice. While there is a clear element of objectivism in Marxism (most obviously encapsulated in the idea of 'historical materialism'), and certainly some forms of Marxism emphasise also a major place for voluntarism (see, for example Thompson, 1963), it becomes problematic in its societal orientation. Marxism focuses on change at a societal level, which involves overturning the current social system and working to impact on social structure. This is not the approach to working with social problems as essentially residual, and hence it entails practice at a 'level' in society which conflicts with the social work practice paradigm – the assumptions which underlie it. While, therefore, one can acknowledge the attractions of Marxism (to some) as a form of analysis of society, it is not of great relevance as a recipe for the conduct of practice.

The discipline of social work, then, requires (in addition to a form of epistemic validity) an additional fundamental criterion, that of practice validity. Knowledge is more or less relevant and useful to social work, to the extent that it is consistent with its underlying assumptions. Where it is not, it is (to that extent) of limited or even no practical use for social work. The complete denial of any degree of objectivism (which is a relativist position) is, therefore, problematic in terms of social work (however acceptable it may be in other areas of study). A knowledge form which requires action at the level of social structure and social change is likewise problematic, and so on (Sheppard, 1995a, 1998).

Essentialism and the discipline of social work

The notion of practice validity has caught the attention of a number of thinkers in social work (such as Parton, 2000; Parton and O'Byrne, 2000; Jeffries, 1996; Clifford, 1998; Houston, 2001; Cooper, 2001), many of whom regard it to be quite fundamental to the understanding of the relationship between social work practice and its knowledge – and hence the discipline of social work.

Parton, in particular, however, while accepting its importance as an 'anchor' for social work, nevertheless regards social work to be essentially ambiguous and uncertain. It is, he thinks, furthermore, subject to change. The result is that this *essentialist* notion of practice validity put forward through the practice paradigm – that is as a core foundation for the discipline of social work – is not one which he regards to be valid. While committing himself to the idea that the test for knowledge should (at least in part) be some abstract understanding of practice, this practice, and hence its assumptions, is neither clear nor unchanging.

Parton (2000; Parton and O'Byrne, 2000) argues social work must be considered in its social, political and historical context. Thus, in the last quarter century welfarism has been rethought, social work has played a less central part than previously, and it has emerged (in its state form) as a proceduralised and legalised bureaucratic service. This he compares with the more humanistic traditions of social work, of which Jordan (1978, 1979, 1987) wrote (of informal client–practitioner relationships) of 'natural settings' (of people's normal living situations) and 'negotiating' rather than 'imposing' solutions.

That social work *situations* can contain ambiguous elements, I think most people would agree (indeed, some of the discussion of reflexivity in this book is predicated in the difficulties presented by ambiguity). However, we should distinguish this from the definition of its *nature*, which needs be less ambiguous (and, again, has been the subject of much of this book). What needs to be understood is that the degree of ambiguity, or change, as compared with continuity, or essential content, of social work, depends on the level of analysis which is conducted. While the concept of practice validity is disarmingly simple at base (who, after all, could argue that knowledge for social work needs to be valid in relation to practice?), it is a highly abstract idea. If we examine the process by which it was developed and which is incorporated into much of the thinking in this book, we find that this is achieved by using (predominantly, but not entirely) social philosophy to examine key dimensions of social work. This is the level of analysis, or abstraction, required.

None of this, it should be emphasised, is to call into question the quality of Parton's (and other) work. Rather, it suggests their level of abstraction is not sufficiently great. Theirs is a focus on policy and practice, developed using social, political and historical contexts. At this level, some, at least, of their analysis clearly holds true. Social work has been the subject of change. There can be little doubt that much of it has become more bureaucratised, and so on. What Parton is referring to here, however, is largely (but not completely) about the manner by which social work's central functions have been carried out. However, it is apparent, through all recent legislation (in the UK anyway) that even in state social work, the practice paradigm (and hence the essentialist notion of practice validity) has been reaffirmed. Social work is carried out with the three fundamental characteristics (a core of objectivism, a limited voluntarism and a consensus-order orientation, veering towards an individualised–personalised form of practice). It is, therefore, both possible to accept some of Parton's arguments about change, while nevertheless affirming that it is not inconsistent with an underlying, essentialist, notion of practice validity.

Essentialism and the process of judgement and decision making

Some writers have sought to present social work in postmodernist (Jeffries, 1996), relativist (Taylor and White, 2001) and constructivist (Cooper, 2001; Parton, 1999, 2000) terms, of a sort we have discussed earlier. From such a perspective, of course, a key aspect of the practice paradigm (and hence practice validity) – the core of objectivism – is not valid. How can it be, if all knowledge and understanding is constructed and relativist?

If we take Parton (2000), for example, he argues that terms like child abuse are socially constructed, and reflect the fact that child care behaviours, and appropriate parenting actions, are differently constructed in different societies and over different time periods. With this empirical statement (of differing definitions of 'adequate' parenting) there can be no real dispute. However, in relation to social work this position is hugely problematic.

There are very serious (indeed fatal) objections to this relativist/constructivist position, and we have noted these earlier. However, the greatest problem, in terms of the idea of social work and its form as a discipline, is that relativism does not reflect the assumptions of social work. One may make the observation, from the perspective of a relativist if you like, that child abuse is an entirely relative concept, merely reflecting the norms and mores of a society at any particular time or place. Within the assumptions of relativism (which as we have noted is problematic), such a statement make sense. But such a statement lies *outside the discipline of social work* because it lacks practice validity. It denies the possibility of any objectivism, when this lies at the core of social work.

We can understand this clearly, as we have seen earlier, by considering the implications for anti-racist social work or for feminist perspectives. These positions would lack any authority at all *vis-à-vis* alternative positions (such as those of the white supremacist), because there would be no criteria by which to prefer one to the other. The same, it should be said, would be the case for the even more fundamental commitments of social work, to the dignity and worth of humans, a position which underlies anti-racist and feminist positions.

These positions are only coherent, *can* only be coherent, if there is a core of objectivism assumed in social work.

The same applies to substantive areas of practice. The 'objective reality' of certain conditions is enshrined in the legislation which gives the very form and meaning to areas of social work. For example, under the Mental Health Act 1983, there is no debate about the legitimacy of the term 'mental disorder'. We have a notion of an existent mental disorder in that Act, a condition which is real and can be manifested in some human beings. Likewise, the notion that 'significant harm' can be perpetrated on a child is not a matter for discussion in the Children Act 1989. It is a term used to describe a situation which is real and can be manifested in interactions (for example) between parents and their children.

As an *outsider* (that is operating outside the discipline of social work, for example as a sociologist), it is perfectly possible to adopt constructivist positions. When, however, reflecting the 'internal world' of social work, there must be a core of objectivism. While, therefore, seeking to promote practice validity, those of a relativist disposition are, oddly, necessarily inconsistent with the concept itself, precisely because of their relativism.

Objectivism, judgements and decisions in practice

One of the assumptions enshrined in our account of practical reasoning is that this processes gives the prospect of being able more accurately to assess and intervene in a situation – that is, there would be a more adequate 'fit' between the reality of a situation and the way in which it is viewed by a social worker. More formally, they would be going through a process in which they were seeking to select the hypothesis (or set of hypotheses) which were least likely to be wrong.

Taylor and White (2001) have suggested, however, that practitioners can come to a point where, no matter what they do, they are unable to distinguish between the plausibility of alternative accounts. Is this, for example, an accidental injury, arising from a young child falling off a chair and hitting their head on the ground, or is it non-accidental, because the child was pushed?

They draw on the (rather famous) Louise Woodward trial (in which a British nanny was accused of murder when looking after a child in the US, through shaking the child). They use this as an example of the impossibility of choosing between alternative explanations, even when backed up by medical examination and judgements. Instead of making a rational judgement based on the evidence, they suggest, the judge was forced to make practical moral judgement – one, in other words, based on morals. 'I am morally certain that allowing the defendant on this evidence to remain convicted of second degree murder would be a miscarriage of justice (Zobel, 1998, pp. 11–13).

One may first comment that, as many philosophers have pointed out, there is no hard and fast division between (on the one hand) 'facts' and (on the other) 'values'. Judgements of value inevitably involve questions of fact, just as facts are intertwined with the values which we have adopted when taking moral positions. To say someone is, for example, courageous or caring is to make a statement of value, while implicitly drawing upon forms of behaviour (which would be made manifest if we were to explore the reasons behind the judgement that an individual was courageous or caring).

However, one case a whole discipline, or form of practice, does not make. The fame of the Louise Woodward case (which, while involving issues at times pertinent in social work, was nevertheless not a social work case) does not mean that it is of general applicability to all, or most, social work situations. Because, in other words, it proves in one case to be impossible to choose between alternative positions, this does not follow for all, or even most, other cases. However, even in the case of Louise Woodward, Zobel (the judge presiding) made a telling statement: 'I view the evidence as disclosing [a] confusion, fright, and bad judgement, rather than [b] rage or malice'. In other words, he had concluded that one explanation, [a], was more plausible than the other, [b]. The criterion of plausibility, therefore, is used in order to make his judgement.

Indeed, his judgement followed logically from his analysis. Because the death flowed from 'confusion, fright and bad judgement', manslaughter was an appropriate verdict, rather than the mandatory life sentence for murder (which by implication would have followed from a verdict based on actions undertaken out of 'rage or malice'). This logical relationship between judgement (based on plausibility) and response (what should follow the judgement) is one which is a model for social work intervention.

Nevertheless, there may, indeed, be circumstances where social workers are confronted by equally plausible accounts. What then? It is appropriate to work on a principle, enshrined in civil proceedings in law courts, of a 'balance of probabilities'. This is really rather obvious, when considered in this way. In most circumstances there will be one way of viewing the situation, taking into account all the accumulated evidence, which will be more plausible (or less implausible) than others. If social workers are careful and rigorous in the conduct of their practice (they are, as we noted earlier, engaged in practical reasoning), then they enable this process of the discovery of plausible accounts. Where however, there really is an absolute 'balance of plausibility' – a perfect balance between alternative accounts – then the burden of proof lies with the 'accuser' (and hence decisions should veer on the side of the accused, such as those who may be considered to manifest poor parenting).

Conclusion

The *idea of practice*, then, ends with social work not just as a form of practice – which it is – but as a discipline in its own right. It is one which exists firmly within the social sciences, but which has its own 'territory'. It encapsulates social exclusion, of course, but has additional essential elements, most particularly knowledge forms which reflect its underlying assumptions, and a practical reasoning which must be at the heart of practice. Social work most definitely has a 'place', both in its social location in the world of practice and its intellectual location in the world of academe.

Bibliography

Adams, R. (2003) *Social Work and Empowerment* (London: Macmillan).

ADSW (Association of Directors of Social Work) (1997) *Social Work into the Millennium: Critical Issues for Social Work Services*. Glasgow, ADSW.

Alcock, P. (1994) 'Back to the future. Victorian values for the 21st century', in C. Murray (ed.) *Underclass: The Crisis Deepens* (London: Institute of Economic Affairs in association with The Sunday Times).

Aldgate, J. and Tunstill, J. (1995*) Making Sense of Section 17* (London: HMSO).

Altman, J.C. (2003) 'Social motherhood revisited', *Affilia, Journal of Women and Social Work* 18, 80–86.

Anderson, C., Hogarty, G., Bayer, T. and Needleman, R. (1984) 'Expressed emotion and social networks of schizophrenic patients', *British Journal of Psychiatry* 144, 247–55.

Anderson, J. (1988) *Foundations of Social Work Practice* (New York: Springer).

Atherton, C.R. and Bolland, K.A. (2002a) 'Postmodernism: a dangerous illusion for social work', *International Social Work* 45 (4), 421–3.

Atherton, C.R. and Bolland, K.A. (2002b) 'Heuristics versus Logical Positivism: solving the wrong problem' , *Families in Society* 83 (1), 7–13.

Atkinson, R. and Davoudi, S. (2000) 'The concept of social exclusion in the European Union: context, development and possibilities', *Journal of Common Market Studies* 38 (3), 427–48.

Bailey, R. and Brake, M. (1975) *Radical Social Work* (London: Edward Arnold).

Bailey, R. and Brake, M. (1980) *Radical Social Work and Practice* (London: Edward Arnold).

Bandura, A. (1982) 'Self efficacy mechanisms in human agency', *American Psychologist* 37, 12–47.

Barry, B. (1965) *Political Argument*, London, Routledge.

Barry, M. (1998) 'Social exclusion and social work: an introduction', in M. Barry and C. Hallett (eds) *Social Exclusion and Social Work* (Lyme Regis: Russell House).

Barry, M. and Hallett, C. (eds) (1998) *Social Exclusion and Social Work: Issues of Theory, Policy and Practice* (Lyme Regis: Russell House).

Barthes, R. (1985) *The Grain of the Voice* (New York: Hill and Wang).

Bartlett, H. (1970) *The Common Base for Social Work Practice* (New York: National Association of Social Workers).

Beck, A., Steer, R., and Garbin, M. (1988) 'Psychometric properties of the Beck Depression Inventory: twenty five years of evaluation', *Clinical Psychology Review* 8, 77–100.

Beck, U. (1992) *Risk Society: Towards a New Modernity* (London: Scope).

Bee, H. and Mitchell, S. (1984) *The Developing Person: A Lifespan Approach*, 2nd edn (Cambridge: Harper and Rowe).

Benn, S.I. (1967) 'Freedom and persuasion', *Australian Journal of Philosophy* 45, 259–75.

Beresford, P. and Wilson, A. (1998) 'Social exclusion and social work: challenges and contradictions of exclusive debate', in M. Barry and C. Hallett (eds) *Social Exclusion and Social Work* (Lyme Regis: Russell House).

Berghman, J. (1995) 'Social exclusion in Europe: policy, context and analytical framework', in G. Room (ed.) *New Poverty in the European Community* (Basingstoke: Macmillan).

Berkowitz, L. (1986) *A Survey of Social Psychology* (London: CBS Publishing).

Berlin, I. (1969) 'Two concepts of liberty', in I. Berlin, *Four Essays on Liberty* (Oxford: Oxford University Press).

Biddle, B.J. (1986) 'Recent developments in role theory', *Annual Review of Sociology* 12, 67–92.

Biddle, B.J. and Thomas, E.J. (1966) *Role Theory: Concepts and Research* (New York: Kreiger).

Biggs, S. (1998) 'The end of the beginning: a brief history of the psychoanalysis of adult ageing', *Journal of Social Work Practice* 12 (2), 135–40.

Blom Cooper, L. (1985) *A Child in Trust* (London: Kingswood Press).

Bowring, F. (2000) 'Social exclusion: limitations to the debate', *Critical Social Policy* 20 (3), 307–20.

Bradshaw, J. (1972) 'The concept of social need', *New Society* 19 (496), 640–642.

Braybrooke, D. (1987) *Meeting Needs* (Princeton NJ: Princeton University Press).

Brown, C. (1994) 'Feminist postmodernism and the challenge of diversity', in A.S. Chambon and A. Irving (eds) *Essays on Postmodernism and Social Work* (Toronto: Canadian Scholars' Press), 33–46.

Brown, C.V. (1995) 'Empowerment in social work practice with older women', *Social Work* 40 (3), 358–64.

Brown, G. (1997), *The Guardian*, 2 August.

Brown, G. and Harris, T. (1978) *Social Origins of Depression* (London: Tavistock).

Budgen, R.P. (1982) *A Critical Examination of the Principle of Self-Determination in Social Work*, Ph.D. thesis, University of East Anglia.

Bulmer, M. and Rees, A. (1996) *Citizenship Today* (London: UCL Press).

Burgess, H. (1992) *Problem-Led Learning For Social Work Education: The Enquiry and Action Approach* (London: Whiting and Birch).

Burgess, H. (1999) 'Reflective practice: action learning sets for managers in social work', *Social Work Education* 18 (3), 257–80.

Burgess, H. and Jackson, S. (1990) 'Enquiry and action learning: a new approach to social work education', *Social Work Education* 9 (3), 3–18.

Burgess, H. and Taylor, I. (1995) 'Facilitating enquiry and action learning groups for social work education', *Groupwork* 8 (2), 117–133.

Burke, A. and Clapp, J. (1997) 'Ideology and social work practice in substance abuse settings', *Social Work* 42 (6), 552–62.

Burr, V. (2003) *Social Constructionism*, 3rd edn (London: Routledge).

Burrel, G. and Morgan, G. (1979) *Sociological Paradigms and Organisational Analysis* (London: Heinemann).

Busch, N. and Valentine, D. (2000) 'Empowerment practice: a focus on battered women', *Affilia: Journal of Women and Social Work* 15 (1), 82–95.

Butrym, Z. (1976) *The Nature of Social Work* (London: Macmillan).

Cabinet Office (1991) *The Citizen's Charter: Raising the Standard*, Cmnd 1599 (London: HMSO).

Carew, R. (1987) 'The place of intuition in social work activity', *Australian Social Work* 40 (3), 5–10.

Carew, R. (1979) The place of knowledge in social work activity', *British Journal of Social Work* 9, 349–64.

Carver, C.S. and Sheier, M.F. (1982) 'Control theory: a useful conceptual framework for personality, social, clinical and health psychology', *Psychological Bulletin* 108, 111–135.

Carver, C.S., Weintraub, J.K. and Scheier, M. (1989) 'Assessing coping strategies: a theoretically based approach', *Journal of Personality and Social Psychology* 56 (2), 267–83.

CCETSW (Central Council for Education and Training in Social Work) (1985) *Policies for Qualifying Training in Social Work: The Council's Propositions* (London: CCETSW).

Chambon, A. and Irving, A. (1994) Essays *on Postmodernism in Social Work* (Toronto: Canadian Scholars' Press).

Cheetham, J. (1992) 'Evaluating the effectiveness of social work: its contribution to the development of a knowledge base', *Issues in Social Work Education* 12 (1), 52–68.

Cheetham, J., Fuller, R., McIvor, J. and Petch, A. (1992) *Evaluating Social Work*

Effectiveness (Buckingham: Open University Press).

Clark, C. (2002) *Social Work Ethics* (London: Macmillan).

Cleaver, H., Unell, I. and Aldgate, J. (1999) *Children's Needs – Parenting Capacity: The Impact of Parental Mental Illness, Problem Alcohol and Drug Use and Domestic Violence on Children's Development* (London: Stationery Office).

Clegg, S. (1979) *The Theory of Power and Organisation* (London: Routledge and Kegan Paul).

Clifford, D. (1998) *Social Assessment Theory and Practice* (Aldershot: Ashgate).

Colton, M., Drury, C. and Williams, M. (1995) *Children in Need* (Aldershot: Avebury).

Comité des Sages (1996) *For a Europe of Civic and Social Rights*. Report of the Comité des Sages chaired by Maria de Loudes Pintasilgo (Luxemburg: OOPEC).

Commission of the European Communities (1992) *Towards a Europe of Solidarity: Intensifying the Fight Against Social Exclusion, Fostering Integration*. COM (92) 542.

Commission of the European Communities (1998) *Non-Monetary Indicators of Poverty and Social Exclusion – Final Report* (Luxemburg: OOPEC).

Compton, B. and Galloway, B. (1989) *Social Work Processes*, 4th edn (London: Wadsworth).

Cooper, B. (2001) 'Constructivism in social work: towards a participative practice viability', *British Journal of Social Work* 31 (5), 201–216.

Cooper, D.E. (1999) *Existentialism: A Reconstruction* (Oxford: Blackwell).

Corby, B. (1982) 'Theory and practice in long-term social work', *British Journal of Social Work* 12, 343–4.

Corrigan, P. and Leonard, P. (1978) *Social Work Practice Under Capitalism* (London: Macmillan).

Cox, R. and Kelly, P. (2002) 'From anti-psychiatry to critical psychology', *Journal of Critical Psychology, Counselling and Psychotherapy* 2 (3), 171–4.

Craig, G. and Mayo, M. (1995) *Community Empowerment: A Reader in Participation and Development* (London: Zed Books).

Crimeen, K. and Wilson, L. (1997) 'Economic rationalism and social justice: a challenge for social workers', *Australian Social Work* 50 (4), 47–52.

Crossley, N. (1998) 'R.D. Laing and the British Anti-Psychiatry movement: a socio-historical analysis', *Social Science and Medicine* 47 (7), 877–99.

Curnock, K. and Hardiker, P. (1979) *Towards Practice Theory* (London: Routledge and Kegan Paul).

Dahrendorf, R. (1987) 'The erosion of citizenship and its consequences for us all', *New Statesman*, 12 June, p. 13.

Dain, N. (1989) 'Critics and dissenters: reflections on anti psychiatry in the

United States', *Journal of the History of the Behavioural Sciences* 25, 3–25.

Davies, M. (1994) *The Essential Social Worker* (Aldershot: Arena).

Davies, M. (2002) *The Blackwell Companion to Social Work* (Oxford: Blackwell).

Delgado, M. (2000) *New Arenas for Community Social Work Practice with Urban Youth* (New York: Columbia University Press).

Derber, C. (1982) 'Managing professionals: ideological proletarianization and mental labor', in C. Derber (ed.) *Professionals as Workers: Mental Labor in Advanced Capitalism* (Boston MA: G.K. Hall).

Dewees, M. (1999) 'The applications of social constructionist principles to teaching social work practice in mental health' *Journal of Teaching in Social Work* 19, 31–46.

DHSS (Department of Health and Social Security) (1974) *Report of the Commission of Inquiry into the Care and Supervision of Maria Colwell* (London: HMSO).

DoH (Department of Health) (1989) *Introduction to the Children Act, 1989* (London: Stationery Office).

DoH (Department of Health) (1991a) *Care Management and Assessment: Practitioners' Guide* (London: HMSO).

DoH (Department of Health) (1991b) *Care Management and Assessment: Managers' Guide* (London: HMSO).

DoH (Department of Health) (1995) *Child Protection: Messages from Research* (London: HMSO).

DoH (Department of Health) (2000) *Framework for the Assessment of Children in Need and their Families* (London: HMSO).

DoH (Department of Health) (2002) *The Integrated Children's System*, CD Rom (London: Department of Health).

Dominelli, L. (2002) *Feminist Social Work Theory and Practice* (New York: Palgrave).

Dominelli, L. and Macleod, E. (1989) *Feminist Social Work* (London: Macmillan).

Donavon, M. (2002) 'Social work and therapy: reclaiming a generic therapeutic space in child and family work', *Journal of Social Work Practice* 16 (2), 113–123.

Donzelot, J. (1988) 'The promotion of the social', *Economy and Society* 17, 395–427.

Dowling, M. (1999) 'Social exclusion, inequality and social work', *Social Policy and Administration* 33 (3), 245–61.

Doyal, L. and Gough, I. (1991) *A Theory of Human Need* (London: Macmillan).

Drakeford, M. (2000) 'Researching social work as a means of social inclusion – notes on the Edinburgh seminar', *British Journal of Social Work* 30 (4), 523–6.

Dunsire, A. (1978) *Control in a Bureaucracy* (Oxford: Martin Robertson).

Durkheim, E. (1897) *Suicide: Studies in Sociology* (Paris: Felix Alcan).

Durkheim, E. (1947) *The Division of Labour in Society* (Glencoe IL: The Free Press).

Edwards, R.B. (1982) 'Mental health as rational autonomy', in R. Edwards (ed.) *Psychiatry and Ethics* (Buffalo NY: Prometheus Books).

Ellerman, A. (1998) 'Can discourse analysis enable reflective social work practice?', *Social Work Education* 17 (1), 35–44.

England, H. (1986) *Social Work as Art* (London: Allen and Unwin).

Etzioni, A. (ed.) (1995) *New Communitarian Thinking* (Charlottesville VA: University of Virginia Press).

Etzioni, A. (1997) *The New Golden Rule. Community and Morality in a Democratic Society* (London: Profile Books).

Etzioni, A. (ed.) (1998) *Essential Communitarian Reader* (London: Rowman and Littlefield).

Etzioni, A. (1997) *The New Golden Rule. Community and Morality in a Democratic Society* (London: Profile Books).

Evans, T. and Harris, J. (2004) 'Citizenship, social inclusion and confidentiality', *British Journal of Social Work* 34, 69–91.

Evetts, J. (2002) 'New directions in state and international professional occupations: top discretionary decision making and acquired regulation', *Work, Employment and Society* 16 (2), 341–53.

Feinberg, J. (1973) *Social Philosophy* (Englewood Cliffs NJ: Prentice Hall).

Feinberg, J. (1977) 'Harm and self-interest', in P.M.S. Hacker and J. Raz (eds) *Law, Morality and Society. Essays in Honour of H.L.A. Hart* (Oxford: Oxford University Press).

Ferguson, H. (2003) 'Welfare, social exclusion and reflexivity: the case of child and woman protection', *Journal of Social Policy* 32 (2), 199–216.

Field, F. (1990) *Losing Out: The Emergence of Britain's Underclass* (Oxford: Blackwell).

Field, F. (1996) 'Britain's underclass: countering the growth', in Institute of Economic Affairs, *Charles Murray and the Underclass: The Developing Debate* (London: Institute of Economic Affairs).

Fischer, J. (1976) *The Effectiveness of Social Casework* (Springfield IL: C.H. Thomas).

Fleming, S. (2004) 'The contribution of psychoanalytical observation in child protection assessments', *Journal of Social Work Practice* 18 (2), 223–38.

Forsythe, B. and Jordan, B. (2002) 'The Victorian ethical foundations of social work in England: continuity and contradiction', *British Journal of Social Work* 32, 847–62.

Fox Harding, L. (1997) *Perspectives in Child Care Policy* (London: Longman).

Friere, P. (1972) *Pedagogy of the Oppressed* (London: Sheed and Ward).

Gadlin, H. and Tizard, J. (1984) 'Family life and the market place', in K.J. Gergen and M.M. Gergen (eds) *Historical Social Psychology* (Hillside NJ: Erlbaum).

Gardiner, D. (1988) 'Improving student learning: setting an agenda for quality in the 1990s', *Issues in Social Work Education* 8 (1), 3–10.

Gardiner, D. (1989) *The Anatomy of Supervision* (London: Falmer).

Garland, B., Yorkston, N., Stone, A. and Frank, J. (1972) 'The structured and scaled instrument to measure maladjustment', *Archives of General Psychiatry* 27, 259–64.

George, V. and Wilding P. (1994) *Welfare and Ideology* (London: Harvester Wheatsheaf).

Giddens, A. (1994) 'Living in a post-traditional society', in U. Beck, A. Giddens and S. Lash (eds) *Reflexive Modernisation: Politics, Tradition and Aesthetics in the Modern Social Order* (Cambridge: Polity).

Gil, D. (1975) 'Unravelling child abuse', *American Journal of Orthopsychiatry* 45, 346–54.

GlenMaye, L. (1998) 'Empowerment of women', in L. Gutierrez, R. Parsons and E.O. Cox (eds) *Empowerment in Social Work Practice: A Sourcebook* (Pacific Grove CA: Brooks/Cole).

Goffman, I. (1959) *The Presentation of Self in Everyday Life* (New York: Doubleday).

Goldman, A.I. (1970) *A Theory of Human Action* (Englewood Cliffs NJ: Prentice Hall).

Goldstein, H. (1973) *Social Work Practice: A Unitary Approach* (Columbia SC: University of Carolina Press).

Goldstein, H. (1981) *Social Learning and Change* (London: Tavistock).

Goldstein, H. (1992) 'If social work has not made progress as a science, might it be an art?', *Families in Society* 73 (1), 48–55.

Goldstein, H. (1999) 'The limits and art of understanding in social work practice', *Families in Society* 80 (4), 385–95.

Gould, N. (1994) 'Anti-racist social work: a framework for action', *Issues in Social Work Education* 14 (1), 2–17.

Gould, N. and Taylor, I. (1996) *Reflective Learning for Social Work* (Aldershot: Arena).

Grobman, L. (1999) 'Beyond internationalisation: multicultural education in the professional writing contact zone', *Journal of Business and Technical Communication* 13, 427–48.

Gusfield, J.R. (1989) 'Constructing the ownership of social problems', *Social Problems* 36 (5), 431–41.

Gutterez, E. and Lewis, E. (1999) *Empowering Women of Colour* (New York: Columbia University Press).

Hagge, J. (1996) 'Ethics, words and the world in Moore's and Miller's accounts of scientific and technical discourse', *Journal of Business and Technical Communication* 10 (4), 461–75.

Haines, J. (1981) *Skills and Methods in Social Work*, rev. edn (London: Constable).

Halmos, P. (1978) *The Personal and the Political: Social Work and Political Action* (London: Hutchinson).

Halstead, J.M. (1999) 'Moral education in family life: the effects of diversity', *Journal of Moral Education* 28 (3), 565–81.

Hamilton, G. (1941) 'The underlying philosophy of social casework', *Family* 23, 139–48.

Hammersley, M. (1983) 'Reflexivity and naturalism in ethnography', in M. Hammersley (ed.) *The Ethnography of Schooling* (Chester: Benrose Press).

Hammersley, M. and Atkinson, P. (1983) *Ethnography: Principles in Practice* (London: Tavistock).

Hanson, N. (1958) *Patterns of Discovery* (Cambridge: Cambridge University Press).

Hardiker, P. (1981) 'Heart and head – the function and role of knowledge in social work', *Issues in Social Work Education* 1, 85–111.

Harris, J. (1998) 'Scientific management, bureau professionalism, new managerialism: the labour process of state social work', *British Journal of Social Work* 28 (6), 839–62.

Harris, J. (2003) *The Social Work Business* (London: Routledge).

Harris, R. (1983) 'Social work and the transfer of learning', *Issues in Social Work Education* 3 (2), 103–17.

Hart, H.L.A. and Honore, T. (1985) *Causation and the Law*, 2nd edn (Oxford: Clarendon Press).

Hartnoll, M. (1998) 'A struggle around an ideal: Kilbrandon or the Kilkenny Cats', in M. Barry and C.Hallett (eds) *Social Exclusion and Social Work* (Lyme Regis: Russell House).

Hayek, F. (1960) *The Constitution of Liberty* (London: Routledge and Kegan Paul).

Heine, S.J. (2001) 'Self as cultural product: an examination of East Asian and North American selves', *Journal of Personality* 69 (6), 881–906.

Heinemann, M. (1981) 'The obsolete scientific imperative in social work research', *Social Service Review* 55, 343–57.

Henderson, A.S. (1977) 'The social network, support and neurosis: the function of attachment in adult life', *British Journal of Psychiatry* 131, 185–91.

Hesletine, M. (1980) 'Ministers and management in Whitehall', *Management Services in Government* 35.

Hollis, F. (1972) *Casework: A Psychosocial Therapy*, 2nd edn (New York: Random House).

Holman, B. (1993) *A New Deal for Social Welfare: A Powerful Analysis of the Contract Culture and Potential Proposals for the Way Forward* (London: Lion Publishing).

Holman, B. (1998) 'Neighbourhoods and exclusion', in M. Barry and C. Hallett (eds) *Social Exclusion and Social Work* (Lyme Regis: Russell House).

Horne, M. (1987) *Values in Social Work* (Aldershot: Gower).

Houston, S. (2001) 'Beyond social constructivism', *British Journal of Social Work* 31 (6), 845–62.

Howe, D. (1980) 'Inflated states and empty theories in social work', *British Journal of Social Work* 10 (3), 317–40.

Howe, D. (1988) *An Introduction to Social Work Theory* (Aldershot: Gower).

Howe, D. (1992) 'Child abuse and the bureaucratisation of social work', *Sociological Review* 40, 491–58.

Howe, D. (1994) 'Modernity, postmodernity and social work', *British Journal of Social Work* 24, 513–32.

Howe, D. (1996) 'Surface and depth in social work practice', in N. Parton (ed.) *Social Theory, Social Change and Social Work* (London: Routledge).

Hudson, A. (1985) 'Feminism and social work: resistance or dialogue?' *British Journal of Social Work* 10 (3), 317–40.

Hughes, J. (1990) *The Philosophy of Social Research*, 2nd edn (London: Longman).

Hugman, R. (2001) 'Post-welfare social work? Reconsidering postmodernism, post-fordism and social work education', *Social Work Education* 20 (3), 321–33.

Hull, C.L. (1943) *Principles of Behaviour* (New York: Appleton).

Humphries, B. (2000) 'Resources for hope: social work and social exclusion', in J. Batsleer and B. Humphries (eds) *Welfare Exclusion and Political Agency* (London: Routledge).

Hurdle, D. and Stromall, L. (2003) 'Psychiatric rehabilitation: an empowerment-based approach to mental health services', *Health and Social Work* 8 (3), 206–13.

Huxley, T. (1902) *Collected Essays* (London: Methuen).

Jamous, H. and Peloille, B. (1970) 'Professions or self-perpetuating systems? Changes in the French university-hospital system', in J. Jackson (ed.) *Professions and Professionalisation* (Cambridge: Cambridge University Press).

Jeffries, A. (1996) 'The social work practice paradigm: a definitive framework for social work education?', *Issues in Social Work Education* 16 (1), 88–105.

Johnston, J. and Wong, M. (2002) 'Cultural differences in beliefs and practices concerning talk to children', *Journal of Speech, Language and Research* 45 (5), 916–26.

Jones, C. (1983) *Social Work and the Working Class* (London: Macmillan).

Jones, C. (2001) 'Voices from the front line: state social workers and New

Labour', *British Journal of Social Work* 31, 547–62.

Jones, C. (2002) 'Poverty and social exclusion', in M. Davies (ed.) *Blackwell Companion to Social Work* (Oxford: Blackwell), pp. 7–18.

Jordan, B. (1978) 'A comment on "Theory and practice in social work"', *British Journal of Social Work* 8, 23–5.

Jordan, B. (1979) *Helping in Social Work* (London: Routledge and Kegan Paul).

Jordan, B. (1987) 'Counselling, advocacy and negotiation', *British Journal of Social Work* 17, 135–46.

Jordan, B. (2001) 'Tough love: social work, social exclusion and the third way', *British Journal of Social Work* 31, 527–46.

Jordan, B. with Jordan, C. (2000) *Social Work and the Third Way: Tough Love as Social Policy* (London: Sage).

Karusu, T. (1999) 'Spiritual psychotherapy', *American Journal of Psychotherapy* 53, 143–62.

Katz, M.M. and Lyerly, S.B. (1963) 'Methods for measuring adjustment and social behaviour in the community', *Psychological Reports* 13, 503–34.

Keane, J. (1988) *Democracy and Civil Society* (London: Verso).

Keith Lucas, A. (1972) *Giving and Taking Help* (Chapel Hill NC: University of North Carolina Press).

Kirk, S. and Reid, W. (2002) *Science and Social Work: A Critical Appraisal* (New York: Columbia University Press).

Kirsch, I. (1985) 'Self-efficacy and expectancy: old wines in new labels', *Journal of Personality and Social Psychology* 49, 824–30.

Kotchnick, B. and Forehand, R. (2002) 'Putting parenting in perspective: a discussion of contextual factors that shape parenting practice', *Journal of Child and Family Studies* 11 (3), 255–69.

Kristensen, H. (1995) 'Social exclusion and spatial stress: the connections', in G. Room (ed.) *New Poverty in the European Community* (Basingstoke: Macmillan).

Kruglanski, A. and Freund, T. (1983) 'The freezing and unfreezing of lay inferences: effects on impressional primacy, ethnic stereotyping and numerical anchoring', *Journal of Experimental Psychology* 19, 448–64.

Kuhn, T.S. (1970) *The Structure of Scientific Revolutions* (Chicago IL: University of Chicago Press).

Kymlicka, W. and Norman, W. (1995) 'Return of the citizen: a survey of recent work on citizenship theory', in R. Beiner (ed.) *Theorizing Citizenship* (Albany NY: State University of New York Press).

Labour Party (1991) *Citizen's Charter. Labour's Better Deal for Consumers and Citizens* (London: The Labour Party).

Lakatos, I. (1978) *Philosophical Papers, Volume I: The Methodology of Scientific Research Programmes* (Cambridge: Cambridge University Press).

Langan, M. and Lee, P. (1989) *Radical Social Work Today* (London: Unwin Hyman).

Laswell, H. (1952) 'The threat to privacy', in R. McIvor (ed.) *Conflict and Loyalties* (New York: Harper and Row).

Lazarus, R.S. (1993) 'Coping theory and research: past, present and future', *Psychosomatic Medicine* 55, 234–47.

Lazarus, R.S. and Folkman, S. (1984) *Stress, Appraisal and Coping* (New York: Springer).

Lee, J. (2001) *Empowerment Approach to Social Work Practice* (New York: Columbia University Press).

Lefcourt, H.M. (1991) 'Locus of control', in J.P. Robinson, P.R. Shaver and L.S. Wrightsman (eds) *Measures of Personality and Social Psychology Attitudes* (London: Academic Press).

Leonard, P. (1975) 'Towards a paradigm or radical practice', in R. Bailey and M. Brake (eds) *Radical Social Work* (London: Routledge).

Leonard, P. (1997) *Postmodern Welfare: Reconstructing an Emancipatory Project* (London: Sage).

Levitas, R. (1999) *The Inclusive Society? Social Exclusion and New Labour* (London: Palgrave Macmillan).

Lindesmith, A.R. (1968) *Addiction and Opiates* (New York: Aldine).

Linn, M.W., Sculthorpe, W.B., Evje, M., Slater, O.H. and Goodman, S.P. (1969) 'A social dysfunction rating scale', *Journal of Psychiatric Research* 6, 299–306.

Lister, R. (1997) *Citizenship: Feminist Perspectives* (Basingstoke: Macmillan).

Lister, R. (1998) 'In from the margins: citizenship, inclusion and exclusion', in M. Barry and C. Hallett (eds) *Social Exclusion and Social Work* (Lyme Regis: Russell House).

Lukes, S. (1974) *Power: A Radical View* (London: Macmillan).

Lupton, D. (1999) *Risk* (London: Routledge).

Lynn, E. (1999) 'Value base in social work education', *British Journal of Social Work* 29 (6), 939–53.

McBeath, G. and Webb S. (1991) 'Social work, modernity and postmodernity', *Sociological Review* 39 (4), 745–62.

Maccoby, E. and Martin, J. (1983) 'Socialisation in the context of the family: parent–child interaction', in M.E. Hetherington (ed.) *Handbook of Child Psychology, Volume 4: Socialisation, Personality and Personal Development* (New York: Wiley).

McDermott, F.E. (ed.) (1976) *Self-Determination in Social Work* (London: Routledge and Kegan Paul).

Macdonald, G. and Sheldon, B. (1992) 'Contemporary studies of the effectiveness of social work', *British Journal of Social Work* 22 (6), 615–43.

Macdonald, G. and Sheldon, B. (1998) 'Changing one's mind: the final frontier?', *Issues in Social Work Education* 18, 3–25.

Macdonald, G. and Winkley, A. (1999) *What Works in Child Protection?* (London: Barnardo's).

Macdonald, G., Sheldon, B. and Gillespie, J. (1992) 'Contemporary studies of the effectiveness of social work', *British Journal of Social Work* 22, 615–43.

McInnes-Miller, M. and Weiling, E. (2002) 'Points of connection and disconnection: a look at feminism and postmodernism in family therapy', *Journal of Feminist Family Therapy* 14 (2), 1–19.

McLoyd, V. (1998) 'Socioeconomic disadvantage and child development', *American Psychologist* 53, 185–204.

Markus, H. and Nurins, P. (1986) 'Possible selves', *American Psychologist* 51, 954–69.

Marsh, P. and Triselliotis, J. (1996) *Readiness to Practice: Social Workers and Probation Officers: Their Training and First Year in Work* (Aldershot: Avebury).

Marshall, T.H. (1950) *Citizenship and Social Class* (Cambridge: Cambridge University Press).

Marshall, T.H (1963) 'Citizenship and social class', in T.H. Marshall (ed.) *Sociology at the Crossroads* (London: Heinemann).

Marshall, T.H. (1965) *Social Policy* (London: Hutchinson).

Martinez-Brawley, E. (1999) 'Social work, postmodernism and higher education', *International Social Work* 42 (3), 333–46.

Martinez-Brawley, E. and Mendez-Bonito, P. (1998) 'At the edge of the frame: beyond science and art in social work', *British Journal of Social Work* 28 (2), 197–21.

Maslow, A.H. (1954) *Motivation and Personality*, 2nd edn (New York: Harper and Row).

Medawar, P. (1979) *Advice to a Young Scientist* (New York: Harper and Row).

Meinert, R. (1998) 'Consequences for professional social work under conditions of postmodernity', *Social Thought* 18, 41–54.

Meir, D. and Bell, W. (1959) 'Anomie and differential access to life goals', *American Sociological Review* 24, 189–202.

Merton, R.K. (1957) *Social Theory and Social Structure* (New York: The Free Press).

Merton, R. (1968) 'Role theory', in R. Blau and N. Goodman (eds) *Social Roles and Social Institutions* (Boulder CO: Westview Press).

Midgely, M. (1984) 'On being terrestrial', in S.C. Brown (ed.) *Objectivity and Cultural Divergence* (London: Cambridge University Press).

Miller, C. (1979) 'A humanistic rationale for technical writing', *College English* 40, 610–617.

Miller, D. (1976) *Social Justice* (Oxford, Clarion).

Miller, W. and Neusess, C. (1978) 'The welfare state illusion and the contradictions between labour and capital', in J. Holloway and S. Picotto (eds) *State and Capital* (London: Edward Arnold).

Milne, A.J.M. (1968) *Freedom and Rights* (London: Allen and Unwin).

Moore, P. (2000) 'Pluralism, instrumental discourse and the limits of social construction', *Journal of Business and Technical Communication* 14 (1), 74–83.

Morgan, G. (1980) *Organisation and Society* (London: Macmillan).

Morgan, M., Calnon, M. and Manning, N. (1985) *Sociological Approaches to Health and Illness* (London: Croom Helm).

Morris, W. (ed.) (1981) T*he American Heritage Dictionary of the English Language* (Boston MA: Houghton Mifflin).

Mullaly, R. (1998) *Structural Social Work: Ideology, Theory and Practice* (Oxford: Oxford University Press).

Murray, C. (1994) *Underclass: The Crisis Deepens* (London: Institute of Economic Affairs in association with The Sunday Times).

Nagel, J. (1994) 'Constructing ethnicity: creating and recreating ethnic identity and culture', *Social Problems* 41 (1), 152–76.

Nahri, K. (2002) 'Social workers' conceptions of how the local environment is related to social exclusion', *European Journal of Social Work* 5 (3), 255–67.

Nasser, M. (1995) 'The rise and fall of anti-psychiatry', *Psychiatric Bulletin* 19 (12), 2–6.

NISW (National Institute for Social Work) (1982) *Social Workers: Their Role and Tasks (The Barclay Report)* (London: Bedford Square Press).

Oliver, D. and Heater, D. (1994) *The Foundations of Citizenship* (Hemel Hempstead: Wheatsheaf).

Paley, J. (1987) 'Social work and the sociology of knowledge', *British Journal of Social Work* 17, 169–86.

Palmer, N. (2002) 'Reflections on art in social work practice: metaphor from the drawing of a swan', *Affilia, Journal of Women and Social Work* 17 (2), 191–205.

Pardeck, J.T. and Murphy, J.W. (1993) 'Postmodernism and clinical practice: a critical analysis of the disease model', *Psychological Reports* 72, 1187–1194.

Pardeck, J.T., Murphy, J.W. and Chung, J.M. (1994a) 'Some implications of postmodernism on social work practice', *Social Work and Social Sciences Review* 39 (4), 343–6.

Pardeck, J.T., Murphy, J.W. and Chung, J.M. (1994b) 'Social work and postmodernism', *Social Work and Social Sciences Review* 5 (2), 113–123.

Parton, N. (1979) 'The natural history of child abuse: a study in social problem management', *British Journal of Social Work* 9, 431–53.

Parton, N. (1985) *The Politics of Child Abuse* (Basingstoke: Macmillan).

Parton, N. (1994a) 'The nature of social work under conditions of (post)modernity', *Social Work and Social Sciences Review* 5 (2), 93–113.

Parton, N. (1994b) '(Post)social work: a response to Pardeck, Murphy and Chung', *Social Work and Social Sciences Review* 5 (2), 124–6.

Parton, N. (1994c) 'Problematics of government, (post)modernity and social work', *British Journal of Social Work* 24 (1), 9–32.

Parton, N. (1996) *Social Theory, Social Work and Social Change* (London: Routledge).

Parton, N. (ed.) (1997) *Child Protection and Family Support: Tensions, Contradictions and Possibilities* (New York: Routledge).

Parton, N. (1999) 'Social work: what kinds of knowledge?', paper given to the ESRC *Theorising Social Work* Seminars, available at www.elsc.orh.uk/socialcareresource/twsr/seminar/parton.htm.

Parton, N. (2000) 'Some thoughts on the relationship between theory and practice in social work', *British Journal of Social Work* 30 (4), 449–64.

Parton, N. and O'Byrne, P. (2000) *Constructive Social Work: Towards a New Practice* (Basingstoke: Macmillan).

Payne, M. (1997) *Modern Social Work Theory* (London: Macmillan).

Payne, M. (1998) 'Why social work? Comparative perspectives on social issues and response formation', *International Social Work* 41 (4), 443–53.

Pease, B. (2002) 'Rethinking empowerment: a postmodern reappraisal for emancipatory practice', *British Journal of Social Work* 32, 135–47.

Penz, P. (1986) *Consumer Sovereignty and Human Interest* (Cambridge: Cambridge University Press).

Perlman, H.H. (1957) *Social Casework: A Problem Solving Process* (Chicago IL: University of Chicago Press).

Perlman, H.H. (1968) *Persona: Social Role and Personality* (Chicago IL: University of Chicago Press).

Peters, R.S. (1960) *The Concept of Motivation* (London: Routledge).

Pfohl, S. (1977) 'The "discovery" of child abuse', *Social Problems* 24, 310–24.

Philp, M. (1979) 'Notes on the form of knowledge in social work', *Sociological Review* 27 (1), 83–111.

Pierson, C. (1991) *Beyond the Welfare State? The New Political Economy of Welfare* (Cambridge: Polity).

Pierson, J. (2002) *Tackling Social Exclusion* (London: Routledge).

Pincus, A. and Minahan, A. (1973) *Social Work Practice: Model and Method* (Itasca IL: Peacock).

Pinsoff, W.M. (2002) 'The death of "till death us do part": the transformation of pair bonding in the twentieth century', *Family Process* 41 (2), 135–57.

Plant, R. (1991) 'Social rights and the reconstruction of welfare', in G. Andrews (ed.) *Citizenship* (London: Lawrence and Wishart).

Plant, R., Lesser, H. and Taylor Gooby, P. (1982) *Political Philosophy and Social Welfare* (London: Croom Helm).

Pocock, D. (1995) 'Searching for a better story: harnessing modern and postmodern positions in family therapy', *Journal of Family Therapy* 17 (2), 149–69.

Pollit, C. (1990) *Managerialism and the Public Services* (Oxford: Blackwell).

Popper, K. (1963) *Conjectures and Refutations* (London: Routledge and Kegan Paul).

Powell, W. (2002) 'Doing it artfully', *Families in Society* 82 (1), 23–34.

Pritchard, C. (1992) 'Children's homicide as an indicator of effective child protection: a comparative study of Western European countries', *British Journal of Social Work* 22 (6), 663–84.

Pritchard, C. (2004) *The Child Abusers* (Maidenhead: Open University Press).

QAA (Quality Assurance Agency, Higher Education Funding Council) (2000) *Social Work Benchmarking Document* (Gloucester: QAA).

Ragg, N. (1977) *People Not Cases* (London: Routledge and Kegan Paul).

Rawls, J. (1973) *A Theory of Justice* (London: Oxford University Press).

Reid, W.J. (1977) *The Task Centred System* (New York: Columbia University Press).

Reid, W.J. and Epstein, L. (1972) *Task Centred Casework* (New York: Columbia University Press).

Rein, M. and White, S. (1981) 'Knowledge for practice', *Social Services Review* 55, 1–14.

Ringel, S. (2003) 'The reflective self: a path to creativity and intuitive knowledge in social work practice education', *Journal of Teaching in Social Work* 23 (3 / 4), 15–28.

Robbins, S., Chatterjee, P. and Kanda, E. (1999) 'Ideology, scientific theory and social work practice', *Families in Society* 80 (4), 374–84.

Robinson, W.S. (1951) 'The logical structure of Analytic Induction', *American Sociological Review* 16, 812–18.

Rojek, C., Peacock, G. and Collins, S. (1988) *Social Work and Received Ideas* (London: Routledge).

Rose, N. (1985) *The Psychological Complex: Psychology, Politics and Society in England, 1869–1939* (London: Routledge and Kegan Paul).

Rose, S.M. (2000) 'Reflections on empowerment-based practice' *Social Work* 45 (5), 403–12.

Ruch, G. (2002) 'From triangle to spiral: reflective practice in social work education and research', *Social Work Education* 21 (2), 199–216

Runciman, W.G. (1972) *Relative Deprivation and Social Justice* (Harmondsworth: Penguin).

Runciman, W.G. (1990) 'How many classes are there in contemporary British society?' *Sociology* 24 (3), 38.

Rutter, M. (1981) *Maternal Deprivation Reassessed* (Harmondsworth: Penguin).

Rutter, M. (1999) 'Psychosocial adversity and child psychopathology', *British Journal of Psychiatry* 171, 480–93.

Rycroft-Malone, J., Seers, K., Titchen, A., Harvey, G., Kitson, A. and McCormack, B. (2004) 'What counts as evidence in evidence-based practice?', *Journal of Advanced Nursing* 47, 81–90.

Sackett, D., Rosenberg, W. and Grey, J. (1996) 'Evidence-based medicine. What it is and what it isn't', *British Medical Journal* 312, 71–2.

Salzer, B. (1995) 'It is no surprise to see the atomisation of society reflected in our audiences', *Chronicles of Higher Education*, 21 July, p. 85.

Sarafino, E.P. (1998) *Health Psychology* (Chichester: John Wiley).

Sartre, J.-P. (1965) *Existentialism and Humanism* (London: Methuen).

Sayce, L. (1998) 'Stigma, discrimination and social exclusion: what's in a word?', *Journal of Mental Health* 7 (4), 331–43.

Schön, D. (1983) *The Reflective Practitioner* (New York: Basic Books).

Schön, D. (1987) *Educating the Reflective Practitioner* (San Fransisco: Jossey Bass).

Schurr, R.A. (1973) *Radical Non Intervention: Rethinking the Delinquency Problem* (Englewood Cliffs NJ: Prentice Hall).

Schwartz, W. (1977) 'Social groupwork: the interactional approach', in J.S. Turner (ed.) *Encyclopaedia of Social Work, Vol. 11* (New York: National Association of Social Workers).

Scottish Office (H.M. Government) (1999) *Aiming for Excellence: Modernising Social Work Services in Scotland* (White Paper), Cm 4288 (London: Stationery Office).

Seebohm Report (1968) *Report of the Committee on Local Authority and Allied Personal Social Services (Seebohm Report)*, Cmnd 3703 (London: HMSO).

Sen, A. (1984) *Resources, Values and Development* (Oxford: Blackwell).

Servian, R. (1996) *Theorising Empowerment: Individual Power and Community Care* (London: Policy Press).

Sheldon, B. (1978) 'Theory and practice in social work: a re-examination of a tenuous relationship', *British Journal of Social Work* 8, 1–21.

Sheldon, B. (1986) 'Social work effectiveness experiments: reviews and implications', *British Journal of Social Work* 16 (2), 223–47.

Sheldon, B. (1994) 'Social work effectiveness research: implications for probation and juvenile justice services', *Howard Journal of Criminal Justice* 33, 218–35.

Sheppard, M. (1990) *Mental Health: The Role of the Approved Social Worker* (Sheffield: JUSSR, University of Sheffield Press).

Sheppard, M. (1991) *Mental Health Work in the Community: Theory and Practice in Social Work and Community Psychiatric Nursing* (London: Taylor and Francis).

Sheppard, M. (1992) 'Client satisfaction, brief intervention and interpersonal skills', *Social Work and Social Sciences Review* 3 (2), 124–50.

Sheppard, M. (1993) 'Client satisfaction, extended intervention and interpersonal skills in community mental health', *Journal of Advanced Nursing* 18, 246–59.

Sheppard, M. (1995a) *Care Management and the New Social Work: A Critical Analysis* (London: Whiting and Birch).

Sheppard, M (1995b) 'Social work, social science and practice wisdom', *British Journal of Social Work* 25, 265–93.

Sheppard, M. (1997a) 'Social work practice in child and family care: a study of maternal depression', *British Journal of Social Work* 27 (6), 815–47.

Sheppard, M. (1997b) 'The preconditions for social work as a distinctive discipline', *Issues in Social Work Education* 17 (1), 82–9.

Sheppard, M. (1998) 'Practice validity, reflexivity and knowledge for social work', *British Journal of Social Work* 28 (5), 763–83.

Sheppard, M. (2001) (with Kelly, N.) *Social Work Practice with Depressed Mothers in Child and Family Care* (London: Stationery Office).

Sheppard, M. (2004a) (with Grohn, M.) *Prevention and Coping in Child and Family Care* (London: Jessica Kingsley).

Sheppard, M. (2004b) *Appraising and Using Social Research in the Human Services* (London: Jessica Kingsley).

Sheppard, M. and Ryan, K. (2003) 'Practitioners as rule-using analysts', *British Journal of Social Work* 33 (2), 157–77.

Sheppard, M., Newstead, S., Di Caccavo, A. and Ryan, K. (2000) 'Reflexivity and the development of process knowledge in social work: a classification and empirical study', *British Journal of Social Work* 30, 465–88.

Sheppard, M., Newstead, S., Di Caccavo, A. and Ryan, K. (2001) 'Comparative hypothesis assessment and quasi-triangulation as process knowledge assessment strategies in social work practice', *British Journal of Social Work* 31, 863–85.

Shulman, L (1999) *The Skills of Helping*, 3rd edn (Itasca IL: Peacock).

Sibeon, R. (1990) *Towards a New Sociology of Social Work* (Aldershot: Avebury).

Silver, H. (1994) 'Social exclusion and social solidarity: three paradigms', *International Labour Review* 133, 531–78

Sinclair, I. (1992) 'Social work research: its relevance to social work and social work education', *Issues in Social Work Education* 11 (2), 65–80.

Siporin, M. (1988) 'Clinical social work as an art form', *Social Casework* 68, 177–83.

Smale, G. (1988) *Community Social Work: A Paradigm for Change* (London: National Institute for Social Work).

Smale, G., Tuson, G. and Marsh, P. (1993) *Empowerment, Assessment, Care Management and the Skilled Worker* (London: Department of Health, HMSO).

Smale, G., Tuson, G. and Statham, D. (2000) *Social Work and Social Problems: Working Towards Social Inclusion and Social Change* (London: Macmillan).

Smith, C. and White, S. (1997) 'Parton, Howe and postmodernity: a critical comment on mistaken identity', *British Journal of Social Work* 27 (2), 275–96.

Smith, G. (1980) *Social Need* (London: Routledge and Kegan Paul).

Snyder, M. (1984) 'When beliefs create reality', in L. Berkowitz (ed.) *Advances in Experimental Social Psychology, Vol. 17* (London: Academic Press).

Snyder, M. and Campbell, B. (1980) 'Testing hypotheses about other people: the role of hypotheses', *Personal and Social Psychology Bulletin* 6, 421–26.

Snyder, M. and Swan, W. (1978) 'Hypothesis-testing processes in social interaction', *Journal of Personality and Social Psychology* 36, 1202–12.

Sokal, A. and Briemont, J. (1998) *Fashionable Nonsense: Postmodern Intellectuals' Abuse of Science* (New York: Picador).

Spector, M. and Kituse, J. (1977) *Constructing Social Problems* (London: Cummings).

Spicker, P. (1997) 'Exclusion', *Journal of Common Market Studies* 35 (1), 133–43.

Srole, L. (1956) 'Social integration and certain corollaries: an exploratory analysis', *American Sociological Review* 21, 709–16.

Stedman-Jones, G. (1971) *Outcast London: A Study of the Relationship between Classes in Victorian Society* (Oxford: Clarendon Press).

Steetler, C. (2001) 'Updating the Steetler model of research utilisation to facilitate evidence-based practice', *Nursing Outlook* 49 (6), 272–8.

Stevenon, O. and Parsloe, P. (1978) *Social Services Teams: The Practitioners' View* (London: HMSO).

Sudbery, J. (2002) 'Key features of therapeutic social work: the use of relationships', *Journal of Social Work Practice* 16 (2), 149–62.

Summerson Carr, E. (2003) 'Rethinking empowerment theory using a feminist lens: the importance of process', *Affilia, Journal of Women and Social Work* 18 (1), 8–20.

Taylor, C. (1973) 'Neutrality in political science', in A. Ryan (ed.) *The Philosophy of Social Explanation* (London: Oxford University Press).

Taylor, C. (1991) 'What's wrong with negative liberty?', in D. Miller (ed.) *Liberty* (Oxford: Oxford University Press).

Taylor, C. and White, S. (2001) 'Knowledge, truth and reflexivity: the problem of judgement in social work', *Journal of Social Work* 1 (1), 30–60.

Taylor, I. (1993) 'Self-directed learning and social work: a critical analysis', *Issues in Social Work Education* 13 (1), 3–24.

Taylor, R., Huxley, P. and Johnson, D. (1984) 'The role of social networks in the maintenance of schizophrenic patients', *British Journal of Social Work* 14, 129–40.

Taylor Gooby, P. (1994) 'Postmodernism and social policy: a great leap backwards?', *Journal of Social Policy* 23 (3), 385–404.

Thoburn, J. (1995) *Paternalism or Partnership* (London: HMSO).

Thoits, P.A. (1986) 'Social support as coping assistance', *Journal of Consulting and Clinical Psychology* 54 (4), 416–23.

Thompson, E.P. (1963) *The Making of the English Working Class* (London: Gollancz).

Thompson, G. (1987) *Needs* (London: Routledge).

Thyer, B. (1993) 'Social work theory and practice research: the approach of logical positivism', *Social Work and Social Sciences Review* 4 (1), 5–26.

Thyer, B. and Gomory, T. (2001) 'What is the role of theory in social work practice?', *Journal of Social Work Education* 37 (1), 69–78.

Towle, C. (1969) 'Social work: cause and function', in H.H. Perlman (ed.) *Helping: Charlotte Towle on Social Work and Social Casework* (Chicago IL: University of Chicago Press).

Townsend, P. (1979) *Poverty in the United Kingdom: A Survey of Household Resources and Standard of Living* (London: Allen Lane).

Wachholtz, S. and Mullaly, B. (2000) 'The politics of the textbook: a content analysis of the coverage and treatment of feminist, radical and anti-racist social work scholarship in American introductory social work textbooks published between 1988 and 1997', *Journal of Progressive Human Services* 11 (2), 51–76.

Wallace, C. and Bruce, S. (1983) 'Accounting for action: defending the common sense heresy', *Sociology* 17, 97–111.

Wagner, D. (1989) 'Radical movements in the social services: a theoretical framework', *Social Services Review* 63, 264–84.

Walker, A. and Walker, C. (eds) (1997) *Britain Divided: The Growth of Social Exclusion in the 1980s and 1990s* (London: Child Poverty Action Group).

Walker, S. (2001) 'Tracing the contours of postmodern social work', *British Journal of Social Work* 31 (1), 29–39.

Walter, U. (2003) 'Toward a third space: improvisation and professionalism in social work', *Families in Society* 84 (3), 317–22.

Watson, D. (1978) 'Social services in a nutshell', in N. Timms and D. Watson (eds) *Philosophy in Social Work* (London: Routledge and Kegan Paul).

Webb, D. (1981) 'Themes and continuities in radical and traditional social work', *British Journal of Social Work* 11, 143–58.

Weber, M. (1949) *Essays in Sociology* (London: Oxford University Press).

Weber, M. (1969) *The Theory of Social and Economic Organisation* (Glencoe IL: The Free Press).

Weick, A. (2000) 'Hidden voices' *Social Work* 45, 395–402

Weiss, R. (1974) 'The provisions of social relationships', in Z. Rubin (ed.) *Doing Unto Others* (Englewood Cliffs NJ: Basic Books).

Weiss, R. (1978) 'Couple relationships', in M. Corbin (ed.) *The Couple* (New York: Penguin).

Weissman, M. and Paykel, E. (1974) *The Depressed Woman: A Study of Social Relationships* (Chicago IL University of Chicago Press).

White, S. (1997) 'Beyond retroduction? – hermeneutics, reflexivity and social work practice', *British Journal of Social Work* 27, 739–54.

White, V. and Harris, J. (2001) *Developing Good Practice in Community Care: Partnership and Participation* (London: Jessica Kingsley).

Whittaker, J.K. and Garbarino, J. (1983) *Social Support Networks: Informal Helping in the Human Services* (New York: Aldine).

Wilding, P. (1982) *Professional Power and Social Welfare* (London: Routledge and Kegan Paul).

Wilkes, R. (1981) *Social Work and Undervalued Groups* (London: Tavistock).

Winch, P. (1958) *The Idea of Social Science and its Relationship to Philosophy* (London: Routledge and Kegan Paul).

Winch, P (1964) 'Understanding a primitive society', *American Philosophical Quarterly* 1, 307–24.

Woolgar, S. and Pawlich, D. (1985) 'How shall we move beyond Constructivism?', *Social Problems* 33, 159–62.

Wright Mills, C. (1960) *Images of Man* (New York: George Brazilier).

Young, I.M. (1990) 'Polity and group difference: a critique of the ideal of universal citizenship', *Ethics* 99, 250–74.

Younghusband, E. (1951) *Social Work in Britain. Supplementary Report* (Edinburgh: Constable).

Znaniecki, F. (1934) *The Method of Sociology*, New York, Rinehart.

Zobel, H. (1998) Commonwealth of Massachusetts, Criminal no. 97–0433. *Commonwealth* v *Louise Woodward*. Available at http/courttv.com.trials/ woodward/week6.html#nov10.

Websites

http://www.icms.com.au/social99/Highlights.asp (1999) *Promoting Inclusion, Redressing Exclusion: The Social Work Challenge*. 26th Annual Conference of the Australian Association of Social Workers.

http://www.elsc.org.uk/socialcareresource/tswr/seminars.htm (2000) *Researching*

Social Work as a Means of Social Inclusion. Economic and Social Research Council Sponsored Conference, Edinburgh.

http://www.ifsw.org/Info/SWAD2003-1.info.html (2003) *Disability, Human Rights and Social Work: Social Workers Promoting Inclusion of People with Disabilities,*. International Federation of Social Workers Action Day.

http://www.lancs.ac.uk/users/acadreg/pubs/00ass.htm (2004)

http://www.stockport.ac.uk/CourseSearch/course_search_page (2004)

http://www.anglia.ac.uk/health/social_prospectus/structureandsequence oftheprograme.htm (2004)

Author index

Subject index